English and Reading Workout for the

ACT®

Second Edition

Melissa Hendrix
and the Staff of the Princeton Review

PrincetonReview.com

Random House, Inc. New York

The Princeton Review, Inc.
111 Speen Street, Suite 550
Framingham, MA 01701
Email: editorialsupport@review.com

ISBN: 978-0-307-94594-5
ISSN: 2157-6025

ACT is a registered trademark of ACT, Inc., which does
not sponsor or endorse this product.

The Princeton Review is not affiliated with Princeton
University.

Editor: Meave Shelton
Production: Berryville Graphics, Inc.

Printed in the United States of America on partially
recycled paper.

10 9 8 7 6 5 4 3 2 1

Second Edition

Editorial
Rob Franek, Senior VP, Publisher
Mary Beth Garrick, Director of Production
Selena Coppock, Senior Editor
Calvin Cato, Editor
Kristen O'Toole, Editor
Meave Shelton, Editor

Random House Publishing Team
Tom Russell, Publisher
Nicole Benhabib, Publishing Director
Ellen L. Reed, Production Manager
Alison Stoltzfus, Managing Editor

Acknowledgments

The Princeton Review would like to thank the following individuals for their help on this book:

Brian Becker, Stacy Baker Boatman, Krista Correa, Rob Hennen, Amy Forsyth, Michelle McCannon, Henry Price, Patrick Tyrell, Christopher Anton, Elizabeth Owens, Stephen Ronkowski, and particularly Melissa Hendrix.

Contents

Part I
Orientation

Chapter 1
Introduction to the English and Reading Tests

WELCOME

The ACT is an important part of college admissions. Most schools require their applicants to submit either SAT or ACT scores, but no school will mandate which particular test to take—they just want to see good scores. For a long time, different schools would accept only one or the other. If you wanted to apply to schools in the Midwest, you took the ACT, but if you wanted to apply to schools on the East or West Coast, you took the SAT.

The good news is that these rules are obsolete. All schools that require a standardized test will take either the ACT or SAT.

This is good news indeed for test-takers. While there are many similarities between the two tests, many students find they do better on one than on the other. The expert advice of The Princeton Review is to take whichever test you do better on. While you can certainly take both, you should focus your efforts on one for substantive score improvement. True improvement takes hard work, and it can be tough to become an expert on both tests. And since schools will accept scores for either one, you won't win any brownie points for punishing yourself.

Since you bought this book, we assume you've already made the decision to boost your ACT score. This book provides a strategic and efficient way to improve your scores, specifically on English and Reading. For a more thorough review of content and exhaustive practice, we recommend *Cracking the ACT* and *1,296 ACT Practice Questions*.

For more on admissions, see The Princeton Review's *The Best 377 Colleges* or visit our website, PrincetonReview.com

See The Princeton Review's companion book, *Math and Science Workout for the ACT*.

FUN FACTS ABOUT THE ACT

The ACT is nothing like the tests you take in school. In your English class, you may learn grammar, but do you have to fix underlined portions? You may have to read a lot, but do you write papers or take speed tests on comprehension?

All of the content review and strategies we teach in the following lessons are based on the specific structure and format of the ACT. Before you can beat a test, you have to know how it's built.

Structure

The ACT is made up of four multiple-choice tests and an optional Writing test.

The five tests are always given in the same order.

English	Math	Reading	Science	Writing
45 minutes	60 minutes	35 minutes	35 minutes	30 minutes
75 questions	60 questions	40 questions	40 questions	1 Essay

Scoring

When students and schools talk about ACT scores, they mean the composite score, a range of 1–36. The composite is an average of the four multiple choice tests, each scored on the same 1–36 scale. Neither the Writing test score nor the combined English plus Writing score affect the composite.

It's All About the Composite

Whether you look at your score online or wait to get it in the mail, the biggest number on the page is always the composite. While admissions offices will certainly see the individual scores of all five tests (and their sub-scores), schools will use the composite to evaluate your application, and that's why it's the only one that matters in the end.

The composite is an average: Let the full weight of that sink in. Do you need to bring up all four scores equally to raise your composite? Do you need to be a superstar in all four tests? Should you focus more on your weaknesses than your strengths? No, no, and absolutely not. The best way to improve your composite is to shore up your weaknesses but exploit your strengths as much as possible.

> To improve your ACT score, use your strengths to lift the composite score as high as possible.

You don't need to be a rock star on all four tests. Identify two, maybe three tests, and focus on raising those scores as much as you can to raise your composite. Work on your weakest scores to keep them from pulling you down. Think of it this way: If you had only one hour to devote to practice the week before the ACT, put that hour to your best subjects.

English and Reading Scores

These two make a good pair. Every student is different, but many students begin with English as one of their higher scores and Reading as one of the lower. There is no content to review for Reading. Instead, it's entirely skill-based. If Reading ever had a child with Math, the result would be English. For the most part, English is rules-based, like Math. Review the right rules, and your score zooms. But English also requires comprehension and analysis, skills similar to those used for Reading.

Time

Time is your enemy on the ACT. You have less than a minute per question on either the English or Reading—and it's not as if there's extra time for reading the passages. The Princeton Review's strategies are all based on this time crunch. You can think of both the English and Reading tests as open-book tests, but you can neither waste all your time reading the whole book nor skip it altogether.

STRATEGIES

You will raise your ACT score not by working harder but by working *smarter*, and a smart test-taker is a strategic test-taker. You will target specific content to review, you will apply an effective and efficient approach, and you will employ the common sense that frequently deserts many of us when we pick up a number 2 pencil.

Each test on the ACT demands a different approach, and even the most universal strategies vary in their applications. In the chapters that follow, we'll discuss these terms in greater detail customized to English and Reading.

Personal Order of Difficulty (POOD)

If time is going to run out, would you rather it run out on the hardest Reading passage or on the easiest? Of course you want it to run out on the points you are less likely to get right. On the English test, you can't afford to spend too long on questions you find the most time-consuming and never even get to a bunch of questions you'd nail. The trick is to know how to pick your order of passages and questions in Reading, and how to pace yourself in English to get to as many easy questions as you can.

We'll discuss in greater detail what these mean in the individual lessons, but for now, understand that you have to make smart decisions for good reasons quickly as you move through each test.

Now

Does a question look okay? Do you know how to do it? Do it *Now*.

Later

Will this question take a long time to work? Leave it and come back to it *Later*. Circle the question number for easy reference to return.

Never

Test-taker, know thyself. Know the topics that are your worst and learn the signs that flash danger. Don't waste time on questions you should *Never* do. Instead, use more time to answer the Now and Later questions accurately.

Letter of the Day (LOTD)

Just because you don't *work* a question doesn't mean you don't *answer* it. There is no penalty for wrong answers on the ACT, so you should never leave any blanks on your scantron. When you guess on Never questions, pick your favorite two-letter combo of answers and stick with it. For example, always choose A/F or C/H. If you're consistent, you're statistically more likely to pick up more points.

The Best Way to Bubble In
Work a page at a time, circling your answers right on the booklet. Transfer a page's worth of answers to the scantron at one time. It's better to stay focused on working questions rather than disrupt your concentration to find where you left off on the scantron. You'll be more accurate at both tasks. Do not wait to the end, however, to transfer all the answers of that test on your scantron. Go a page at a time.

Process of Elimination (POE)

On English and Reading both, it's more important, and often easier, to know what's wrong and eliminate it rather than try to find out what's right. In fact, on English POE is so strong you may find few Never questions. It's worth the time to eliminate what's wrong and pick from what's left before you move on. On Reading, you may have absolutely no idea what you *have* read, but you'll likely know what you *haven't* and be able to eliminate a few wrong answers. Using POE to get rid of at least one or two wrong answers will substantially increase your odds of getting a question right.

Pacing

The ACT may be designed for you to run out of time, but you can't rush through it as fast as possible. All you'll do is make careless errors on easy questions you should get right and spend way too much time on difficult ones you're unlikely to get right.

To hit your target score, you have to know how many raw points you need. Your goals and strategies depend on the test and your own individual strengths.

On each test of the ACT, the number of correct answers converts to a scaled score of 1–36. ACT works hard to adjust the scale of each test at each administration as necessary to make all scaled scores comparable, smoothing out any differences in level of difficulty across test dates. There is thus no truth to any one test date being "easier" than the others, but you can expect to see slight variations in the scale from test to test.

This is the scale from the free test ACT makes available at www.act.org. We're going to use it to explain how to pick a target score and pace yourself.

English Pacing

Scale Score	Raw Score	Scale Score	Raw Score	Scale Score	Raw Score
36	75	27	62	18	41–42
35	73–74	26	60–61	17	39–40
34	71–72	25	58–59	16	36–38
33	70	24	56–57	15	33–35
32	69	23	54–55	14	30–32
31	67–68	22	52–53	13	28–29
30	66	21	49–51	12	26–27
29	65	20	46–48	11	24–25
28	63–64	19	43–45	10	22–23

For English, there is no order of difficulty of the passages or their questions. The most important thing is to finish, finding all the Now questions you can throughout the whole test and skipping over (LOTD) the Never questions as you go.

Reading Pacing

Scale Score	Raw Score	Scale Score	Raw Score	Scale Score	Raw Score
36	40	27	30	18	18
35	39	26	29	17	16–17
34	38	25	27–28	16	15
33	37	24	26	15	14
32	36	23	24–25	14	12–13
31	35	22	23	13	11
30	34	21	22	12	9–10
29	32–33	20	20–21	11	8
28	31	19	19	10	6–7

When it comes to picking a pacing strategy for Reading, you have to practice extensively and figure out what works best for you.

Some students are slow but good readers. If you take 35 minutes to do fewer passages, you could get all of the questions right for each passage you do. Use your LOTD for the passages you don't work, and you should pick up a few additional points.

Other students could take hours to work each passage and never get all the questions right. But if you find all the questions you can do on many passages, using your LOTD on all those Never questions, you could hit your target score.

Which is better? There is no answer to that. True ACT score improvement will come with a willingness to experiment and analyze what works best for you.

Be Flexible

The worst mistake a test-taker can make is to throw good time after bad. You read a question, don't understand it, so read it again. And again. If you stare at it really hard, you know you're going to just *see* it. And you can't move on, because really, after spending all that time it would be a waste not to keep at it, right? Actually, that way of thinking couldn't be more wrong.

You can't let one tough question drag you down. Instead, the best way to improve your ACT score is to follow our advice.

1. Use the techniques and strategies in the lessons to work efficiently and accurately through all your Now and Later questions.

2. Know your Never questions, and use your LOTD.

3. Know when to move on. Use POE, and guess from what's left.

Now move on to the lessons and learn the best way to approach the content.

Part II
English

Chapter 2
The ACT
English Test

The English test is not a grammar test. It's also not a test of how well you write. In fact, it tests your editing skills: your ability to fix errors in grammar and punctuation and to improve the organization and style of five different passages. In this chapter, you'll learn the basic strategy of how to crack the passages and review three of the most heavily tested concepts—commas, apostrophes, and strategy questions.

FUN FACTS ABOUT THE ENGLISH TEST

Before we dive into the details of the content and strategy, let's review what the English test looks like. Remember, the five tests on the ACT are always given in the same order, and English is always first.

There are five prose passages on topics ranging from historical essays to personal narratives. Each passage is typically accompanied by 15 questions for a total of 75 questions that you must answer in 45 minutes. Portions of each passage are underlined, and you must decide if these are correct as written or if one of the other answers would fix or improve the selection. Other questions will ask you to add, cut, or re-order text, while still others will ask you to evaluate the passage as a whole.

WRITING

While the idea of English grammar makes most of us think of persnickety, picky rules long since outdated, English is actually a dynamic, adaptive language. We add new vocabulary all the time, and we let common usage influence and change many rules. Pick up a handful of style books and you'll find very few rules that everyone agrees upon. This is actually good news for studying for the ACT: You're unlikely to see questions testing the most obscure or most disputed rules. However, few of us follow ALL of even the most basic, universally accepted rules when we speak, much less when we e-mail, text, or tweet.

The 4 C's: Complete, Consistent, Clear, and Concise

ACT test writers will never make you name a particular error. But with 75 questions, they can certainly test a lot of different rules—and yes, that's leaving out the obscure and debated rules. You would drive yourself crazy if you tried to learn, just for the ACT, all of the grammar you never knew in the first place. You're much better off with a common sense approach. That's where the 4 C's come in.

Good writing should be in *complete* sentences; everything should be *consistent*; the meaning should be *clear*. The best answer, free of any errors, will be the most *concise*.

Grammar Review

The 4 C's make sense of the rules you should specifically study. Focus your efforts on heavily tested topics that you can identify and know (or can learn) how to fix. In *Cracking the ACT*, we focus on the use of punctuation and conjunctions to link complete and incomplete ideas, verbs, pronouns, apostrophes, and transitions. Can't identify what the question is testing? Apply the 4 C's.

In this book, we teach you how to crack two topics students find the trickiest: commas and apostrophes. We also teach you how to crack strategy questions, another heavily tested category.

But first, you need to know how crack the test and apply our 5-step Basic Approach.

HOW TO CRACK THE ENGLISH TEST

The Passages

As always on the ACT, time is your enemy. With only 45 minutes to review 5 passages and answer 75 questions, you can't read a passage in its entirety and then go back to do the questions. For each passage, work the questions as you make your way through the passage. Read from the beginning until you get to an underlined selection, work that question, and then resume reading until the next underlined portion and the next question.

The Questions

Not all questions are created equal. In fact, ACT divides the questions on the English test into two categories: Usage and Mechanics, and Rhetorical Skills. These designations will mean very little to you when you're taking the test. All questions are worth the same amount of points, after all, and you'll crack most of the questions the same way, regardless of what ACT calls them. Many of the Rhetorical Skills questions, however, are those on organization and style, and some take longer to answer than other questions do. Since there is no order of difficulty of the passages or of the questions, all that matters is that you identify your *Now, Later, Never* questions and make sure you finish.

The Basic Approach

While some of the Rhetorical Skills questions come with actual questions, the majority of the 75 questions provide only 4 answer choices and little direction of what to do. So allow us to tell you *exactly* what to do.

Step 1: Identify the Topic

For each underlined portion, finish the sentence and then look at the answers. The answers are your clues to identifying what the question is testing. Let's start off with this first question.

For the first episode of its new radio

series, CBS decided to adapt H.G. <u>Wells' *The*</u>
₁

<u>*War of the Worlds'*</u>, the story of a Martian
₁

invasion of Earth.

1. **A.** NO CHANGE
   B. Wells' *The War of the World's*,
   C. Wells' *The War of the Worlds*,
   D. Wells *The War of the Worlds*,

Do any of the words change? No. What is the only thing that does change? Apostrophes. So what must be the topic of the question? Apostrophes.

Always identify the topic of the question first. Pay attention to what changes versus what stays the same in the answers.

Step 2: Use POE

You may have chosen an answer for question 1 already. If you haven't, don't worry: We'll review all the rules of apostrophes later in the lesson. But let's use question 1 to learn the next step, POE. To go from good to great on the English test, you can't just fix a question in your head and then find an answer that matches. Instead, after you've identified what's wrong, eliminate all the choices that do not fix the error.

For question 1, no apostrophe is needed for *Worlds*. Cross off choices (A) and (B).

1. **A.** NO CHANGE
   B. Wells' *The War of the World's*,
   C. Wells' *The War of the Worlds*,
   D. Wells *The War of the Worlds*,

Now compare the two that remain, choices (C) and (D). Do you need the apostrophe for *Wells*? Yes, you do, so choice (C) is the correct answer. Here's where you could have messed up if you didn't use POE: If you fixed it in your head and looked for your answer, you could have missed the absence of the apostrophe in choice (D) and chosen incorrectly. POE on English isn't optional or a backup when you're stuck. You have to first eliminate wrong answers and then compare what's left.

Let's go onto the next step.

Step 3: Use the Context

Even though you may struggle with time on the English test, you can't skip the non-underlined text in between questions in order to save yourself a few minutes. Take a look at this next question.

> In order to tell the story in traditional
> ———
> 2
> radio play format, however, the young
>
> director Orson Welles decided to present it
>
> as an unfolding news story and hired actors
>
> to portray radio reporters "stunned" by the
>
> horrific events unfolding before their eyes.

2. **F.** NO CHANGE
   G. Rather than
   H. Therefore, to
   J. Thus, to

Don't forget to apply the first two steps. The transition word is changing in the answers. Transitions test the correct direction to match the flow of the sentence. How do you know which direction to use? Read the entire sentence for the full context. The information that follows indicates Welles' direction would be a departure; the word *however* also helps. Eliminate all answers that are not *consistent* with the clues in the non-underlined portion and only choice (G) remains.

Always finish the sentence before attacking the question, and don't skip from question to question. The non-underlined text provides context you need.

Let's move on to the next step.

Step 4: Trust Your Ear, But Verify

Your ear can be pretty reliable at raising the alarm for outright errors and clunky, awkward phrasing.

You should, however, always verify what your ear signals by confirming the actual error. Steps 1 and 2 will help with that: Use the answers to identify the topic, and use POE heavily.

But remember to be careful of errors your ear *won't* catch. Using the answers to identify the topic will save you there as well.

Let's try another question.

Any listener who tuned in after the

program's start believed that the United

States faced an alien invasion in their skies.   **3. A.** NO CHANGE
₃   **B.** there skies.
         C. it's skies.
         D. its skies.

Need a Pronoun Refresher?
Check out the box
on page 22.

That sounded pretty good to us, how about you? But before we circle NO CHANGE and go on our merry way, look at the answers to identify the topic and confirm there is no error. Only the pronoun changes, so the question is testing pronouns. *Their* is a plural pronoun, but all countries take the singular verb and pronoun, including the *United States*. Cross off choices (A) and (B)—(B) isn't even the right type of pronoun, plural or not. Since we need a possessive pronoun, cross off choice (C) as well. Choice (D) is the correct answer.

Let's move on to our last step.

Step 5: Don't Fix What Isn't Broken
Read the next question.

In retrospect, it seems strange that so

many could have been fooled by what surely

could not have been all that convincing a   **4. F.** NO CHANGE
₄   **G.** all that believable or credible a
radio play.   radio play.
₄   **H.** all convincing.
         J. considered convincing by most who listened to it.

Go to Step 1, and identify the topic. *Everything* seems to be changing in the answers for question 4: What the question is testing isn't obvious at all. You can't confirm what you can't identify, so leave "NO CHANGE," and apply the 4 C's.

Does one of the answers fix something you missed?

Does one of the answers make the sentence better by making it more concise?

If the answer to both questions is *No* for all three other answers, the correct answer choice is (F), NO CHANGE.

NO CHANGE *is* a legitimate answer choice. Don't make the mistake of assuming that all questions have an error that you just can't spot. If you use the five steps of our Basic Approach, you'll catch errors your ear would miss, and you'll confidently choose NO CHANGE when it's the correct answer.

THREE TO KNOW

We've chosen three types of questions to tackle in this book. Commas and apostrophes are heavily tested, and most students find them devilishly confusing. Strategy questions are among the most heavily tested Rhetorical Skills questions.

COMMAS

Find a reason to use a comma, not a reason to take it out. There are four reasons to use a comma on the ACT. If you can't justify a comma by one of these rules, it shouldn't be used. In other words, if a choice offers no commas, it's right unless you can name the reason to add a comma.

1. Stop Punctuation

ACT tests the correct way to link ideas in several ways. If two ideas are complete (that is, each could stand apart as a complete sentence), use Stop punctuation in between: a period, a semi-colon, a question mark, or an exclamation mark.

A comma on its own can never come in between two complete ideas. On their own, coordinating conjunctions (*for, and, nor, but, or, yet, so*)—or FANBOYS, as we like to call them—can never come in between two complete ideas. But a comma paired with one of the FANBOYS becomes Stop punctuation.

Consider the following incorrect sentence:

Orson Welles wanted listeners to know the upcoming broadcast was a work of fiction he made sure that the program began with a disclaimer.

If you break this sentence in between *fiction* and *he*, you'll see that the two ideas could each be its own sentence. Two complete ideas have to be properly linked, and here are three ways to fix.

Orson Welles wanted listeners to know the upcoming broadcast was a work of fiction. He made sure that the program began with a disclaimer.

Orson Welles wanted listeners to know the upcoming broadcast was a work of fiction; he made sure that the program began with a disclaimer.

Orson Welles wanted listeners to know the upcoming broadcast was a work of fiction, and he made sure that the program began with a disclaimer.

On the ACT, any of these would be fine. In fact, ACT rarely makes you choose the nuanced difference among them. The particular FANBOYS word adds an element of direction that could affect the answer, but there is no structural difference among a period, a semi-colon, or a comma + FANBOYS. All are Stop punctuation, and all could work above.

2. Go Punctuation

An incomplete idea can't stand on its own. A comma is one way to link the incomplete idea to a complete idea to form one sentence.

Consider the following examples.

Once the broadcast began, listeners who tuned in late believed the Martian invasion to be real.

Many people reportedly tried to flee, desperate to escape certain destruction.

In the first example, *Once the broadcast began* is incomplete. In the second example, *desperate to escape certain destruction* is incomplete. In each case, a comma links the incomplete idea to the complete idea.

3. Lists

Use a comma to separate items on a list.

The chilling broadcast of The War of the Worlds *was a long, tense hour for many listeners.*

Long and *tense* are both describing *hour*. If you would say *long and tense* then you can say *long, tense.*

Welles went on to direct such classics as Touch of Evil, The Magnificent Ambersons, *and* Citizen Kane.

Whenever you have three or more items on a list, always use a comma before the "and" preceding the final item. This is a rule that not everyone agrees on, but if you apply the 4 C's, the extra comma makes your meaning *Clear*. On the ACT, always use the comma before the "and."

4. Unnecessary Info

Use a pair of commas around unnecessary info.

It did not occur to Welles, however, that a great number of people would tune in after the broadcast had started.

If information is necessary to the sentence in either meaning or structure, don't use the commas. If the meaning would be exactly the same but less interesting, use a pair of commas—or a pair of dashes—around the information.

Try a few questions.

CBS hoped to draw on highbrow viewers

who were more interested in serious literary
<u>   </u>
                         5

material, than in the songs and jokes that
<u>   </u>
     5

dominated most radio programs.

5. A. NO CHANGE
   B. serious, literary material, than
   C. serious literary, material than
   D. serious literary material than

Here's How to Crack It

Step 1 identifies commas as the topic. Run through the four reasons to use a comma and see if any is in play, and use Step 2, POE. Choice (D) offers no commas at all, so find a reason to *not* pick it. There are no FANBOYS included, so it's not Stop punctuation. The two commas in choice (B) would make the information in between them unnecessary; the information is necessary, so eliminate (B). Compare choices (A) and (C). Each has one comma but in a different placement. Is this a list? Is there a separate complete idea embedded in the sentence to link an incomplete idea to? No, and no. The correct choice is (D).

No other station reported the <u>invasion,</u>
                                   6

<u>but listeners</u> still believed the program to be
      6

breaking news.

6. F. NO CHANGE
   G. invasion but listeners
   H. invasion, listeners
   J. invasion, but, listeners

Here's How to Crack It

Step 1 identifies commas as the topic. With the presence of *but*—one of our FANBOYS—decide first if the two ideas are complete on either side of , *but*. They are complete, so use Step 2, POE, to eliminate wrong answers. The correct choice is (F).

APOSTROPHES

Apostrophes make your writing more concise. They have two uses, possession and contraction.

Possession

To show possession with single nouns, add *'s*, and with plural nouns, add just the apostrophe. For tricky plurals that do not end in *s,* add *'s*.

Consider the following examples:

The career of Orson = Orson's career
The actions of the boys = the boys' actions
The voices of the men = the men's voices

To show possession with pronouns, never use apostrophes. Use the appropriate possessive pronoun.

His *direction*
Their *fear*
Its *legacy*

Quick and Dirty Pronoun Lesson

Pronouns vary by number, gender, and case, that is, the function they perform in the sentence.

	1st person	2nd person	3rd person
Subject	I, we	you	she, he, it, they
Object	me, us	you	her, him, it, them
Possessive	my, mine, our, ours	your	her, hers, his, its, their, theirs

Contractions

Whenever you see a pronoun with an apostrophe, it's (it is) a contraction, which means the apostrophe takes the place of at least one letter.

Consider the following examples.

It is a classic. = ***It's*** *a classic.*
They are fans of the production. = ***They're*** *fans of the production.*
Who is the star of the play? = ***Who's*** *the star of the play?*

Because these particular contractions sound the same as some possessive pronouns, these questions can be very tricky on the ACT. You can't use your ear: You have to know the above rules.

Try a question.

While some suspect the reports were at best wildly overstated, the young directors₇ notoriety₇ soared.

7. **A.** NO CHANGE
   B. director's notoriety,
   C. directors' notoriety,
   D. director's notoriety

Here's How to Crack It

Step 1 identifies apostrophes and commas as the topic. Use Step 2, POE, to eliminate wrong answers. *Director* is singular, so eliminate choice (C). The *notoriety* does belong to the *director*, so you need an apostrophe and can therefore eliminate choice (A). Between choices (B) and (D), decide if there is a reason to use a comma. In fact, the added comma would make *the young director's notoriety* unnecessary, which makes no sense. The correct choice is (D).

RHETORICAL SKILLS STRATEGY

Many Rhetorical Skills questions look just like the Usage and Mechanics questions, accompanied by four answer choices. But others feature a bona fide question. Of those, Strategy questions are among the most common and confusing.

Strategy questions come in many different forms, but they all revolve around the *purpose* of the text. Among the different types of Strategy questions, expect to see questions asking you to add and replace text, determine if text should be added or deleted, evaluate the impact on the passage if text is deleted, or judge the overall effect of the passage on the reader.

Try a question.

Many of them, assuming that what they were hearing was genuine on-the-scene coverage, panicked; they were very frightened.
8

8. If all of the choices below are true, which of them best uses specific detail to convey the panic that the broadcast of *The War of the Worlds* caused?

F. NO CHANGE.
G. the highways were clogged with cars full of people seeking escape, and train stations were crowded with mobs willing to buy tickets to anywhere far away.
H. many felt that they had never encountered anything as terrifying in their lives and fully believed that what they were hearing was the absolute truth.
J. they did not stop to think that what they were hearing might be fiction; instead they leaped to the unlikely conclusion that an interplanetary invasion was indeed occurring.

Here's How to Crack It

Identify the purpose of the proposed text. According to the question, one of these choices *uses specific detail to convey the panic that the broadcast of* The War of the Worlds *caused*. We don't even need to go back into the passage: Find an answer choice that fulfills the purpose. Answer choices (F), (H), and (J) all may be true, but they do not offer any *specific detail* conveying the panic. Only (G) does that, and it is our correct answer.

Try another.

In addition to directing the production, Orson Welles also acted as the narrator of *The War of the Worlds.* [9]

9. At this point, the writer is considering adding the following true statement:

> In the 1970s, Orson Welles made television commercials for a winery.

Should the writer add this sentence here?

A. Yes, because it explains that Welles became famous outside of radio.
B. Yes, because it explains why many people forgot he directed and narrated *The War of the Worlds*.
C. No, because it doesn't explain why Welles stopped directing.
D. No, because it distracts the reader from the main point of this paragraph.

Here's How to Crack It

Whenever the strategy question asks if you should add or delete new text, evaluate the reasons in the answer choices carefully. The reason should correctly explain the purpose of the selected text. Here, choice (D) is correct because there is no reason to add text that is irrelevant to the topic.

Try another.

In the 1930s, most American households owned a radio. After all, it seems likely that most people would have questioned why all of the other radio stations continued to play their regular programs if such a disaster of global proportions were underway.

10. Given that all choices are true, which one provides the best opening to this paragraph?

F. NO CHANGE
G. Soon the reports of panic were dismissed as overblown if not outright false.
H. At the time of the broadcast, fears of a German invasion of Europe were growing.
J. Today, many Americans believe in life on other planets.

Here's How to Crack It

In many strategy questions, the purpose is to add a sentence to open or close a paragraph, or tie two paragraphs together. Use the context of the paragraph, and read through to the end before deciding. Since the author provides a reason why most listeners would have doubted the story, choice (G) provides the best introduction to the paragraph.

Three-to-Know Drill

Part 1A

In the following sentences, cross out the commas IF they are unnecessary or incorrectly placed. Some sentences have more than one comma error, and some sentences are correct as written.

1. The book, you're reading right now, looks really interesting.

2. I always meant to study more for the ACT, but I just couldn't find the time.

3. Jack loved to listen to music, and to play games on his new iPhone, which he had purchased the day before.

4. Every time, I go on Twitter, there's always something interesting next to something really annoying.

5. When I see an action movie, I love the explosions, but not the romantic subplot.

6. Every, single time I work out I feel like I'm going to puke.

7. The Flyers won the game in overtime, but they should have won it earlier.

8. My grandparents used to listen, to the radio, but now they just watch TV.

9. Of all the cities, I've visited, my favorites are probably Paris, France, and San Francisco, California.

10. Squash is not well known in the United States, yet it is one of the most popular sports, in Egypt.

11. Next time I go to the store, I'm going to get peanut butter, jelly, and, bread.

12. It seemed like the characters' treatment of their dog in the movie was exceedingly, inhumane, and hurtful.

13. On sunny summer days, history, museums don't seem so appealing.

14. Jazz, whether you like that style of music or not, was one of the most important cultural movements of the twentieth century.

15. Sometimes, when Americans, who love Chinese food, go to China, they find, ironically, that they don't like the food.

Part 1B

Add commas if necessary. If you add commas, state why you need them.

1. We'd like to hire you for the job and we hope you can start Monday.

   Why?

   _____

2. If you'd like to lose weight try eating better drinking more water and exercising regularly.

   Why?

   _____

3. The Philadelphia Phillies my favorite baseball team won the World Series in 2008.

   Why?

   _____

4. We took a scary drive on a dark stormy night.

   Why?

   _____

5. When used properly commas can really help to improve the clarity of a sentence.

   Why?

   _____

6. The lecturer's style was a little dull but so informative.

   Why?

   _____

7. I don't typically like Thai food yet I must admit I could drink Thai iced teas all day long.

   Why?

   _____

8. Some people still buy CDs but most have switched to digital music mainly for the convenience.

   Why?

   _____

9. I prefer a walk in the park to a walk around a city block.

Why?

_____

10. Around here you're out of luck if you won't buy your groceries at A&P Shop-Rite or Pathmark.

Why?

_____

11. The author Philip Roth wrote some of my favorite books.

Why?

_____

12. Sometimes I think plums the red ones especially are the best fruits in the world.

Why?

_____

13. Ice hockey is a fun challenging sport and it's great to watch.

Why?

_____

14. I don't think I could go five minutes without checking my e-mail or updating my Facebook status.

Why?

_____

15. When I was in college I had nothing but time but not anymore now that I'm working.

Why?

_____

Part 2A

In the following sentences, cross out any apostrophes that don't belong. If a word is spelled or used incorrectly because of an apostrophe error, write the correct word in the margin.

1. My arteries' seemed to get more and more clogged with every trip to the donut shop.

2. The pie was delicious when I first made it, but it's not so great anymore.

3. I absolutely did not expect them to be here on time, but they're they are.

4. If this device needs them, then why are there no battery's included?

5. I know the car seems out of her price range, but I'm pretty sure it's hers'.

6. It was time to go back to class, but the teacher didn't want to interrupt the children's game.

7. Do you have any idea who's letter this is?

8. Thank you so much for the cookies. Their delicious.

9. There's no dog in the world whose as much fun as ours'.

10. The politician ran on the idea that he was the people's candidate.

Part 2B

In the following sentences, add any apostrophes that are missing. If a word is spelled or used incorrectly because of an apostrophe error, write the correct word in the margin.

1. I need to start exercising more if I want to improve my arteries health.

2. St. Louis seems close to Chicago, but its actually five hours away by car.

3. I prefer red grapes, but there never available at the grocery store.

4. Because of all the corrosion, I cannot read the part where it lists this batteries charge.

5. There are two hamburgers here: one is his, and the other is hers.

6. The childrens treehouse was marked with a sign that said, "No Girls Allowed."

7. I cannot tell whose on the phone: I do not recognize the voice.

8. Were going to the concert later, so were trying to relearn some of the lyrics.

9. I think I see your car across the street, and ours is over there.

10. I thought the singer was terrible, and I had no idea why he was chosen as the peoples choice.

Part 2C

Choose the correct word from the parentheses.

1. My parents didn't give us permission, but (we're/were) going anyway.

2. I don't want to start a movie now: (it's/its) almost midnight!

3. My (adversary's/adversaries) favorite team was losing, and I was delighted.

4. (Who's/whose) child is this, and (who's/whose) responsible for him?

5. My wallet feels full right now, but most of the bills are (one's/ones).

6. The cat guarded (it's/its) toy, as if to suggest, "(It's/Its) mine."

7. These (dictionary's/dictionaries) seem identical to me, so I'm not sure which one to get.

8. I thought my essay was pretty good, but (her's/hers) was much better.

9. Were you the one looking for the lost sunglasses? (They're/There) over (they're/there).

10. You can say (it's/its) (society's/societies) fault all you want: I still insist (it's/its) (your's/yours).

Part 3A

Find the correct answer using only the information given in the question.

1. Which of the following choices would most effectively communicate the parents' <u>skeptical attitude</u> toward the narrator's plans?
   A. Enthusiastically,
   B. Distracted by other tasks,
   C. Because they were older,
   D. Despite their clear doubts,

2. Which of the following begins this paragraph and conveys the <u>importance of this album</u>?
   F. The Mars Volta's debut album was just like the debut albums of many other bands: underappreciated.
   G. It's hard to choose a single Mars Volta album to represent the band's huge range.
   H. The Mars Volta's debut album showed that a band could write complex, unique music but still sell records.
   J. There was a time when it seemed like progressive rock would never reach the major labels again.

3. Given that all the choices are true, which one best develops the paragraph's focus on <u>the place of radio in Welles' career</u>?

   A. Welles' voice performances over the airwaves well outnumber his appearances in film.
   B. Though he is best known for film, Welles was initially a famed director in the theater.
   C. Welles performed in thousands of radio broadcasts, but many of them are lost today.
   D. Many Americans considered radio their main news source during the Second World War, and Welles was no exception.

4. Given that all the choices are true, which one would most clearly suggest the <u>songwriting collaboration</u> between Lennon and McCartney?

   F. listened to the song.
   G. liked the song more than he thought he would.
   H. thought about the song a lot the next day.
   J. heard one part of the song, then added his own.

5. Given that all the choices are true, which one is most relevant to the writer's intention to help readers <u>hear the sound</u> produced by the car horn?

   A. almost like two trumpets playing dissonant notes.
   B. as if the driver were honking in a panic.
   C. like the horn on one of the other cars in the traffic jam.
   D. just like a horn I remembered hearing on the road in Italy.

Part 3B

Using only the information given in the question, cross off the answer choices that could NOT be the correct answer. Any of the remaining answers could be the correct answer, but without the essay, it's impossible to pick for certain.

15. Suppose the writer's goal had been to write a brief <u>persuasive essay encouraging students to question what they are taught in school</u>. Would this essay fulfill that goal?

   A. Yes, because the essay lists examples of Harleen questioning what her teachers taught her.
   B. Yes, because the essay focuses on scientific discoveries made by students outside the classroom.
   C. No, because the level of strictness varies depending on the type of school one attends.
   D. No, because the essay gives only one example of a student who disagreed with his teachers.

30. Suppose the writer's goal had been to write an essay that details how religious study influences the work of famous philosophers. Would this essay successfully fulfill that goal?

   F. Yes, because the essay makes clear that Walter Benjamin's study of Jewish tradition influenced his philosophical writings.
   G. Yes, because the essay suggests that Benjamin was very devout.
   H. No, because the essay outlines only a single philosopher's engagement with religious writings and tradition.
   J. No, because the essay demonstrates that Benjamin's study of Jewish texts had no influence on his philosophical writings.

45. Suppose the writer's goal was to draft an essay that would show the connection between economic conditions and voting patterns. Would this essay fulfill that goal?

   A. Yes, because it links Franklin Roosevelt's New Deal to the economic depression in the 1930s.
   B. Yes, because it details a historical event and focuses on one president's rise to power.
   C. No, because it is focused mainly on the rise of the Republican party in American politics.
   D. No, because it shows the economic conditions in the 1930s but does not show those conditions in later decades.

60. Suppose the author intended to write an essay that shows that athletes' skills often bear no relation to the environment in which those athletes are raised. Would this essay successfully fulfill that goal?

   F. Yes, because the essay describes Robyn Regehr's long, successful career in the NHL.
   G. Yes, because the essay shows that Robyn Regehr became a professional hockey player even though he was born in Brazil.
   H. No, because the author focuses on Robyn Regehr and his career rather than on athletes in general.
   J. No, because the essay reveals that Regehr's family returned to Canada when he was seven.

75. Suppose the author intended to write a sketch of a painter that would show that painter's contributions to the art world. Does this essay successfully accomplish that goal?

   A. Yes, because it outlines Kehinde Wiley's career as an artist and his unique position among twentieth-century artists.
   B. Yes, because it details how Kehinde Wiley became interested in art history and eventually chose to become an artist.
   C. No, because it does not succeed in showing that Kehinde Wiley has contributed in any substantial way to the art world.
   D. No, because it doesn't adequately list Kehinde Wiley's inspirations, models, and awards.

THREE-TO-KNOW DRILL ANSWERS AND EXPLANATIONS

Part 1A

1. The book/ you're reading right now/ looks really interesting.
2. I always meant to study more for the ACT, but I just couldn't find the time.
3. Jack loved to listen to music/ and to play games on his new iPhone, which he had purchased the day before.
4. Every time/ I go on Twitter, there's always something interesting next to something really annoying.
5. When I see an action movie, I love the explosions/ but not the romantic subplot.
6. Every/ single time I work out I feel like I'm going to puke.
7. The Flyers won the game in overtime, but they should have won it earlier.
8. My grandparents used to listen/ to the radio, but now they just watch TV.
9. Of all the cities/ I've visited, my favorites are probably Paris, France/ and San Francisco, California.
10. Squash is not well known in the United States, yet it is one of the most popular sports/ in Egypt.
11. Next time I go to the store, I'm going to get peanut butter, jelly, and/ bread.
12. It seemed like the characters' treatment of their dog in the movie was exceedingly/ inhumane/ and hurtful.
13. On sunny summer days, history/ museums don't seem so appealing.
14. Jazz, whether you like that style of music or not, was one of the most important cultural movements of the twentieth century.
15. Sometimes, when Americans/ who love Chinese food/ go to China, they find, ironically, that they don't like the food.

Part 1B

1. We'd like to hire you for the job↓ and we hope you can start Monday.

   Why? Stop.

2. If you'd like to lose weight↓ try eating better↓ drinking more water↓ and exercising regularly.

   Why? Go, List.

3. The Philadelphia Phillies↓ my favorite baseball team↓ won the World Series in 2008.

   Why? Unnecessary information

4. We took a scary drive on a dark, stormy night.

   Why? List.

5. When used properly, commas can really help to improve the clarity of a sentence.

   Why? Go.

6. The lecturer's style was a little dull but so informative.

   Why? No commas necessary.

7. I don't typically like Thai food, yet I must admit I could drink Thai iced teas all day long.

   Why? Stop.

8. Some people still buy CDs, but most have switched to digital music, mainly for the convenience.

   Why? Stop, Go.

9. I prefer a walk in the park to a walk around a city block.

   Why? No commas necessary.

10. Around here, you're out of luck if you won't buy your groceries at A&P, Shop-Rite, or Pathmark.

    Why? Go, List.

11. The author Philip Roth wrote some of my favorite books.

    Why? No commas necessary.

12. Sometimes I think plums, the red ones especially, are the best fruits in the world.

    Why? Unnecessary information

13. Ice hockey is a fun, challenging sport, and it's great to watch.

    Why? List, Stop.

14. I don't think I could go five minutes without checking my e-mail or updating my Facebook status.

   Why? No commas necessary

15. When I was in college, I had nothing but time but not anymore now that I'm working.

   Why? Go.

Part 2A

1. My arteries seemed to get more and more clogged with every trip to the donut shop.
2. The pie was delicious when I first made it, but it's not so great anymore.
3. I absolutely did not expect them to be here on time, but ~~they're~~ ^{there} they are.
4. If this device needs them, then why are there no ~~battery's~~ ^{batteries} included?
5. I know the car seems out of her price range, but I'm pretty sure it's hers.
6. It was time to go back to class, but the teacher didn't want to interrupt the children's game.
7. Do you have any idea ~~who's~~ ^{whose} letter this is?
8. Thank you so much for the cookies. ~~Their~~ ^{They're} delicious.
9. There's no dog in the world who's as much fun as ours.
10. The politician ran on the idea that he was the people's candidate.

Part 2B

1. I need to start exercising more if I want to improve my **arteries'** health.
2. St. Louis seems close to Chicago, but **it's** actually five hours away by car.
3. I prefer red grapes, but **they're** never available at the grocery store.
4. Because of all the corrosion, I cannot read the part where it lists this **battery's** charge.
5. There are two hamburgers here: one is his, and the other is hers.
6. The **children's** treehouse was marked with a sign that said, "No Girls Allowed."
7. I cannot tell **who's** on the phone: I do not recognize the voice.
8. **We're** going to the concert later, so **we're** trying to relearn some of the lyrics.
9. I think I see your car across the street, and ours is over there.
10. I thought the singer was terrible, and I had no idea why he was chosen as the **people's** choice.

Part 2C

1. My parents didn't give us permission, but **we're** going anyway.
2. I don't want to start a movie now: **it's** almost midnight!
3. My **adversary's** favorite team was losing, and I was delighted at his agony.
4. **Whose** child is this, and **who's** responsible for him?
5. My wallet feels full right now, but most of the bills are **ones**.
6. The cat guarded **its** toy, as if to suggest, "**It's** mine."
7. These **dictionaries** seem identical to me, so I'm not sure which one to get.
8. I thought my essay was pretty good, but **hers** was much better.
9. Were you the one looking for the lost sunglasses? **They're** over **there**.
10. You can say **it's society's** fault all you want: I still insist **it's yours**.

Part 3A

1. D
2. H
3. A
4. J
5. A

Part 3B

15. B, C
30. G
45. A, B
60. F
75. B, D

Summary

o   Identify what the question is testing by changes in the answer choices.

o   Use POE heavily.

o   Don't skip the non-underlined text: Use it for context.

o   Trust your ear, but verify by the rules.

o   NO CHANGE is a legitimate answer choice.

o   Good writing should be complete, consistent, clear, and concise.

o   There are only four reasons to use a comma. Name the reason to add a comma, and always be biased toward a choice with no commas.

o   Use an apostrophe with nouns to show possession. Use an apostrophe with pronouns to make a contraction. Be careful of your ear with contractions, since possessive pronouns will sound the same as a pronoun with a contraction.

o   Strategy questions always involve a purpose. Identify the purpose in the question, and pick an answer choice consistent with that purpose.

Chapter 3
English Practice
Test 1

ACT ENGLISH TEST
45 Minutes—75 Questions

DIRECTIONS: In the five passages that follow, certain words and phrases are underlined and numbered. In the right-hand column, you will find alternatives for each underlined part. In most cases, you are to choose the one that best expresses the idea, makes the statement appropriate for standard written English, or is worded most consistently with the style and tone of the passage as a whole. If you think the original version is best, choose "NO CHANGE." In some cases, you will find in the right-hand column a question about the underlined part. You are to choose the best answer to the question.

You will also find questions about a section of the passage or the passage as a whole. These questions do not refer to an underlined portion of the passage but rather are identified by a number or numbers in a box.

For each question, choose the alternative you consider best and blacken the corresponding oval on your answer document. Read each passage through once before you begin to answer the questions that accompany it. For many of the questions, you must read several sentences beyond the question to determine the answer. Be sure that you have read far enough ahead each time you choose an alternative.

PASSAGE I

What You See Isn't What You Get

Two freshmen stand, looking uncertainly at what appears to be a pleasant seating area just ahead. There are two tables: one is occupied by a young woman but the other is empty. <u>Nevertheless,</u> no one else seems to be considering walking in.
[1]

That's because the seating area is actually a life-size <u>painting on the wall</u> of one of the campus buildings.
[2]

A life-size seating area that's only a painting? That's John Pugh's specialty: <u>large-scale public art that is available for anyone to see.</u> He employs the trompe l'oeil, or "trick of the
[3]
eye," style. His paintings are strikingly realistic, <u>having carefully included shadows and reflections, making his</u>
[4]
paintings appear to be three-dimensional, as well as numerous details. The cafe scene includes not only the young woman <u>and</u>
[5]
also a statute, a framed piece of art, and a small cat, peering around a corner. [6]

1. Which of the following alternatives to the underlined portion would NOT be acceptable?
   - A. However,
   - B. Therefore,
   - C. Still,
   - D. And yet,

2. F. NO CHANGE
   - G. painting, on the wall,
   - H. painting, on the wall
   - J. painting; on the wall

3. A. NO CHANGE
   - B. large-scale public art
   - C. public art for everyone
   - D. art that is public and freely available

4. F. NO CHANGE
   - G. always including a variety of
   - H. due to Pugh's inclusion of
   - J. being careful to include

5. A. NO CHANGE
   - B. nor
   - C. or
   - D. but

6. If the writer were to delete the question "A life-size painting that's only a painting?" from this paragraph, the essay would primarily lose:
   - F. an acknowledgement that Pugh's work might seem unusual to some.
   - G. a statement of the writer's central thesis for the remainder of the essay.
   - H. an argumentative and persuasive tone.
   - J. nothing, because the question simply confuses the main idea.

In another of his paintings, a wave looms across the entire front of a building. The painting is immense, the wave looks like it's about to crash, and three children appears to stand
<u>7</u>

directly in its path. <u>Being life-size and incredibly life-like,</u> a
<u>8</u>
group of firefighters ran over to save the "children" shortly before the piece was completed. When the men got close enough to realize it was only a painting, they had a good laugh. No one seems to mind being fooled by Pugh's paintings. Most people, like the firefighters, are just impressed by Pugh's skill. [9]

Pugh believes that by creating public art, he can
<u>10</u>
communicate with a larger audience than if his art were in a
<u>10</u>
gallery. Many of his pieces, including the café scene described
<u>10</u>
above, use the existing architecture. One of his other pieces

created the illusion that part of a building's wall has collapsed,
<u>11</u>
revealing an ancient Egyptian storeroom in the middle of Los Gatos, California. Like the café scene, the Egyptian scene includes a human figure. [A] In this case, however, the woman is not part of the scene. [B] Instead, she appears to be a passer-by, peering in to the revealed room. [C] Cities around the world have commissioned works from Pugh. [D] It is Pugh's ability to create an apparent mystery in the middle

---

7. A. NO CHANGE
   B. appeared
   C. appear
   D. was appearing

8. F. NO CHANGE
   G. Stopping their truck in the middle of traffic,
   H. Appearing young enough to be swept away,
   J. Like so many of Pugh's other works,

9. If the writer were to remove the quotation marks around the word "children," the paragraph would primarily lose:

   A. an explanation of why the firemen were so concerned about the wave.
   B. a rhetorical device that lessens the reader's fear.
   C. a way to distinguish between the painted wave and the real children.
   D. emphasis on the fact that the children were painted, not real.

10. Given that all the choices are true, which one best conveys the theory behind Pugh's method as discussed in the remainder of the paragraph?

   F. NO CHANGE
   G. Pugh prefers incorporating his work into the pre-existing environment to simply adding his art without regard for its surroundings.
   H. Drawing his inspiration from many different cultures, Pugh enjoys startling the viewer by placing objects in an unexpected context.
   J. The firefighters may not have been upset at Pugh's trick but they were certainly startled, just like so many other people who see Pugh's work.

11. A. NO CHANGE
   B. is creating
   C. creates
   D. creating

of everyday life that makes his work speak to so much people.
                                                        —12—
After all, who doesn't appreciate being tricked once in a while?

13

12. **F.** NO CHANGE
    G. more
    H. most
    J. many

13. If the writer were to divide this paragraph into two, the most logical place to begin the new paragraph would be at Point:

    A. A.
    B. B.
    C. C.
    D. D.

Question 14 asks about the preceding passage as a whole.

---

14. Suppose the writer's goal had been to write a passage exploring some of the current trends in the art community. Would this essay accomplish that goal?

    F. Yes, because it looks at a variety of styles popular among muralists throughout the Los Angeles area.
    G. Yes, because is considers some of the reasons for Pugh's preference for large-scale public art.
    H. No, because it only explores Pugh's artistic vision without considering the broader context of the art world.
    J. No, because it details a number of incidents in which people have been confused by Pugh's artwork.

PASSAGE II

Leaving the Nest

My mother flew out with me and stayed for a few days, to make the transition easier for me. We went shopping and bought odds and ends for my dorm room—pillows, small decorative items, even a few pots and pans—to make it feel more like home. It felt more like a vacation than anything else.

Then suddenly her brief stay was over. Her plane was leaving for San Juan, and I realized I wasn't going with her. She was going home, but I already was home. This strange new city was my home now. Sitting on my bed in the dorm room that remained half-empty, it hit me. I had just turned eighteen. I was about to start college in a new place, with a new language, a new culture. I had just said my first real farewell to a mother whom I had never before been away from for more than a weekend. I had to learn how to live on my own, with mi

familia so many miles away and me all by myself.

During high school, I had fantasized about moving to the United States someday. I was born in a sleepy, rural village in southern Puerto Rico. My high school class had fifty people in it, and the small town where I grow up was a very close-knit community. I had spent hours imagining what it would be like to be surrounded not by a few dozen people but by a few million.

Living in such a small town, I was used to knowing everyone and having everyone know me. The very first

15. **A.** NO CHANGE
    B. pans; to make
    C. pans: to make
    D. pans. To make

16. **F.** NO CHANGE
    G. As I sat on the bed in my half-empty dorm room,
    H. Nervously looking around the half-empty dorm room,
    J. Looking around the half-empty dorm room from my bed,

17. Which of the following choices is most logically supported by the first part of the sentence?

    A. NO CHANGE
    B. who had always done my laundry, prepared my meals, and kissed me goodnight.
    C. whom I hoped was having a pleasant flight back to San Juan and then on to our village.
    D. who had herself spent some years living in the United States in her twenties, before I was born.

18. **F.** NO CHANGE
    G. and no one with me.
    H. not with me any more.
    J. DELETE the underlined portion and end the sentence with a period.

19. **A.** NO CHANGE
    B. grew
    C. grown
    D. growth

20. Given that all the choices are true, which provides the best transition to the topic discussed in the rest of the paragraph?

    F. NO CHANGE
    G. The idea of being surrounded by so many people, and being able to meet and talk with any of them seemed like a dream come true.
    H. When the time came to apply to colleges, I picked several, all in major metropolitan areas in the continental United States.
    J. I had considered applying to colleges in San Juan but decided that it was still too close to home, too familiar, too easy.

acceptance received by me was from this school, located in the
———————————
21
middle of a city with millions of inhabitants. My parents

were so proud that I get this opportunity to see the world
————
22
outside of our village. They had spent enough time outside

of Puerto Rico in the United States to know that the English
————————————
23
language was not the only thing that was different. We

celebrated the weekend before I left, inviting all the neighbors

over to my parents home. We played music and ate and danced
—————
24

past midnight. 25

As the memory faded; I looked around my new room
——————————
26
again. Sure, it was small and a little bit dingy. True, I didn't
know anyone yet. None of that mattered, though. I had finally
made it. My new roommate would be arriving the next day.
Hopefully she would be a new friend and even if she wasn't,
my classes were starting in a few days. I had literally millions
of people to meet; surely a few of them would become my new
friends. I smiled, suddenly feeling nervous but excited, not
—————————
27

21. **A.** NO CHANGE
    B. acceptance I received
    C. acceptance, I received,
    D. acceptance, receiving by me

22. **F.** NO CHANGE
    G. will get
    H. was getting
    J. had to get

23. The best placement for the underlined portion would be:
    A. where it is now.
    B. after the word time.
    C. after the word language.
    D. after the word different (and before the period).

24. **F.** NO CHANGE
    G. parents's
    H. parent's
    J. parents'

25. At this point, the writer is considering adding the following true statement:

    My favorite dance has always been la bomba.

    Should the writer make this addition here?

    A. Yes, because it adds a detail that helps explain the personality of the narrator.
    B. Yes, because it provides a smooth transition to the following paragraph.
    C. No, because it gives the false impression that the narrator will study dance in college.
    D. No, because it would be an unnecessary digression from the main point of the paragraph.

26. **F.** NO CHANGE
    G. faded, and I looked
    H. faded, I looked
    J. faded. I looked

27. Which of the following alternatives to the underlined portion would NOT be acceptable?
    A. excitement nervous
    B. nervously excited
    C. nervous excitement
    D. excitedly nervous

lonely any more. I was eighteen, in the city, and <u>had to face</u>
₂₈

the world. [29]

28. Which choice most effectively expresses the narrator's confidence about her new life?

    F. NO CHANGE
    G. ready to take on
    H. all alone in
    J. about to enter

29. The writer is considering adding a concluding sentence here. Which of the following would be most logical and best express one of the main ideas of the essay?

    A. Still, I knew I would miss Puerto Rico and my friends I had left behind.
    B. Little did I know that my new roommate would become a lifelong friend.
    C. My dreams of living in the big city were finally going to become a reality.
    D. I hoped that my classes would be as exciting as my move had been.

PASSAGE III

Dual Personalities

[1]

When Lois Lane finds herself in serious danger, she looks
to Superman for help. When she needed help with an article,
on the other hand, she calls on Clark Kent. Of course, as the
reader knows, the two men are actually the same person.

30. **F.** NO CHANGE
    G. in need of
    H. she was needing
    J. needed

[2]

The tradition of giving superheroes alternate names and
characters, or "alter-egos" goes back as far as superhero stories
do. Today, when it's a commonplace writing technique.
Batman fights crime by night, but he poses as millionaire Bruce

31. **A.** NO CHANGE
    B. where
    C. because
    D. DELETE the underlined portion.

Wayne at day. Spider-Man protects the streets of New York—

32. **F.** NO CHANGE
    G. for
    H. by
    J. DELETE the underlined portion.

when he's not busy going to school as Peter Parker. [33]

33. At this point, the writer is thinking about adding the following
true statement:

> Wonder Woman, on the other hand, is always herself,
> since she comes from a tribe of warrior women.

Should the writer make this addition here?

   A. Yes, because it provides a balance for the previous examples of Batman and Spider-Man.
   B. Yes, because it emphasizes the author's earlier claim that the alter-ego is commonplace.
   C. No, because it strays from the primary focus of the passage by providing irrelevant information.
   D. No, because it poses the unnecessary hypothetical that no superhero really needs an alternate identity.

[3]

Each of the superheroes have something in his (or her)
back-story to explain the dual character. They all have a few
things in common too, though. Superheroes have a certain
image—the costume and the name, for example; that helps

34. **F.** NO CHANGE
    G. has
    H. is having
    J. are having

35. **A.** NO CHANGE
    B. for example,
    C. for example.
    D. for example—

them maintain their authority. If Batman didn't fight crime, he would probably do something else to deal with his past. Peter
<u>36</u>

Parker isn't a very awe-inspiring <u>name, but</u> Spider-Man is. At
<u>37</u>
the same time, the hero often has friends and family members

who are somehow completely unaware of their loved <u>ones'</u>
<u>38</u>

other identity. <u>Providing</u> the superheroes with everyday names
<u>39</u>

and jobs helps <u>in their</u> attempts to fit in with the people around
<u>40</u>
them.

[4]

Stan <u>Lee, creator of Spider-Man,</u> and dozens of other
<u>41</u>
superheroes, has often commented on what he believes makes
a true hero. His opinion is that in order for the reader to care
about the hero, the hero has to be flawed. <u>Do you agree with</u>
<u>42</u>
<u>him?</u> According to Lee, without some kind of flaw, the hero
<u>42</u>

wouldn't really seem human. Lee builds <u>tension, in his stories,</u>
<u>43</u>
by putting those human flaws and the hero's quest into conflict.
It is that tension, perhaps, that makes his storylines so gripping.
Even Superman, the least "normal" of all the heroes, has to
deal with the tension between his love for Lois Lane and her

36. Given that all the choices are true, which one provides the best support for the statement in the preceding sentence?

  F. NO CHANGE
  G. Batman, who lost his parents when he was young, were younger, he might have a harder time.
  H. Batman were just a regular-looking man, it would be harder for him to strike fear into the heart of criminals.
  J. Batman needed to, he could probably fight criminals without his gadgets since he knows several martial arts.

37. Which of the following alternatives to the underlined portion would NOT be acceptable?

  A. name; on the other hand,
  B. name, because
  C. name, although
  D. name; however,

38. F. NO CHANGE
  G. one's
  H. individuals
  J. individuals'

39. A. NO CHANGE
  B. Assuming
  C. Offering
  D. Allowing for

40. F. NO CHANGE
  G. it's
  H. his
  J. one's

41. A. NO CHANGE
  B. Lee creator of Spider-Man,
  C. Lee creator of Spider-Man
  D. Lee, creator of Spider-Man

42. Which choice provides the most logical and effective transition to the rest of this paragraph?

  F. NO CHANGE
  G. Why would anyone want a hero to be less than perfect?
  H. Are you familiar with Lee's various characters?
  J. What kind of flaw could a superhero have?

43. A. NO CHANGE
  B. tension in his stories
  C. tension in his stories,
  D. tension, in his stories

love for Superman, not Clark Kent. 44

44. The writer is considering deleting the preceding sentence. Should this sentence be kept or deleted?

F. Kept, because it provides a specific example of the theory being discussed throughout the paragraph.

G. Kept, because it demonstrates that the ultimate superhero will not seem human under any circumstances.

H. Deleted, because it takes away from the persuasiveness of the point made in the previous sentences.

J. Deleted, because it switches the focus from the more "human" superheroes to the "least" human of them.

Question 45 asks about the preceding passage as a whole.

45. While reviewing this essay, the writer thinks of some additional information and writes the following sentence:

Even though many readers feel that Lane's ignorance is hard to believe, the Clark Kent persona provides a valuable, and time-honored, element to the Superhero story: the alter-ego.

If the writer were to include this sentence in the essay, the most logical place to add it would be after the last sentence in Paragraph:

A. 1.
B. 2.
C. 3.
D. 4.

PASSAGE IV

Curly Hair: The Circular Trend

Is curly hair a blessing or a curse? Passing trends, which can last a day or a decade, typically influence hairstyles, which can vary dramatically; every bit as much as clothing. Some
<u>dramatically; every bit as much as clothing.</u> Some
[46]
segment of the population will therefore always be fighting the natural tendency of their hair, unless the fashion becomes natural hair.

[47] In the 1950s, curls were in, and the average American woman spent countless hours pinning, rolling, and curling her hair every week. Without blowdryers or curling irons, women were left with few options, maintaining properly stylish

hair-dos <u>to work hard</u> and a great deal of time. By the mid-
[48]
1960s, a lot of women started to wonder whether all that work was really necessary. Suddenly, natural hair was all the rage. Women began to grow <u>they're</u> hair out and allow it to remain in
[49]
its natural state, whether curly or straight. For a brief moment, it looked like women would be able to embrace their natural hair, whether straight or curly, light or dark, or <u>having length or</u>
[50]
<u>being short.</u>
[50]

The change <u>was short-lived, however, and didn't last for</u>
[51]
long, perhaps unsurprisingly. The desire to have long, natural hair somehow turned into the desire to have long, straight hair. During the 1970s, the movie and television <u>star Farrah Fawcett</u>
[52]
popularized a look that involved long hair that seemed naturally straight and feathered—cut into layers designed to frame the

46. **F.** NO CHANGE
    G. dramatically, being every
    H. dramatically, every
    J. dramatically. Every

47. Given that all of the following statements are true, which one, if added here, would most clearly and effectively introduce the main subject of this paragraph?
    A. Some people don't care for curly hair because it is considered more difficult to style than straight hair is.
    B. As far back as the Renaissance, people have faked having curly hair by wearing wigs and using curlers.
    C. Curly hair has bounced in and out of the American fashion scene for at least the last fifty years.
    D. Clothing styles also change frequently, and sometimes influence hairstyles in a direct, easily visible way.

48. **F.** NO CHANGE
    G. was hardly work
    H. with hard work
    J. by working hard

49. **A.** NO CHANGE
    B. their
    C. there
    D. her

50. **F.** NO CHANGE
    G. and regardless of length.
    H. which can be long or short.
    J. long or short.

51. **A.** NO CHANGE
    B. wasn't fated to continue, though, so it
    C. predictably enough failed to stick and
    D. DELETE the underlined portion.

52. **F.** NO CHANGE
    G. star, Farrah Fawcett
    H. star, Farrah Fawcett,
    J. star Farrah Fawcett,

face—yet slightly messy. [53] Women who had

naturally curly hair <u>were suddenly</u> the ones to suffer now, as
₅₄
they painstakingly ironed their hair to achieve that "natural"
look. The fashions of the 1980s, however, turned everything
around yet again. Big was in, and that went for hair as well as
clothes. Curly hair became incredibly popular, and <u>the main
₅₅
fashion goal was to make one's hair as curly and as big as
₅₅
possible.</u> Women who didn't have natural curls got "permanent
₅₅

waves," or "perms" to create the rampant curls <u>modeled</u> by
₅₆
their pop icons, such as Cyndi Lauper and Gloria Estefan.

[1] By the middle of the 1990s, however, the perm had
lost its appeal, and straight hair was back in fashion where it
remains today. [2] Some <u>commentator's</u> have recently claimed
₅₇
that curly hair is making a comeback, but only time will
tell. [3] Instead of using an iron, women can have their hair
chemically straightened in a sort of "reverse perm." [4] While
it's hard to know what the trend of tomorrow will be, one thing
seems certain: no style lasts forever. [58]

53. The writer is considering deleting the phrase "cut into
layers designed to frame the face" from the preceding sentence (adjusting the punctuation as needed). Should this
sentence be kept or deleted?

  A. Kept, because it contrasts the style popularized by Fawcett with earlier styles.
  B. Kept, because it defines the word used immediately
before the phrase.
  C. Deleted, because it fails to adequately explain the term
it is intended to modify.
  D. Deleted, because it digresses from the main point of the
paragraph.

54. F. NO CHANGE
  G. suddenly we're
  H. sudden were
  J. sudden we're

55. A. NO CHANGE
  B. the curlier, the better.
  C. it.
  D. it didn't seem possible to have hair that was too curly, or
too big to be fashionable.

56. Which of the following alternatives to the underlined portion would NOT be acceptable?

  F. worn
  G. displayed
  H. imitated
  J. popularized

57. A. NO CHANGE
  B. commentators
  C. commentators'
  D. commentators's

58. For the sake of the logic and coherence of this paragraph,
Sentence 3 should be placed:

  F. where it is now.
  G. before Sentence 1.
  H. after Sentence 1.
  J. after Sentence 4.

Question 59 asks about the preceding passage as a whole.

59. Suppose the writer had been instructed to write an essay discussing modern attitudes towards curly hair. Would this essay meet that requirement?

A. Yes, because it explains why some women prefer to wear their hair straight, regardless of current fashions.

B. Yes, because it analyzes the reasons behind changes in fashion that affect the popularity of curly hair.

C. No, because it focuses more on the changeability of fashions than the attitudes towards them.

D. No, because it focuses primarily on the popularity of straight hair and the effort of style maintenance.

PASSAGE V

Marie Curie: Physicist, Chemist, and Woman

Marie Curie is famous today for two main reasons: her scientific discoveries and her defiance of gender stereotypes. She, along with her husband, identified two new elements, polonium and radium. She then coined the term "radioactive"
[60]

and developed a theory to explain the phenomenon. Curie first began to research radioactivity after noticing that the amount of radiation produced by a sample depended wholly on the quantity of uranium in the sample.
[61]

Curie was proficient in the fields of physics and chemistry, though her education was somewhat unusual, which prevented [62] her from attending university due to a lack of money, Curie [62] initially studied in a laboratory run by her cousin. Determined to pursue her love of science, Curie eventually enrolled at the University of Paris, where she later became the first female [63] professor.

60. The writer is considering deleting the underlined phrase and adjusting the punctuation accordingly. If the phrase were removed, the paragraph would primarily lose:

F. a specific detail that provides information about the result of some of Curie's research.

G. an explanation of how Curie was able to make such a variety of important scientific discoveries.

H. information that identifies the reason Curie was awarded two Nobel prizes.

J. a definition of radioactivity included by the writer and necessary to the paragraph as a whole.

61. Given that all of the choices are true, which provides the most effective transition from this paragraph into the rest of the essay?

A. NO CHANGE

B. Due to her discoveries, she was both the first woman to receive a Nobel Prize and the first person to receive two Nobel Prizes, though her road to success was paved with difficulties.

C. Although physics and chemistry are treated as separate fields, like so many other branches of science, the two are so interconnected in some areas that it can be difficult to tell them apart.

D. Curie's husband, Pierre, was also a noted scientist who wrote several famous pieces on magnetism, including one that detailed the relationship between temperature and paramagnetism.

62. F. NO CHANGE
G. unusual, prevented
H. unusual. Prevented
J. unusual prevented her

63. A. NO CHANGE
B. like
C. when
D. DELETE the underlined portion.

While Curie is widely given recognition and credit for
<u>
</u>₆₄ discovering radioactivity, this is not entirely accurate. Henri
Becquerel, a French scientist, has that honor. When Curie
made her discovery, Becquerel had already saw that rays,
₆₅
functioning much like X-rays but produced by uranium salt,
existed; however, he did not identify the underlying process.
Becquerel of radioactivity was performing
₆₆

experimental involving photographic paper, and the discovery
₆₇
was accidental. He realized that something was exposing the
photographic paper to rays even before he placed the paper in
the sunlight. Nevertheless, further experiments revealed that
₆₈
the substance emitting rays was the fluorescent substance,
potassium uranyl sulfate.

However, Becquerel didn't identify the underlying
scientific principal, namely, that the rays were produced not by
₆₉
a molecular interaction but by the atom itself. Curie was

the first to make this discovery; it was she that isolated, and
₇₀
identified radium and polonium. The earliest scientist to
realize that there was an element in the fluorescent substance
more reactive than uranium, Curie dedicated the next twelve
₇₁
years to developing a method for isolating that substance,

which was not yet known but later came to be identified and is
₇₂
now called "radium."
₇₂

64. F. NO CHANGE
    G. credited and acknowledged as the person responsible for
    H. generally credited with
    J. appreciated often as deserving credit and recognition for

65. A. NO CHANGE
    B. has already seen
    C. had already seen
    D. has already saw

66. The most logical placement of the underlined portion
    would be:

    F. where it is now.
    G. after the word performing.
    H. after the word paper.
    J. after the word discovery.

67. A. NO CHANGE
    B. an experimental
    C. experimentally
    D. an experiment

68. F. NO CHANGE
    G. Subsequently, further
    H. Further
    J. In contrast, further

69. A. NO CHANGE
    B. principle namely,
    C. principal namely,
    D. principle: namely,

70. F. NO CHANGE
    G. isolated
    H. isolated it
    J. isolated—

71. A. NO CHANGE
    B. uranium;
    C. uranium
    D. uranium:

72. F. NO CHANGE
    G. we now know as radium.
    H. scientists and laypeople alike are familiar with today
       under the name "radium."
    J. people in the present day refer to under the name of
       "radium."

Curie was progressive for a chemist; much less for a
<u>73</u>

woman. Women in science would of often had a difficult
<u>74</u>

time, and Curie was no exception. She was refused a position at Krakow University due to her gender, and was ultimately denied membership in the French Academy of Sciences. However, the general consensus is that Curie was not bitter about these rejections. Instead, she worked as hard as she
<u>75</u>

could even when she wondered whether she would ever be
<u>75</u>

recognized. She was a woman who knew her own worth, even
<u>75</u>

when others did not: a trait as valuable today as during the eighteenth century.

73. A. NO CHANGE
B. chemist,
C. chemist; moreover,
D. chemist so

74. F. NO CHANGE
G. might of
H. have
J. has

75. Given that all the choices are true, which one provides the most consistent description of Curie's personality as described in this paragraph?

A. NO CHANGE
B. became somewhat reclusive in her later years, preferring her work to society.
C. spent many years in her eventually successful attempt to identify the source of Becquerel's mysterious rays.
D. was generally described by those who knew her as persistent, friendly, and humble.

END OF TEST 1
STOP! DO NOT TURN THE PAGE UNTIL TOLD TO DO SO.

Chapter 4
English Practice
Test 1
Answers and
Explanations

ENGLISH PRACTICE TEST 1 ANSWERS

1.	B		39.	A
2.	F		40.	F
3.	B		41.	D
4.	H		42.	G
5.	D		43.	B
6.	F		44.	F
7.	C		45.	A
8.	G		46.	H
9.	D		47.	C
10.	G		48.	H
11.	C		49.	B
12.	J		50.	J
13.	C		51.	D
14.	H		52.	F
15.	A		53.	B
16.	G		54.	F
17.	A		55.	B
18.	J		56.	H
19.	B		57.	B
20.	H		58.	H
21.	B		59.	C
22.	H		60.	F
23.	D		61.	B
24.	J		62.	H
25.	D		63.	A
26.	H		64.	H
27.	A		65.	C
28.	G		66.	J
29.	C		67.	D
30.	G		68.	H
31.	D		69.	D
32.	H		70.	G
33.	C		71.	A
34.	G		72.	G
35.	D		73.	B
36.	H		74.	H
37.	B		75.	D
38.	G			

SCORE YOUR PRACTICE TEST

Step A
Count the number of correct answers: _____. This is your ***raw score***.

Step B
Use the score conversion table below to look up your raw score. The number to the left is your ***scale score***: ___31_____ .

English Scale Conversion Table

Scale Score	Raw Score	Scale Score	Raw Score	Scale Score	Raw Score
36	75	27	62	18	41–42
35	73–74	26	60–61	17	39–40
34	71–72	25	58–59	16	36–38
33	70	24	56–57	15	33–35
32	69	23	54–55	14	30–32
31	67–68	22	52–53	13	28–29
30	66	21	49–51	12	26–27
29	65	20	46–48	11	24–25
28	63–64	19	43–45	10	22–23

ENGLISH PRACTICE TEST 1 EXPLANATIONS

Passage I

1. **B** The question asks you to find the answer choice that is NOT acceptable as a replacement for the underlined portion—remember, that means the passage is correct as written. Look at the answer choices—they are all transition words, so you need to find the one that can't be used to connect the two ideas. The original word, *Nevertheless*, is used to connect two different ideas. Choices (A), (C), and (D) are all used in the same way. Choice (B), *Therefore*, is used to connect two similar ideas, so it can't be used to replace *Nevertheless*.

2. **F** When you see answer choices "stacked" like this, using all (or mostly all) the same words with Stop and Go punctuation changing in the same spot, check for Complete/Incomplete on either side of that spot. In this case, *That's because the seating area is actually a life-size painting* is a complete idea, and *painting on the wall of one of the campus buildings* is incomplete. Since Stop punctuation can only separate complete ideas, eliminate (J). There's not a good reason to insert a comma either after *painting* or *wall*, so the best answer choice is (F).

3. **B** The answer choices here all say the same thing in slightly different ways, but none contains an obvious grammatical error. Remember your fourth "C," concise! *Public* denotes the same idea as *for anyone/everyone* and *freely available*, so there's no need to say both—eliminate (A), (C), and (D).

4. **H** Here you have three answer choices with different "-ing" forms of verbs, and one without. Whenever you see a 3/1 split in the answer choices, take a look at the one that is different. We know ACT doesn't like the "-ing" form—it's not concise—and (H) has no grammatical errors; therefore, it's the best answer.

5. **D** The answer choices are all transition words, but this time ACT is testing idioms—specifically the "*not only, ___ also*" construction. The proper word to use is *but*, answer choice (D).

6. **F** To identify what the essay would lose by deleting the sentence, you must first determine the purpose of that sentence. In this case, the author asks, "A life-size painting that's just a painting?" rhetorically, anticipating the reader's possible surprise at such a notion. (F) is the only answer choice that expresses that purpose.

7. **C** You need to find the correct form of the verb here. Eliminate (A) and (D)—they are singular forms and don't agree with the plural subject, *children*. (B) is the correct plural form but the wrong tense—the correct answer choice has to be consistent with the other present-tense verbs in the passage: *looms, is*, and *looks*—that is choice (C).

8. **G** Here again you see a 3/1 split with three "-ing" verbs and one without, so check the one without. Unfortunately, (J) actually creates an error, because in this question, the answer choices are all modifying phrases, and ACT wants a modifying phrase to be right next to the thing that it describes. That means you need to find the phrase that describes a *group of firefighters*. (F) describes the image of the wave, (H) describes the children, and (J) describes the painting itself, leaving (G) as the only possible choice.

9. **D** The author is using the quotation marks to emphasize the fact that there weren't really any children there to rescue, so if you take out the quotation marks, you will lose that emphasis—choice (D). Choice (A) might seem tempting, but the firefighters' concern was for the "children," not the wave, and in any case, the quotations don't explain anything.

10. **G** The remainder of the paragraph talks about how Pugh uses his art to transform the appearance of an existing building, which agrees with (G). There is no comparison with gallery displays as in (F), nor is there discussion of multi-cultural influence on his work, as in (H). Choice (J) refers to the preceding paragraph.

11. **C** The correct form of the verb needs to be consistent with the preceding sentence: *use* is present-tense, so eliminate (A). Remember, ACT doesn't like "-ing" verbs, so you should only choose one if you have eliminated every other answer choice. In this case, even though (B) and (D) are both present-tense, (C) is as well, and it isn't an "-ing" verb, making it the best answer.

12. **J** There is no comparison being made here, so eliminate (G) and (H). The author is trying to express a large number of people, so you have to use *many*—answer choice (J).

13. **C** A good place to begin a new paragraph is a point where there is a shift in focus or topic. Prior to point C the author is describing one of Pugh's works; after point C the discussion turns to the high demand for his work and his worldwide popularity. (A), (B), and (D) all separate sentences that belong together.

14. **H** The question asks about "trends" in the plural, and only one artist and one style was discussed in the essay—eliminate (F) and (G). (J) is incorrect because although the essay does talk about people being confused by Pugh's art, that's not the reason the essay doesn't accomplish the stated goal—it's a problem of scope, as outlined in (H).

Passage II

15. **A**   On the ACT, a semicolon is used in exactly the same way as a period, so you can eliminate (B) and (D)—they can't both be correct! *Besides, to make it feel more like home* is an incomplete idea, and Stop punctuation can only be used to separate two complete ideas. The colon in (C) comes after a complete idea, which is correct, but saying *to make it feel more like home* after it is awkward. You'll need a dash to be consistent with the rest of the sentence and set off the unnecessary *pillows, … pots and pans* from the rest of the sentence—answer choice (A).

16. **G**   The answer choices here all say the same thing in slightly different ways, but none contains an obvious grammatical error. Remember your fourth "C"—concise! (G) is the only answer choice that doesn't use an "-ing" form of the verb (which ACT doesn't like), and has no grammatical errors, so it's the best choice.

17. **A**   You need to find an answer choice that agrees with *I had just said my first real farewell to a mother.* The sentence as written accomplishes this by explaining that she had never been away from her mother *for more than a weekend.* Choices (B), (C), and (D) all introduce new and off-topic information.

18. **J**   When you see DELETE or OMIT as an answer choice, do that first. If you can take out the underlined portion without creating an error, chances are you've found your answer. In this case, deleting *and me all by myself* doesn't create an error, and leaving it in would be redundant—the narrator has already described herself as *on my own*—so eliminate (F). Choices (G) and (H) are redundant for the same reason.

19. **B**   The correct tense of the verb here needs to be consistent with the non-underlined portion of the passage. The narrator is talking about her life before coming to college, so you must use the past tense, *grew*, to be consistent with the other verbs in the sentence, *had* and *was*. (A), *grow*, is present tense, and (D), *growth*, isn't a verb, so eliminate them. (C), *grown* could be past tense, but needs to be paired with a helping verb.

20. **H**   The task here is to transition from a discussion of the narrator's life in high school to her acceptance at a major university in the United States. (H) begins with her in high school—*when the time came to apply to colleges*—and ends with her applying to several in the United States. (F) and (G) don't talk about applying to college at all, and (J) only talks about applying to college in Puerto Rico.

21. **B**   There are a couple of things changing in the answer choices here—commas and pronouns—work with one first and then the other. Remember that unless you have a reason to use a comma, no punctuation is preferable. Here, we have no reason to use a comma after *acceptance*, so eliminate (C) and (D). Now it's a matter of comparing *acceptance received by me* or *acceptance I received*. They both say the same thing, but the latter is more concise—choose (B).

22. **H** The answer choices are forms of the verb "to get." To choose the correct one, look at the non-underlined portion of the sentence. The narrator says her parents *were* proud, so you need a past-tense verb to agree with that—eliminate (F) and (G). (J) changes the meaning of the sentence, so the only answer choice left is (H), even though it uses the "-ing" form of the verb.

23. **D** The difference being talked about here is between Puerto Rico and the United States, so *in the United States* needs to be placed in the spot that will make that most clear. (A) makes it sound like Puerto Rico is in the United States—eliminate it. Neither (B) nor (C) make it clear that the United States is where things are different—only (D) does.

24. **J** Apostrophes are used to show either possession or contraction. The word after *parents* is *house*, so you want to show possession. The narrator is referring to the house that belongs to both of her parents, and with a plural noun that ends in "s," all you need to do is add an apostrophe—choice (J).

25. **D** Remember that on the ACT, less is more, so you should have a really compelling reason to add something. In an essay discussing the narrator's feelings about being away from her home and family for the first time, it's not really important to know what is her favorite dance—eliminate (A) and (B). The reason it's not important isn't because of any false impression created, so (D) is the best answer choice.

26. **H** Here you see nicely "stacked" answer choices with Stop and Go punctuation changing in the same spot. Check for Complete/Incomplete on either side: *As the memory faded* is Incomplete, so no matter what, you're not going to be able to use Stop punctuation—that can only connect two complete ideas. Eliminate (F), (G), and (J), and you're done.

27. **A** You're looking for the answer choice that can NOT be used in place of the underlined portion—remember, that means the sentence is correct as written. Choices (B), (C), and (D) all express either how the narrator was feeling or what she was feeling; (A) is the only choice that makes no sense—you wouldn't feel "excitement nervous"—and is therefore the one to choose.

28. **G** The assignment here is to *emphasize the narrator's confidence*, so the correct answer choice must do exactly that. (G), *ready to take on*, does that much more effectively than *had to face, all alone in*, or *about to enter*.

29. **C** Make sure to read the question carefully—the goal here is to not only pick a logical concluding sentence but also the one that *best expresses one of the main ideas of the essay*. A main idea is one that recurs throughout the essay, so you can eliminate (B) and (D). While Puerto Rico is certainly mentioned throughout the essay, it wouldn't be logical for the narrator to express her regret at leaving home—the preceding sentence has an upbeat and confident tone, which (C) continues while including another main idea—her dream of living in a large city.

Passage III

30. **G** Three of the answer choices offer a form of the verb "to need," and one offers no verb at all—that's a 3/1 split, and on the English test, you always want to check the "1" first. That makes the sentence read *When in need of help with an article, she calls on Clark Kent*, which is a present-tense sentence that is consistent with the first: *When Lois Lane finds herself in serious danger, she looks to Superman for help.* The verbs in (F), (H), and (J) are all past-tense, so (G) is the best answer.

31. **D** DELETE is an answer choice, so do that first—if you don't create an error by taking out the underlined portion, it's probably the correct choice. In this case, taking out the question word *when* leaves *Today it's a commonplace writing technique*—a perfectly good complete sentence. Leaving *when*, *where*, or *because* in there would make the sentence incomplete, so you shouldn't choose (A), (B), or (C).

32. **H** You've got DELETE as an option, so try it. This time, it creates an error: *...he poses as millionaire Bruce Wayne day* doesn't make sense, so eliminate (J). Now your choices are all prepositions, which means ACT is testing idioms. To express the notion that something occurs during the day, you need to say *by day*—answer choice (H).

33. **C** To decide whether to make the addition here, take a look at the main theme of the passage—Dual Personalities—and what's going on in the paragraph. The author is talking about the *tradition of giving superheroes alternate names and characters*, so adding a sentence about a superhero that doesn't need an alter-ego would be a bad idea—eliminate (A) and (B). (D) is incorrect because the sentence poses no hypothetical situation.

34. **G** The correct verb here needs to agree in number with the subject, *Each*. Careful—*of the superheroes* is a prepositional phrase, so it's not the subject, but it can make the wrong verb sound correct. To avoid confusion, you should cross out prepositional phrases you find inserted between a verb and its subject, one of ACT's favorite tricks. Now you know the subject is *Each*, a singular noun, so it needs a singular verb—eliminate (F) and (J). (G) and (H) are both singular and present-tense, but beware the "-ing" form! They both say the same thing, but (G) is more concise, making it the better answer choice.

35. **D** The phrase *the costume and the name, for example* is unnecessary. Unnecessary info can be offset by either a pair of commas or a pair of dashes, but you can't open with one and close with another. The dash used in the non-underlined text means a dash must be used here.

36. **H** You need to provide support for the preceding sentence, which states that impressive costumes and names help superheroes maintain their authority. Only (H) addresses anything to do with this theme by stating that it would be more difficult for Batman to fight crime if he lacked those things.

37. **B**   You need to find the answer choice that can NOT be used to replace the underlined portion in the passage. A quick glance at the answer choices might give you the impression that Stop/Go punctuation is being tested here, but look closer; the words changing after the punctuation are all transition words, and that typically means ACT is testing direction. Remember, when NO CHANGE is not an answer choice, the sentence in the passage is correct as written, and that gives you an important clue: The transition word used is *but*, an opposite-direction transition—that means a suitable replacement will also have to use one. *On the other hand*, *although*, and *however* in (A), (C), and (D) are all opposite-direction transitions, but *because* in (B) is same-direction, and so can NOT be used—making (B) the correct answer.

38. **G**   There are two things changing here: apostrophes showing possession and word choice between *one* and *individual*. In the sentence, the *loved one/individual* with the *other identity* refers back to *the hero*, so you know you need to choose a singular noun, and to show possession, you need to add an *'s*. Choice (G), *one's*, is the only one that offers that construction.

39. **A**   The superheroes are given these alter-egos by their creators in order to help the characters fit into a societal context. *Providing* best communicates this meaning; there is no assumption being made as in (B), and (C) and (D) make it seem as if the fictional characters had a choice in the matter.

40. **F**   This is a pronoun question, so find the noun that's being replaced. In this case, it's the superheroes who are making the attempts, and *superheroes* is plural. That helps a lot, since, apostrophes or not, you can eliminate (G), (H), and (J)—they're all singular pronouns and can't be used to replace a plural noun.

41. **D**   This is a comma question, so keep your comma rules in mind. There is unnecessary information in this sentence: *creator of Spider-Man and dozens of other superheroes*. This needs to be set off with commas—one after *Lee* (eliminate (B) and (C)) and one after *superheroes*. The only answer choice that offers this without adding additional, unnecessary commas is (D).

42. **G**   The rest of the paragraph discusses the reasons Stan Lee gives his superheroes human flaws, so if you're going to introduce that sort of discussion with a rhetorical question, the natural choice for that question would be one that asks, "Why?" Choice (G) is the only one that asks that question.

43. **B**   This question is testing comma usage, but none of the situational rules seem to apply—there's no introductory idea, list, or unnecessary information. Therefore, the issue is whether there is a definite need to pause at any point in *Lee builds tension in his stories by putting those human flaws and the hero's quest into conflict*. If it helps, you can take an exaggerated pause at the spots ACT suggests putting commas. If the pause creates a little tension, you probably need the comma; if the pause just seems irritating or awkward, you don't. This sentence is a little on the long side, but it doesn't need the commas—answer choice (B).

44. **F** The sentence should be kept, since it's giving an example of what the entire previous paragraph is talking about—eliminate (H) and (J). (G) is the direct opposite of what's happening in the sentence: The ultimate superhero does in fact have human feelings.

45. **A** This sentence fits best with the discussion in the first paragraph about Lois Lane's misconception that Superman and Clark Kent are two different individuals. It also introduces the concept of the alter-ego, the subject of the second paragraph, so it functions nicely as a transition sentence as well.

Passage IV

46. **H** Here you have nicely "stacked" answer choices with Stop and Go punctuation changing in the same spot—check for Complete/Incomplete on either side. *Passing trends… vary dramatically* is Complete, and *every bit as much as clothing* is Incomplete. You'll need Go punctuation to connect these two— eliminate (F) and (J). (G) uses the less-concise "-ing" form of the verb, making (H) the best answer.

47. **C** The assigned task is to introduce the main subject of the paragraph, which begins by talking about curly hair being the fashion in the 1950s and the progression towards "natural" hair by the mid-1960s. (A) is addressed in the paragraph, but it's not a main subject. The Renaissance is never mentioned, so eliminate (B), and (D) introduces a new topic—clothing styles—so the best answer is (C).

48. **H** The answer choices here are all very similar and don't contain any obvious errors. You'll need to check the non-underlined portion on either side and make sure the answer is consistent with both. To the left you have *maintaining properly stylish hair-dos*, and to the right you have *and a great deal of time*. (F) and (J) aren't consistent with both, and (G) is not only inconsistent, but it also contradicts the preceding sentence—these hairdos took a lot of work.

49. **B** There are pronouns changing in the answer choices, and an apostrophe in the sentence as written. If you're in doubt about whether to you need the contraction or a pronoun, expand out the contraction: In this case, *they're* becomes "they are," which doesn't make sense—eliminate (A). The noun being replaced here is *Women*, which is plural, so you need a plural pronoun—eliminate (D). (B) is the possessive, plural pronoun you're looking for, but watch out for its sound-alike, *there*, in (C).

50. **J** All the answer choices basically say the same thing, and none creates a grammatical error, so pick the one that says what they all do in the most concise way. That's (J)—*long or short*.

51. **D** DELETE is an answer choice, so try that first. Taking out the underlined portion leaves *The change didn't last long, perhaps unsurprisingly.* That is a complete sentence, and the meaning hasn't changed, so it's the best answer.

52. **F**   This question is testing comma usage, so keep your comma rules in mind. It might be tempting to think of *Farrah Fawcett* as unnecessary information, but if you remove it from the sentence, it is no longer clear who *the movie and television star* is. Because it's necessary, no commas are needed, which corresponds with answer choice (F), NO CHANGE.

53. **B**   Be careful—the question is asking whether the phrase inside the dashes *should* be deleted, not whether it *can* be. In this case, the author is using the phrase inside the dashes to define a term with which the reader may not be familiar, and you know ACT likes things to be clear. Therefore, the phrase should be kept—eliminate (C) and (D). (A) is incorrect because there is no contrast made to an earlier style.

54. **F**   There are two things changing here: apostrophes showing contraction and word choice between *sudden* and *suddenly*. You need the adverb *suddenly*, so eliminate (H) and (J). (G) is incorrect because we're is a contraction of "we are," which wouldn't make sense in the sentence.

55. **B**   Three of the answer choices say the same thing in slightly different ways, while one just says *it*. While you may be tempted to read *it* in the slang sense of "something really popular," remember there's no slang on the ACT—eliminate (C). Now you're left with the three answer choices that don't contain errors, but all say the same thing—pick the one that's most concise, (B).

56. **H**   You need to find the answer choice that can NOT replace the underlined portion in the sentence, and since NO CHANGE isn't an option, you know the sentence in the passage is correct. The option here is to find an alternate word for *modeled*, so this is just a vocabulary question. (F), (G), and (J) all work as replacements in the context of the sentence, so select (H), the one that does NOT. If this question tricked you, you may have picked *imitated*, since the sentence talks about women imitating the pop icons, but the pop icons are the ones doing the modeling.

57. **B**   If you're unsure about whether an apostrophe is showing possession or expansion, expand it out. In this case, "commentator is" wouldn't make sense, so if you need an apostrophe at all, it would be to show possession. However, look at the word after the underlined portion: *have.* Only nouns can be possessed, and *have* is not a noun; therefore, you can't use an apostrophe here at all—eliminate (A), (C), and (D).

58. **H**   Sentence 3 talks about how women can now have their hair chemically straightened. Both sentence 2 and sentence 4 talk about curly hair, so eliminate (F) and (J). Sentence 3 would naturally follow sentence 1, which transitions from the previous paragraph and introduces the idea of straight hair being the fashion now, so (H) is a better answer choice than (G).

59. **C**   The essay mentions the "modern" preference for straight hair, but that's a long way from *discussing modern attitudes toward curly hair*—eliminate (A) and (B). (D) is incorrect for the same reason: The primary focus is not on the popularity of straight hair.

Passage V

60. **F** The phrase *polonium and radium* names the *two new elements* discovered by the Curies. It doesn't provide an explanation as (G) claims, nor does it offer the reason Marie Curie won the Nobel Prize, as in (H). (J) is incorrect because the phrase does not define radioactivity—it simply lists two radioactive elements—leaving (F) as the best answer choice.

61. **B** The assigned task is to *provide the most effective transition* to the rest of the essay. The next paragraph talks about some of the problems Curie encountered in her academic and professional career, so an *effective transition* will need to incorporate that theme, as (B) does. (A) only provides a specific detail about Curie's research, (C) doesn't mention Curie at all, and (D) talks only about Curie's husband, Pierre.

62. **H** Here you see nicely "stacked" answer choices with Stop and Go punctuation changing in the same spot, but before checking for Complete/Incomplete on either side to see which kind of punctuation you need, notice you have one answer choice with *which* in it, and three without. Whenever you see a 3/1 split like that on the English test, check the "1" first. In (F), the idea after the comma would be *which prevented her from attending university due to a lack of money, Curie initially studied in a laboratory run by her cousin*, which doesn't make sense—eliminate (F). The remaining three answer choices all have *prevented* as the first word in the second idea, but (J) has *prevented her*, which creates another error—eliminate (J). Now it's down to a choice between a period and a comma. The ideas on either side are both complete (make sure to read the entire sentence!), so you need Stop punctuation—answer choice (H).

63. **A** You're given the option to DELETE the underlined portion, so try that first. Taking out *where* in this case leaves you with a comma joining two complete ideas, so eliminate (D). *Like* doesn't make sense, so eliminate (B). Both *when* and *where* might seem to work, but keep in mind that the two things happening in the sentence are Curie enrolling at the University of Paris and becoming the first woman professor there. Those two things didn't happen simultaneously, so you can't use *when* to connect them—choose (A).

64. **H** All the answer choices here say basically the same thing, and none creates a grammatical error, so pick the one that says what they all do in the most concise way. That's (H)—*generally credited with*.

65. **C** There are two things changing in the answer choices: We have *seen* vs. *saw* and *has* vs. *had*. Start with whichever seems easier, and eliminate answer choices that don't agree. The correct form of the verb (regardless of whether you use *has* or *have*) is *has/have seen*, so delete (A) and (D). To figure out which tense you need, check the non-underlined rest of the passage for context. In the same sentence, you have past-tense verbs: *made, existed, did*—(C) is past-tense and therefore consistent with the rest of the sentence.

66. **J**   Here it's really just a matter of inserting the underlined portion, *of radioactivity*, in each of the places in the answer choices; the only place it makes any sense at all is after *discovery*, answer choice (J).

67. **D**   This question is basically just testing word choice. If you happen to notice that there's a 3/1 split in the answers—one noun and three modifiers—then you could probably save a step or two, but from the context of the (now altered) passage, you know that *Bequerel was performing* [something] *involving photographic paper*, not *performing* [in some manner] involving photographic paper. If you need a thing, you need a noun, and the only choice you have is (D).

68. **H**   There are transition words changing in the answer choices, which can often be an indication that ACT is testing direction, but notice the 3/1 split—three answer choices with transitions and one without. If you try the one without, you're left with *Further experiments revealed… potassium uranyl sulfate*, which is a perfectly good sentence, and more concise than the other three. There's no real need for a transition at all here, so (H) is the best answer.

69. **D**   This is another word choice question with some punctuation thrown in to confuse the issue—start easy! *Principal* means something that is highest in rank or value; *principle* means a fundamental assumption. In the context of the sentence, you need to use *principle*—eliminate (A) and (C). Using a colon after *principle* might seem obviously preferable to the comma after *namely*, which seems awkward, but remember that ACT mandates that a colon must follow a complete idea, and must itself be followed by a list, definition, expansion, or explanation of that complete idea; make sure to check that. *However, Bequerel… principle* is a complete idea, and the idea after the colon is a definition (as evidenced by the introductory word *namely*)—pick (D).

70. **G**   You have a 3/1 split of sorts here: All the answer choices have *isolated* by itself with some kind of punctuation, and one that adds *it*—that's probably a good place to start. Adding the pronoun *it* here, though, creates an error: The pronoun is not replacing any noun—eliminate (H). The action in the idea after the semicolon is *she* (Curie) *isolated and identified* the two elements, so there's no need for any punctuation in between the two verbs—choose (G).

71. **A**   The answer choices have Stop and Go punctuation changing in the same spot and all use the same word, so check for Complete/Incomplete on either side: Before the punctuation you have *The earliest scientist to realize that there was an element in the fluorescent substance more reactive than uranium*—an incomplete idea, and afterward you have *Curie dedicated the next twelve years to developing a method for isolating that substance, which was not yet known but later came to be identified and is now called "radium,"* which is a complete idea, so you need Go punctuation to separate them—eliminate (B) and (D), which has a colon, which you know has to follow a complete idea. You definitely need to pause after the incomplete idea, so leave the comma where it is—answer choice (A).

72. **G**   You know ACT is testing Concise when all the answer choices here say basically the same thing, and none creates a grammatical error. That's what's happening here, so pick the one that says what they all do in the most concise way. That's (G)—*we now know as radium*.

73. **B** Here you see Stop and Go punctuation changing in the same spot and nicely "stacked" answer choices, so check for Complete/Incomplete on either side: Before the punctuation you have *Curie was progressive for a chemist*—a complete idea, and afterward you have *much less for a woman*, which is an incomplete idea, so you need Go punctuation to separate them—eliminate (A) and (C). (D) is awkward and doesn't really make sense—choose (B).

74. **H** There are two things changing in the answer choices here: word choice and helping verbs. It's incorrect to say *would of* or *might of*—it's "would have" and "might have." Eliminate (F) and (G). Helping verbs need to agree with the subject in number, just like regular verbs. In this case, the subject is *Women*, which is plural, so choose (H), *have*.

75. **D** The correct answer choice will provide *the most consistent description of Curie's personality as described in this paragraph*. There is no mention in the paragraph of her seeking recognition as in (A), and likewise in (B), no proof that she became reclusive. (C) doesn't talk about her personality at all, leaving (D) as the best answer choice.

Chapter 5
English Practice
Test 2

ACT ENGLISH TEST

45 Minutes—75 Questions

DIRECTIONS: In the five passages that follow, certain words and phrases are underlined and numbered. In the right-hand column, you will find alternatives for each underlined part. In most cases, you are to choose the one that best expresses the idea, makes the statement appropriate for standard written English, or is worded most consistently with the style and tone of the passage as a whole. If you think the original version is best, choose "NO CHANGE." In some cases, you will find in the right-hand column a question about the underlined part. You are to choose the best answer to the question.

You will also find questions about a section of the passage or the passage as a whole. These questions do not refer to an underlined portion of the passage but rather are identified by a number or numbers in a box.

For each question, choose the alternative you consider best and blacken the corresponding oval on your answer document. Read each passage through once before you begin to answer the questions that accompany it. For many of the questions, you must read several sentences beyond the question to determine the answer. Be sure that you have read far enough ahead each time you choose an alternative.

PASSAGE I

A Day in the City

When I woke up this morning, I made myself a bowl of cereal and sat, listening to the traffic. Some of my friends ask me how I can stand living somewhere so noisy. It's true that

1. Which of the following alternatives to the underlined portion would NOT be acceptable?
   A. cereal and sat while listening
   B. cereal, sat listening
   C. cereal, sat, and listened
   D. cereal before sitting and listening

there's always some kind of noise in my neighborhood—taxi drivers honking their horns, kids playing their radios so loud that the bass makes my teeth vibrate, or people yelling in the street. I know that some people wouldn't like it, but to me, these are the sounds of life. [3]

2. F. NO CHANGE
   G. neighborhood, taxi drivers honking
   H. neighborhood; taxi drivers honking
   J. neighborhood taxi drivers honking

3. If the writer were to delete the preceding sentence, the essay would primarily lose:
   A. a contrast to the positive tone of the essay.
   B. an explanation for the narrator's trip to the park.
   C. information that shows the author's attitude toward the place she lives.
   D. nothing at all; this information is not relevant to the essay.

It's Saturday, so this morning I decided to go to the park. The train is the fastest way to go but I took the bus instead.

4. F. NO CHANGE
   G. Since today it is finally
   H. Allowing for it being
   J. The day of the week is

When I ride the bus, you get to see so much more of the city. It can be kind of loud on the bus, with some people talking

5. A. NO CHANGE
   B. one is riding
   C. you ride
   D. they are riding

on their phones, others chatting sociable with their friends, and
<u>6</u>
others playing music. Just like the traffic's sounds, though, the

noise on the bus represents people working, relaxing, and living.
<u>7</u>

     Once I get to the park, I pick a bench over near the play

area. The city added the bench so they could play while their
<u>8</u>

parents sit nearby, obviously I like to sit there because there's a
<u>9</u>
great big oak tree for shade. I can see and hear almost

everything from there. I sit there watching, and listening to the
<u>10</u>
people around me. People-watching is one of my favorite

things to do, I like listening even better. The park is the best
<u>11</u>
place because you get to see and hear everything. The only

problem is that there's so much to see and hear!

     That's why people get so tired after a little while. That way,
<u>12</u>
I can pay more attention to the sounds and not get distracted by

what I see. With my eyes closed, I can pick out parts of

two old men's familiar conversation. One of them is telling the
<u>13</u>
other about something his grandson said. I can't hear the rest,

but whatever it was must have been hilarious because his

friends' laugh is so loud, it startles me.
<u>14</u>

     Later that night, after I've ridden the bus back home, I think

about those old men. When I'm old, I hope that I too will have

a friend who will sit in the park with me, and who will enjoy

listening to the sounds of the city as much as I do.

6. F. NO CHANGE
   G. sociably, with
   H. sociable with,
   J. sociably with

7. A. NO CHANGE
   B. people, working;
   C. people; working
   D. people, working,

8. F. NO CHANGE
   G. kids
   H. because they
   J. that it

9. A. NO CHANGE
   B. nearby.
   C. nearby,
   D. nearby, because

10. F. NO CHANGE
   G. there, watching, and listening,
   H. there, watching and listening
   J. there watching and listening,

11. A. NO CHANGE
   B. do, nevertheless,
   C. do, but
   D. do, however

12. Which choice most effectively introduces the idea discussed in this rest of the paragraph?

   F. NO CHANGE
   G. I close my eyes
   H. the park is interesting
   J. some people like quiet

13. Which choice would emphasize the narrator's curiosity and interest in the old men's conversation in the most logical and effective way?

   A. NO CHANGE
   B. noisy chatter.
   C. animated discussion.
   D. entertaining stories.

14. F. NO CHANGE
   G. friends's
   H. friends
   J. friend's

Question 15 asks about the preceding passage as a whole.

15. Suppose the writer's assignment was to write an essay analyzing one reason people might choose to live in a large city. Would this essay fit that description?

A. Yes, because it discusses the convenience of public transportation.

B. Yes, because it explains the narrator's enjoyment of one of the city's parks.

C. No, because it focuses on one detail of city living that most people dislike.

D. No, because it only discusses why the narrator prefers listening to watching.

PASSAGE II

The Bridge They Said Couldn't Be Built

Visible in the fog as well as the sun, the Golden Gate
Bridge is a symbol of San Francisco. The bridge was once
famous for having the longest suspension span in the world;
even today, its suspension span is the second longest in the
United States. It is open to cars and pedestrians alike, and has
only been shut down three times in that seventy-year history.
_____
16
The amount of concrete needed to anchor the bridge was

enough to construct a sidewalk five feet wide, all the way
_____
17
from San Francisco to New York City. Since the Golden Gate
opened, almost two billion cars have crossed the bridge and it
has been featured in countless movies.

The fame of the Golden Gate Bridge wasn't always assured.
[A] When Joseph Strauss announced his intention of building
the bridge, people flocked to support him. A combination of
_____
18
factors made building a bridge in that location difficult: cold,
stormy seas below, foggy and damp weather, and winds that
regularly reach speeds of 60 miles per hour.

[B] After two years of discussion, the voters approved a
bond: that raise $35 million, all dedicated to building the
_____
19

bridge. Even then, there were many skeptics whom believed
_____
20
that it couldn't be done.

Strauss, a veteran bridge builder, refused to give up.
Construction began in 1933 and ended in 1937, and lasted a
_____
21

16. F. NO CHANGE
    G. their
    H. its
    J. DELETE the underlined portion.

17. A. NO CHANGE
    B. sidewalk five feet wide
    C. sidewalk—five feet wide
    D. sidewalk, five feet wide

18. Which choice provides the conclusion that relates to the rest of the paragraph in the most logical way?
    F. NO CHANGE
    G. many said it was impossible.
    H. some admired his vision.
    J. he had already built other bridges.

19. A. NO CHANGE
    B. bond, that
    C. bond; that
    D. bond that

20. F. NO CHANGE
    G. that
    H. who
    J. DELETE the underlined portion.

21. A. NO CHANGE
    B. being completed by 1937,
    C. ending four years later
    D. DELETE the underlined portion.

little more than four years. <u>On May 28, 1937. The bridge, arching grandly</u> over the water, opened to pedestrians. More
22
than 200,000 people walked across the bridge that day to

celebrate <u>the grand achievement.</u>
23

[C] By the time it was completed, the bridge had exceeded everyone's expectations. Not only was it built, it was also ahead of schedule and under budget. To top it off,

it was beautiful. <u>Nevertheless,</u> the Golden Gate Bridge is
24
considered an artistic masterpiece, recognizable all around the world. At its highest point, the bridge rises 746 feet into the <u>air</u>—191 feet taller than the Washington Monument.
25

The name "Golden Gate" refers not to the color of the bridge, which is actually orange, but to the stretch of water below, where the San Francisco Bay connects to the Pacific Ocean. [D] The color, called "International Orange," was chosen partly because it matched the <u>natural surroundings and</u>
26

partly because it would allow the bridge to remain visible on foggy days. [27]

Today, the bridge is divided into six lanes for cars, and pedestrian lanes for people and bicycles. On sunny days, crowds of people flock to the bridge to enjoy the view. Rising out of the sea like a vision from a dream, the Golden Gate Bridge captures the imagination today, just as it did when

22. F. NO CHANGE
G. On May 28, 1937; the bridge arching grandly
H. On May 28, 1937, the bridge, arching grandly
J. On May 28, 1937, the bridge, arching grandly,

23. A. NO CHANGE
B. an achievement that was extremely impressive because it symbolized a significant victory over difficult circumstances.
C. the successful completion of a project that was amazing both because of the obstacles that had been overcome and because of the magnitude of the product that was the result of the project.
D. DELETE the underlined portion and end the sentence with a period.

24. F. NO CHANGE
G. At the time,
H. Regardless,
J. Even today,

25. A. NO CHANGE
B. air;
C. air
D. air, rising

26. F. NO CHANGE
G. nature surrounding
H. nature surrounded
J. natural surrounds

27. The writer is considering deleting the phrase "on foggy days" from the preceding sentence in order to make the paragraph more concise. If the writer were to make this deletion, the sentence would primarily lose information that:

A. explains why the color of the bridge is referred to as "International Orange."
B. demonstrates the ways in which the bridge's color matches the environment.
C. reveals the danger that the bridge can cause for some ships during bad weather, regardless of color.
D. adds a detail that provides a specific situation in which the bridge's visibility is particularly important.

Strauss first envisioned it. [28]

28. The writer is considering adding a sentence that demonstrates the wide variety of the bridge's uses today. Given that all the following statements are true, which one, if added here, would most clearly and effectively accomplish the writer's goal?

F. On weekdays, during the busiest times of day, the direction of certain lanes changes to accommodate rush hour commuters.

G. The weather in San Francisco is often foggy but when the sky is clear, the bright orange of the bridge stands out against its surroundings.

H. The bridge is 1.7 miles long, so some people walk across in one direction but hire a taxi or take the bus to return.

J. People use it to commute to work, to go on day trips to Marin or San Francisco, and even just to enjoy the beauty of the bridge itself.

Question 29 asks about the preceding passage as a whole.

---

29. Upon reviewing the essay, the writer realizes that some information has been omitted. The writer wants to incorporate that information and composes the following sentence:

> The local community began to consider building a bridge to connect the San Francisco peninsula in 1928.

If the writer were to add this sentence to the essay, the most logical place to insert it would be at Point:

A. A
B. B
C. C
D. D

PASSAGE III

Father of a Language

The Italian language wasn't always the single, unified,
 language that it is today. In fact, during the Middle Ages, Italy
wasn't a unified country. Even today, though Italy is politically
unified, each region speaks its own dialect. In some regions,
such as Tuscany, the dialect is virtually identical to the "official"
Italian language. In other regions, such as Venice, however, the
language is still distinct in many ways.

Dante Alighieri, more commonly known simply as Dante,
is sometimes called the "father of the Italian language." He
was born in Florence during the thirteenth century and was
a prolific writer. In approximately 1305, he published an
essay entitled "De Vulgari Eloquentia," or "In Defense of the
Vernacular." About three years later, Dante began work on his
masterpiece: *The Divine Comedy*. Today he is considered one

of the greatest writers of the Western world. 〔32〕 During his

life, however, his work was more controversial. Some of the
 main reasons for this was his decision not to write in Latin, but
in "Italian."

30. F. NO CHANGE
  G. single yet unified,
  H. single, and unified,
  J. single, unified

31. The writer is considering removing the underlined phrase.
The primary effect of the deletion would be the loss of a
detail that:
  A. provides context that may be helpful in understanding
the passage.
  B. creates confusion regarding the writer's point in this
paragraph.
  C. interrupts the flow of the passage without adding any new
information.
  D. provides a grammatically necessary connection.

32. The writer is considering adding the following phrase to
the end of the preceding sentence (changing the period
after "world" to a comma)

  alongside other recognized greats such as Homer,
Shakespeare, and Sophocles.

Should the writer make this addition?

  F. Yes, because it provides necessary context for the sentence's previous statement.
  G. Yes, because it explains the important role the creation
of Italian played in Western literature.
  H. No, because it adds details that distract from the primary
point of the sentence.
  J. No, the list of important writers does not include all
important writers in the Western tradition.

33. A. NO CHANGE
  B. One
  C. Few
  D. Each

At that time, high literature was written not in the various

local languages and in Latin. Dante believed that literature
<u>34</u>

should be available not only to the educated elite <u>who had</u>
<u>35</u>
<u>education</u> but also to the common people. In order to make
<u>35</u>

this dream possible, Dante "created" a new language <u>as he</u>
<u>36</u>
<u>called</u> "Italian." This new language wasn't really new at all;
<u>36</u>
it consisted of bits and pieces from the different languages

already spoken throughout Italy, and drew most heavily on

Dante's native Tuscan dialect. Dante's creation laid the

foundation for the unified language <u>to be spoken</u> in Italy today.
<u>37</u>

    The Divine Comedy is, in some ways, the beginning of

national Italian literature. By writing it in the language spoken

by the Italian <u>people; Dante</u> made *The Divine Comedy*
<u>38</u>

available to the people. <u>Dante for his opinion that literature to</u>
<u>39</u>
<u>anyone should be accessible drew criticism.</u> However, the
<u>39</u>

movement that Dante helped begin led to <u>diminished literacy</u>
<u>40</u>
among the Italian people, which, in turn, eventually led to the

Renaissance.

The title of *The Divine Comedy* <u>confusing some</u> people. At
<u>41</u>
one time, the label of "comedy" was attached to any work not

written in Latin. *The Divine Comedy* wasn't written in

Latin, <u>but</u> it was considered a comedy; however, today it is
<u>42</u>
widely considered a masterpiece of serious literature. Dante's

---

34. **F.** NO CHANGE
    G. for
    H. as
    J. but

35. **A.** NO CHANGE
    B. who had been taught
    C. with a school background
    D. DELETE the underlined portion.

36. **F.** NO CHANGE
    G. and called
    H. that he called
    J. calling

37. **A.** NO CHANGE
    B. spoken
    C. if spoken
    D. to speak

38. **F.** NO CHANGE
    G. people, Dante
    H. people. Dante
    J. people: Dante

39. **A.** NO CHANGE
    B. Dante should be accessible for his opinion that literature to anyone drew criticism.
    C. Dante drew criticism for his opinion that literature should be accessible to anyone.
    D. Dante drew criticism to anyone for his opinion that literature should be accessible.

40. The writer wants to imply that prior to Dante's development of "Italian," illiteracy was common. Which choice best accomplishes that goal?
    F. NO CHANGE
    G. an increase in
    H. a passion for
    J. compulsory

41. **A.** NO CHANGE
    B. confusing
    C. confuses some
    D. that confuses

42. **F.** NO CHANGE
    G. since
    H. because
    J. so

brave decision, while, in defiance of the common beliefs of
43
his time, demonstrated that it was not necessary for a literary

masterpiece to be written in Latin, paved the way for future

writers and readers alike. Nevertheless, *The Divine Comedy*
44
remains a symbol of both literature and innovation today.

43. A. NO CHANGE
    B. and
    C. which,
    D. so that,

44. F. NO CHANGE
    G. In contrast,
    H. However,
    J. DELETE the underlined portion.

PASSAGE IV

Baking Lessons

[1]

Both of my parents worked full-time when I was a little girl, so my grandmother would stay at our house during the day. We would sit in the living room on the couch at my family's house and watch game shows. Our favorite was

The Price is Right. We would call out their answers along with the contestants. When our answers were right, we would

scream with excitement, and when the contestants were wrong, we would moan with disappointment.

[2]

[1] When I got older and started going to school, we couldn't watch our game shows regular. [2] That was okay with me, though, because the one thing I liked better than watching game shows with my grandmother was helping her bake. 49 [3] Watching her in the kitchen was magical: she never seemed to need the recipes but everything she made tasted like heaven.

[3]

[1] As I got older, she let me help with the easy parts, such as sifting the flour and measuring the sugar. [2] At first I would

45. A. NO CHANGE
B. on the couch in the living room at my family's house
C. in the living room at my family's house on the couch
D. at my family's house on the couch in the living room

46. F. NO CHANGE
G. my
H. our
J. her

47. Which of the following alternatives to the underlined portion would NOT be acceptable?

A. excitement, when
B. excitement; when
C. excitement. When
D. excitement, or when

48. F. NO CHANGE
G. as regular.
H. but regularly.
J. as regularly.

49. The writer is considering deleting the preceding sentence. If the sentence were removed, the essay would primarily lose:

A. a transition from the narrator's discussion of watching game shows to the subject focused on in the remainder of the essay.
B. unnecessary information that serves only to detract from the primary subject being discussed in the paragraph.
C. details that are critical to understanding why the narrator took such pleasure in watching game shows with her grandmother.
D. an insight into why the narrator would choose to spend her afternoons watching television with her grandmother.

50. Which of the following alternatives to the underlined portion would NOT be acceptable?

F. during
G. her with
H. out with
J. along

just sit on the kitchen stool and watch, even though I didn't
understand what she was doing. [3] The day she let me separate

the eggs, I felt like I had reached the pinnacle of success. [52]

[4]

Eventually, my parents decided that I could take care of
myself, and my grandmother stopped coming over every day
because I didn't need someone to keep an eye on me anymore.
The love of baking that she had inspired, however, stayed with
me. I started baking by myself, and even if the cookies ended

up burned

sometimes, more often they turned out pretty well. I dropped
in new recipes, and whenever I got to a tricky part, I would call
my grandmother for advice. Sometimes I would call her just to
talk, too. I felt like I could talk to her about anything.

[5]

Last week, I found a recipe book she made for me. It
included her recipes for brownies, cookies, and my favorite,
lemon meringue pie. As I flipped through the pages, I thought

for a moment I could hear her voice, although she's gone, I
know that in the way that matters most, she'll never really be

51. Which of the following would best express the narrator's respect for her grandmother's abilities in the kitchen, and the enjoyment the narrator feels at watching her grandmother bake?
A. NO CHANGE
B. or work on whatever homework I had for the next day.
C. awed by her skills and eager to taste whatever she was creating.
D. confused by all the different steps that went into each dish.

52. Which of the following is the most logical ordering of the sentence in Paragraph 3?
F. NO CHANGE
G. 3, 1, 2
H. 2, 3, 1
J. 2, 1, 3

53. A. NO CHANGE
B. since I was considered old enough to stay home by myself.
C. due to my parents' decision that I didn't need a babysitter.
D. DELETE the underlined portion and end the sentence with a period.

54. Which of the following alternatives to the underlined portion would NOT be acceptable?
F. spoiled
G. burnted
H. ruined
J. burnt

55. A. NO CHANGE
B. auditioned for
C. tried out
D. fell into

56. Which of the following alternatives to the underlined portion would NOT be acceptable?
F. leafed through
G. looked through
H. tossed out
J. read over

57. A. NO CHANGE
B. voice; but
C. voice. Although
D. voice although

gone at all. She was the one which taught me not just about
                                    ____
                                     58
baking,

but about life. I imagine that I will enjoy baking for the rest of
                                                      59
my life.
____
 59

58. F. NO CHANGE
    G. whom
    H. who
    J. whose

59. Given that all the choices are true, which one would provide a concluding sentence that best captures the main idea of the essay?

    A. NO CHANGE
    B. To this day, I love watching game shows and baking delicious food for my family.
    C. Baking is a great way to relax, and it's often less expensive than buying cakes and pastries from a bakery.
    D. Every day, when I enter the kitchen, I remember my grandmother and everything she taught me.

Question 60 asks about the passage as a whole.

---

60. After completing the essay, the writer realizes that she forgot to include some information and composes the following sentence:

    My grandmother passed away ten years ago, but I still think of her every day.

    This sentence would most logically be placed:

    F. at the end of Paragraph 1.
    G. after Sentence 1 in Paragraph 2.
    H. at the beginning of Paragraph 5.
    J. at the end of Paragraph 5.

PASSAGE V

Global Rat-titudes

The relationship between humans and animals have always been complicated. Some cultures have developed entire belief systems around favored animals. For example, cows are treated with reverence in Hindu societies, in part because some followers of the Hindu religion believe that any cow could carry the spirits of one of their ancestors. Certain Native American tribes believe that they're favored animal, the buffalo, had a connection to the divine. The tribes still hunted the buffalo, but carefully, according to such strict rules that the hunt seemed more like a religious ritual. Even in cultures with less formalized belief systems, regular interactions between people and animals still lead to common opinions.

These stories usually develop around the animals that interact with humans most frequently. Therefore, it should not be surprising that so many stories surround the most common of animals: rats. Rats live side-by-side with humans all over the world, regularly interact with people. Human-rat coexistence may be common all around the world, with different cultures respond to that closeness in different ways.

In the United States and Europe, one typical attitude is that the rat is a pest. This could be due to the common belief that

61. A. NO CHANGE
B. should of
C. had
D. has

62. F. NO CHANGE
G. their
H. theirs
J. there

63. A. NO CHANGE
B. so that
C. as to mean
D. because

64. Given that all of the choices are true, which of the following concludes this paragraph with the clearest allusion to the story of "The Pied Piper of Hamlin," which is discussed later in the essay?

F. NO CHANGE
G. it is well-known that other cultures hold religious beliefs about some animals.
H. people still tend to have beliefs, either individual or cultural, relating to animals.
J. folklore and stories relating to humans' relationship with animals abound.

65. Which of the following alternatives to the underlined portion would NOT be acceptable?

A. tales
B. legends
C. narrators
D. fables

66. F. NO CHANGE
G. world and regularly
H. world, regular
J. world, regularly,

67. A. NO CHANGE
B. world,
C. world, but with
D. world, but

68. F. NO CHANGE
G. pest, which is a common opinion.
H. pest, a belief many people share.
J. pest, moreover.

rats spread disease. They <u>don't, at least not directly; but many</u> people don't know that.₆₉ "The Pied Piper of Hamlin," a well-known children's story, is one example of how rats have been portrayed in a <u>different</u> way in Western literature: in that story, ₇₀ rats cause such a problem that a town has to hire a piper to call them all away.

<u>What's really wild is that in</u> many Latin American countries, ₇₁ and some European countries as well, the rat is portrayed in a very different light. The tooth fairy legend is common all over the world, but in Latin America, the "fairy" is a rat! Rats do have <u>very strong teeth,</u> which could explain the association. ₇₂ Clearly, this shows another attitude toward rats that is much more positive.

[1] <u>Yet another</u> attitude toward the rat can be seen in the ₇₃

Chinese *Zodiac*. [2] <u>The Rat is one of the animals, of the</u> zodiac along with the Sheep, the Rooster, the Boar, and eight ₇₄ others. [3] Like the other zodiac animals, the Rat is neither entirely good nor entirely bad. [4] It's described as clever and friendly, but also tricky and not entirely honest. [5] That may be the most accurate description of the rat so far. [6] Whether you like rats or not, it's hard to deny their reputation for cleverness. [7] As many people are discovering these days, rats can even make excellent pets, so long as you remember to latch

69. A. NO CHANGE
    B. don't, at least not directly,
    C. don't: at least not directly,
    D. don't, at least not directly

70. Given that all the choices are true, which one states a detail that most clearly relates to the information conveyed at the end of this sentence?
    F. NO CHANGE
    G. mystical
    H. negative
    J. juvenile

71. A. NO CHANGE
    B. In
    C. Dig this: in the minds of those born and raised in
    D. You'll be shocked to discover that in

72. Given that all the choices are true, which one provides a physical detail about rats that relates most clearly to the preceding sentence?
    F. NO CHANGE
    G. particularly curious natures,
    H. a reputation for excessive chewing,
    J. long and somewhat unusual tails,

73. A. NO CHANGE
    B. China's
    C. Chinese mysticism's
    D. Their

74. F. NO CHANGE
    G. is one of the animals, of the zodiac,
    H. is one of the animals of the zodiac,
    J. is one, of the animals of the zodiac

the cage carefully! ☐75

75. The writer wants to create a concluding paragraph that focuses on one characteristic of rats outside of any specific cultural frame of reference by dividing the preceding paragraph in two. The best place to begin the new paragraph would be at the beginning of Sentence:

A. 4.
B. 5.
C. 6.
D. 7.

END OF TEST 2
STOP! DO NOT TURN THE PAGE UNTIL TOLD TO DO SO.

Chapter 6
English Practice
Test 2
Answers and
Explanations

ENGLISH PRACTICE TEST 2 ANSWERS

1.	B		39.	C
2.	F		40.	G
3.	C		41.	C
4.	F		42.	J
5.	C		43.	C
6.	J		44.	J
7.	A		45.	B
8.	G		46.	H
9.	B		47.	A
10.	H		48.	J
11.	C		49.	A
12.	G		50.	J
13.	D		51.	C
14.	J		52.	J
15.	B		53.	D
16.	H		54.	G
17.	B		55.	C
18.	G		56.	H
19.	D		57.	C
20.	H		58.	H
21.	D		59.	D
22.	H		60.	H
23.	A		61.	D
24.	J		62.	G
25.	A		63.	A
26.	F		64.	J
27.	D		65.	C
28.	J		66.	G
29.	A		67.	D
30.	J		68.	F
31.	A		69.	B
32.	H		70.	H
33.	B		71.	B
34.	J		72.	F
35.	D		73.	A
36.	H		74.	H
37.	B		75.	C
38.	G			

SCORE YOUR PRACTICE TEST

Step A

Count the number of correct answers: _____. This is your *raw score*.

Step B

Use the score conversion table below to look up your raw score. The number to the left is your *scale score*: _____.

English Scale Conversion Table

Scale Score	Raw Score	Scale Score	Raw Score	Scale Score	Raw Score
36	75	27	62	18	41–42
35	73–74	26	60–61	17	39–40
34	71–72	25	58–59	16	36 38
33	70	24	56–57	15	33–35
32	69	23	54–55	14	30–32
31	67–68	22	52–53	13	28–29
30	66	21	49–51	12	26–27
29	65	20	46–48	11	24–25
28	63–64	19	43–45	10	22–23

ENGLISH PRACTICE TEST 2 EXPLANATIONS

Passage I

1. **B** The question asks you to find the answer choice that is NOT acceptable as a replacement for the underlined portion—remember, that means the passage is correct as written. Look at the answer choices—some change words, some change punctuation. In a case like this, you'll need to check each answer choice. (A), (C), and (D) can all be inserted in place of the underlined portion without creating an error, but (B) makes the sentence *When I woke up this morning, I made myself a bowl of cereal, sat listening to the traffic*, which isn't an appropriate way to join two complete ideas and therefore can NOT be used.

2. **F** When you see answer choices "stacked" like this, using all the same words with Stop and Go punctuation changing in the same spot, check for Complete/Incomplete on either side of that spot. In this case, *It's true that there's always some kind of noise in my neighborhood* is complete, and *taxi drivers honking their horns, kids playing their radios so loud that the bass makes my teeth vibrate, or people yelling in the street* is incomplete. Since Stop punctuation can only separate two complete ideas, eliminate (H). You definitely need some kind of pause after *neighborhood*, so (J) can be eliminated. Now you must choose between a comma and a dash. Using a comma would make it seem like the sentence is giving a list of things that are true, when the intention is to list the kinds of noises in the neighborhood. Remember a single dash is the same thing as a colon—it must follow a complete idea and must itself be followed by a list, definition or explanation of the first complete idea. That's what the sentence has as written, so choose (F).

3. **C** The preceding sentence is *I know that some people wouldn't like it, but to me, these are the sounds of life*. This is almost the exact opposite of what (A) says—the narrator is putting a positive spin on what many would find an annoyance. There is no trip to the park mentioned as in (B), and (D) is incorrect because this sentence is very much relevant to the essay—choose (C).

4. **F** None of the answer choices contains a grammatical error, and they all say roughly the same thing, so pick the one that says it with the fewest words—*It's*.

5. **C** Careful—all of these answer choices may seem fit to use, but on the ACT, there is always a reason to choose the best answer choice. In this case the entire sentence reads *When I ride the bus, you get to see so much more of the city*. The underlined portion you select must have a pronoun that is consistent with the non-underlined *you get*, which is (C), *you ride*.

6. **J**   Here you need to choose between *sociable* and *sociably*, but there's punctuation changing as well—start easy! You need the adverb *sociably* because it's describing how the people are chatting—eliminate (F) and (H). (G) is incorrect because there's no need for a pause after *sociably*, so no comma is needed.

7. **A**   The answer choices have "stacked" words with Stop and Go punctuation changing in one spot, so check for Complete/Incomplete on either side of that spot. *Just like the traffic's sounds, though, the noise on the bus represents people* is complete (but awkward), and *working, relaxing, and living* is incomplete, so you need Go punctuation—eliminate (B) and (C). (D) is incorrect because you don't need a comma after *people*—you only need commas to separate the items in the list of things the people are doing.

8. **G**   Here you have a 3/1 split with three answer choices using pronouns and one that uses the noun *kids*, so check that one first. *Kids* makes sense in the context of the sentence and is consistent with the non-underlined *their parents*.

9. **B**   In the answer choices you see Stop and Go punctuation changing after the word *nearby*, so check for Complete/Incomplete on either side of the punctuation. *The city added the bench so kids could play while their parents sit nearby* is complete, and, regardless of whether it begins with *obviously*, or not, *I like to sit there because there's a great big oak tree for shade* is also complete. Two complete ideas must be connected with Stop punctuation—eliminate (A) and (C). While adding the word *because* in (D) makes the second idea incomplete and might make you think it's okay to use a comma, it's still incorrect: To use the word *because*, you need a causal relationship between the ideas, and there is none in this case.

10. **H**   This question is testing proper comma placement. You don't need a comma after either *watching* or *listening*, since the idea being expressed is *watching and listening to the people around me*—eliminate (F), (G), and (J).

11. **C**   In the answer choices you see Stop and Go punctuation changing after the word *do*, so check for Complete/Incomplete on either side of the punctuation. *People-watching is one of my favorite things to do* is complete, and *I like listening even better* is complete as well. Two complete ideas must be connected with Stop punctuation—eliminate (A). You can also eliminate (B) and (D), because even though they respectively add *nevertheless* and *however* after the punctuation change, both of those are transition words that only indicate direction—they don't make a complete idea incomplete. (C), which uses a comma + FANBOYS (but), is the only choice that gives you the Stop punctuation you're looking for.

12. **G**   The following sentence says *That way, I can pay more attention to the sounds and not get distracted by what I see,* so the most logical introduction would be one that has the narrator closing her eyes—(G).

13. **D**   You need to emphasize the narrator's curiosity and interest in the old men's conversation, so the correct answer choice needs to incorporate the narrator's point of view. Choices (A), (B), and (C) are all objective descriptions of the conversation itself or the old men. (D) characterizes the stories as entertaining, meaning *entertaining* to the narrator, and so is the best answer.

14. **J**   Here apostrophes are being used to show possession. You know there are two old men having the conversation, so the laugh that comes in response to the story one of them is telling must come from his *friend*, not his *friends*. To show possession for a singular noun, all you have to do is add *'s*—answer choice (J).

15. **B**   This essay is definitely pro-city living, and really only explores one aspect of what the narrator likes about the city, so you can eliminate (C) and (D). (A) is incorrect, because although public transportation is mentioned, it isn't the convenience the narrator enjoys—it's the sounds and sights of the city.

Passage II

16. **H**   When you see DELETE as an answer choice, try that first. In this case, taking out *that* causes a syntax error—you wouldn't say *…three times in seventy-year history*. You need to find the correct pronoun, so the first step is to identify the noun that the pronoun replaces—it's *bridge*. Since *bridge* is a singular noun, eliminate (G); you can't replace a singular noun with a plural pronoun. The pronoun *that* in the sentence as written is incorrect; you can't use it because there is no prior reference to the seventy-year history.

17. **B**   The sentence is saying the amount of concrete was *enough to construct a sidewalk five feet wide all the way from San Francisco to New York City*. There isn't a reason to use commas here, so eliminate (A) and (D). (C) has a dash (which is the same as a colon) after *sidewalk*, which creates an awkward and unclear construction afterwards.

18. **G**   The sentence immediately following details the various reasons San Francisco Bay is a bad spot for bridge-building, so a logical introduction will introduce this theme. Neither (F), (G), nor (J) do this as well as (G).

19. **D**   Here you see Stop and Go Punctuation changing after the word *bond* in each answer choice, so check for Complete/Incomplete on either side of the punctuation. *After two years of discussion, the voters approved a bond* is complete, and *that would raise $35 million, all dedicated to building the bridge* is incomplete, so eliminate (C). (A) has a colon after a complete idea, but the incomplete idea after it is awkward and unclear. (B) is incorrect because the phrase *that would raise $35 million* is necessary, and thus there is no need for a comma here, much less two.

20. **H** You have the option to DELETE the underlined portion, so try that first. That leaves *Even then, there were many skeptics believed that it couldn't be done*, which is a bad sentence—eliminate (J). Now you have to choose the correct pronoun, so identify the noun that's being replaced—it's *skeptics*. You can't use *that* to replace skeptics: It's singular and *that* can't be used to refer to people, so eliminate (G). If you have trouble deciding between *who* and *whom*, try substituting a different pronoun: There are multiple skeptics, so you can use "they" and "them." You would use the subject-case "they believed it couldn't be done," not the object-case "them believed it couldn't be done." That means you need to use the subject-case *who*—answer choice (H).

21. **D** When DELETE is an option, you should always check that first—you know ACT likes things concise. Taking out the underlined portion leaves *Construction began in 1933 and lasted a little more than four years*. That's a perfectly good sentence, and you're not adding any new information with (A), (B), or (C)—(D) is the best (most concise) answer.

22. **H** The answer choices have "stacked" words with Stop and Go punctuation changing after *1937*, so check for Complete/Incomplete on either side of that spot. *On May 28, 1937* is an incomplete idea, so you know you can't use Stop punctuation—that's only for connecting two complete ideas—eliminate (F) and (G). (H) and (J) both give you the comma you need after *1937*, but (J) goes a little too far by adding another that you don't need after *grandly*.

23. **A** DELETE the underlined portion first, since that's an option. That leaves *More than 200,000 people walked across the bridge that day to celebrate*, which is a complete idea, but is not as clear as it could be (celebrate what?) The better option is (A)—it's a little less concise, but much more clear. (B) and (C) are much too wordy; neither says anything that (A) doesn't.

24. **J** The answer choices are all transition words, which is usually a sign that the question is testing direction. The two sentences on either side are *To top it off, it was beautiful* and *the Golden Gate Bridge is considered an artistic masterpiece*—two similar ideas (although note the shift in tense between the two from past to present.) You can eliminate the two opposite-direction transitions, (F) and (H), and eliminate (G) because it's still past-tense; you want a transition that will make the change to present tense, as *Even today* does.

25. **A** The answer choices all have Stop and Go punctuation (and a dash) changing after the word *air*, so check for Complete/Incomplete before and after the punctuation. Before the punctuation is *At its highest point, the bridge rises 746 feet into the air*, which is complete, and afterward is *191 feet taller than the Washington Monument*, an incomplete idea. Eliminate (B)—you can't use Stop punctuation here. We can do without the extra *rising*, so eliminate (D). We do, however, need some kind of pause after *air*, so eliminate (C).

26. **F** The answer choices are all different word combinations—you just have to pick the correct one. The idiomatic expression for "environment" is *natural surroundings*—answer choice (F). If you're not sure here, you can try substituting each answer choice into the sentence; you should at least be able to eliminate one or two answer choices. Always keep in mind that NO CHANGE is going to be correct about 25 percent of the time it appears, so don't be afraid to pick it—especially if you can't identify an error in the sentence as it's written.

27. **D** The whole sentence says *The color, called "International Orange," was chosen partly because it matched the natural surroundings and partly because it would allow the bridge to remain visible on foggy days.* Saying *on foggy days* provides a detail about when the bridge might be hard to see, so if you take out that portion, you would lose that detail. That most closely matches (D).

28. **J** You need to emphasize the *wide variety of the bridge's uses* here, so the correct answer choice must do that. (F) only talks about commuter traffic, (G) describes the bridge itself, not how it is used, and (H) talks about how some people cross the bridge—none of which describe *a wide variety of uses*. (J) talks about the bridge's multiple uses for commuters and travelers and as a tourist destination in its own right, so it is the best answer choice.

29. **A** The added sentence talks about the original idea for building the bridge, so it belongs somewhere very early in the discussion of its construction—eliminate (C) and (D). Between (A) and (B), the more logical choice for the placement of the original idea for the bridge would be (A), just before the decision to actually build it.

Passage III

30. **J** Here you have nicely "stacked" answer choices with Stop (comma + FANBOYS) and Go punctuation changing after *single*—check for Complete/Incomplete on either side. *The Italian language wasn't always the single* is incomplete, as is *unified, language that it is today.* You'll need Go punctuation to connect these two—eliminate (H). Remember your comma rules; there's no reason to use a comma after *unified*—eliminate (F) and (G), leaving (J) as the best answer choice.

31. **A** The phrase *during the thirteenth century* introduces the time period the passage will be talking about, so that's what you lose if you take it out—there's no confusion created as in (B), no interruption as in (C), and it's not grammatically necessary as (D) claims; (A) is the best answer.

32. **H** Remember that less is more on the ACT; any time you have the option to add anything, make sure you have a compelling reason to do so. In this case, the sentence (not to mention the passage as a whole) is talking about Dante Alighieri, so adding a list of other writers doesn't add anything necessary to the essay. If you're still unsure, you can check the reasons given in the answer choices and eliminate those that don't agree with the passage: You can eliminate (F) as previously stated, there's no discussion of the creation of Italian as (G) states, and the reason you aren't adding the list isn't because it's not exhaustive, as (J) claims—it's because it's unnecessary.

33. **B** The underlined portion acts as the subject of the singular verb *was* in the non-underlined portion. Choices (A) and (C) are plural. Choice (D) doesn't fit the context of the sentence.

34. **J** The meaning of the sentence is not to say that literature was not written in the local languages and also not in Latin; the idea is that high literature was written in Latin instead of the local languages. To express that, you need to say *literature was written not in the various local languages but in Latin*— answer choice (J).

35. **D** DELETE is an answer choice, so try that first. Taking out the underlined portion leaves *Dante believed that literature should be available not only to the educated elite but also to the common people.* That is a complete sentence, and the meaning hasn't changed, so (D) is the best answer.

36. **H** Three of the answer choices use *called* and one uses *calling*, so you should check that one first, but remember that ACT doesn't really like the "-ing" form of verbs, and you should only pick it when all the other answer choices have an actual error. In this case, however, it doesn't make sense in the sentence—Dante was not literally calling out the word "Italian"—you can eliminate (J), and also (F) and (G), which make the sentence read the same way.

37. **B** Three of the answer choices use *spoken* and one uses *speak*, so you should check that one first. However, *to speak* doesn't make sense in the context of the sentence, so eliminate (D). There's no need to include *to be* or *if* as in (A) and (C); (B) makes the most sense—and it's the most concise—so it's the best answer choice.

38. **G** The answer choices all have Stop and Go punctuation (plus a colon) changing after the word *people*, so check for Complete/Incomplete on either side to see which you need. In this case, *By writing it in the language spoken by the Italian people* is incomplete, and since Stop punctuation can only connect two complete ideas, you can now eliminate (F) and (H). You can also eliminate (J), since a colon can only follow a complete idea. That leaves (G) as the only possible choice.

39. **C** All of the answer choices use the exact same words, just in different orders—you'll need to select the one that is most clear. Dante thought literature should be available to everyone, and was criticized for that opinion. The answer choice that expresses that idea in the most clear fashion is (C).

40. **G**   Remember when ACT gives you a task to accomplish with an answer choice, you must read very literally—an answer choice that does the thing you want is a better choice than one that "could" do the thing you want. In this case, we need an answer choice that will imply that illiteracy changed from more common to less common. Be careful! If you just look at the words in the answer choices, *diminished* might seem the perfect candidate, but the passage is talking about *literacy*, not illiteracy. Therefore, you want the answer choice that says that literacy became more common, which would *imply* that illiteracy became less common—answer choice (G). Both (H) and (J) might conceivably accompany an increase in literacy, neither state that as clearly as (G) does.

41. **C**   A good place to start here is to decide which verb form you need—always keeping in mind ACT's opinion of the "-ing" form. *Confuses* agrees with the subject, *title*, so eliminate (A) and (B). The use of *that* in (D) makes the sentence an incomplete idea, so the best answer choice is (C).

42. **J**   There are transition words changing in the answer choices, but not punctuation, which will typically mean ACT is testing direction. Make sure you read enough to get the proper context! The two ideas we have to connect are *The Divine Comedy wasn't written in Latin* and *it was considered a comedy*. The sentence prior to this says *the label of "comedy" was attached to any work not written in Latin*, so you're going to need a same-direction transition—eliminate (F). (G), (H), and (J) are all same-direction transitions, but (G) and (H) have the relationship wrong—*The Divine Comedy* wasn't written in Latin as a result of being considered a comedy; it was the other way around. Note that in this case, (G) and (H) are "same" answer choices: *since* and *because* mean the exact same thing in this context, which means one cannot be more correct than the other; therefore, you cannot select either one.

43. **C**   The answer choices all feature different transition words, but there's some punctuation changing as well. In fact, three of the answer choices use a comma and one doesn't—start there. In this instance, *and* causes an error, so eliminate (B). All the other answer choices end in a comma, which means the phrase *in defiance of the common beliefs of his time* is unnecessary since it's set off by a pair of commas—it may help to cross it out or simply ignore it to help answer the question. Without the unnecessary phrase (and its commas), the sentence now reads *Dante's brave decision, while demonstrated that it was not necessary for a literary masterpiece to be written in Latin, paved the way for future writers and readers alike*. That's not correct, so eliminate (A), and substituting *so that* for *while* doesn't help either—eliminate (D). That leaves answer choice (C), *which* as the correct answer.

44. **J**   You have the option to DELETE the underlined portion, so try that first. You're left with a complete sentence, so it's at least possible to take out that word without creating an error. However, notice that the other choices are all transition words, so it may be a good idea to assess whether a transition is needed here. The prior sentence (now) reads *Dante's brave decision, which, in defiance of the common beliefs of his time, demonstrated that it was not necessary for a literary masterpiece to be written in Latin, paved the way for future writers and readers alike*, and then you have *The Divine Comedy remains a symbol of both literature and innovation today*. No transition is really needed here, and even if one were, it wouldn't be an opposite-direction one, as are (F), (G), and (H).

Passage IV

45. **B** The answer choices are all different arrangements of the same three modifying phrases. On the ACT, (and in good writing in general), a modifying phrase must be placed next to the thing it's modifying. In this case, the words right before the underlined portion are *We would sit*, and the phrase that most directly modifies that is *on the couch*, so the correct answer choice must start with that phrase. Only (B) matches that description.

46. **H** You have possessive pronouns changing in the answer choices, so to choose the correct one, you'll need to find the context in the non-underlined part of the passage. The answers being called out belong to the narrator and her grandmother, and since the passage is written in the first person, you need to use *our*, answer choice (H). If you're still unsure, notice that using *our* is consistent with the following sentence: *When our answers were right....*

47. **A** You need to find the answer choice that is NOT a suitable replacement for the correctly-written underlined portion in the passage. The answer choices all have Stop and Go punctuation changing after the word *excitement*, so you should check for Complete/Incomplete on either side. Notice the sentence as written uses Stop punctuation (comma + FANBOYS), so you know the two ideas are complete. (B) and (C) both use different forms of Stop punctuation, and so can be used as replacements, and (D), even though it uses Go punctuation, inserts the word *or* into the second idea, making it incomplete, and so is also correct. What can NOT be used as a replacement is (A), which uses a comma to separate two complete ideas.

48. **J** The first decision to make here is whether you need *regular* or *regularly*. The verb *watch* is being modified, so you need the adverb *regularly*—eliminate (F) and (G). (H) is incorrect because it uses the correct adverb but the wrong conjunction—the narrator and her grandmother don't watch the shows *as regularly* as they did prior to school starting.

49. **A** The sentence *That was okay with me, though, because the one thing I liked better than watching game shows with my grandmother was helping her bake* introduces the main idea of the essay, and so serves as a transition between the discussion of the two activities the narrator enjoys with her grandmother. That's not unnecessary or detracting information as in (B), and (C) and (D) can be eliminated because they only talk about watching television.

50. **J** You need to find the answer choice that is NOT a suitable replacement for the correctly-written underlined portion in the passage. (F), (G), and (H) all keep the original meaning of the sentence, but *help along* has a different meaning, and *help along the easy parts* doesn't really make sense; therefore (J) is NOT a suitable replacement.

51. **C**   (C) describes the narrator as *awed* and *eager to taste*, which accomplishes both tasks: expressing both respect and enjoyment. (A) and (D) express lack of understanding and confusion, and (B) talks about homework.

52. **J**   The three sentences describe a progression in the amount of help the narrator was allowed to give her grandmother in the kitchen: *At first* she only sat and watched (sentence 2). *As [she] got older*, she helped with the easier tasks (sentence 1). Finally, she reaches *the pinnacle of success* when she gets to separate the eggs (sentence 3).

53. **D**   Whenever DELETE is an option, you should try that first. In this case, taking out *because I didn't need someone to keep an eye on me anymore* does not create an error or change the meaning; in fact, it gets rid of redundancy because the narrator has already said *my parents decided that I could take care of myself.* (B) and (C) are both redundant and wordy as well—pick (D).

54. **G**   You need to find the answer choice that is NOT a suitable replacement for the correctly-written underlined portion in the passage. (F), (H), and (J) can all be used in place of *burned* in this context, but (G), *burnted*, far from being a replacement, can NOT be used—it's not even a word.

55. **C**   The answer choices all have different pairs of words; notice the second word in each is a preposition. When you see prepositions changing, that's a good sign that ACT may be testing idioms. In this case, in order to express the idea of "attempted something for the first time," you need to use *tried out*, answer choice (C)

56. **H**   You need to find the answer choice that is NOT a suitable replacement for the correctly-written underlined portion in the passage. Notice the answer choices all have different pairs of words, and the second word in each is a preposition: That's a good sign that ACT is testing idioms. In the context of the sentence, *flipped through* means, "quickly read the contents of a book." (F), (G), and (J) all convey that same meaning, but *tossed out* in (H) would imply she threw the book away, and so can NOT be used as a replacement.

57. **C**   The answer choices all have Stop and Go punctuation changing after the same word: *voice.* Check for Complete/Incomplete on both sides. *As I flipped through the pages, I thought for a moment I could hear her voice* is complete, as is *although she's gone, I know that in the way that matters most, she'll never really be gone at all.* You need to use Stop punctuation to separate two complete ideas—eliminate (A) and (D). (B) is incorrect because the transition word *but* makes the second idea incomplete, so you can't use it with a semicolon.

58. **H** When you see pronouns changing in the answer choice, find the noun that's being replaced: *She* (referring to the narrator's grandmother). Eliminate (F) because you can't use *which* to refer a person. (J) is the possessive pronoun *whose*, so look at the word that follows it; only nouns can be possessed. You can't possess *taught*, so eliminate (J). In this case, the pronoun is the subject of the verb *taught*, so you need *who*—answer choice (H).

59. **D** The main focus of the passage isn't baking; it's the relationship between the narrator and her grandmother—eliminate (A). (B) and (C) have the same problem. (D) is the only answer choice that mentions the narrator's grandmother.

60. **H** This sentence doesn't fit in the narrative of either paragraph 1 or 2, so eliminate (F) and (G). It should also come before the narrator says *Although she's gone* so that it's clear to the reader that her grandmother has passed away—(H) is the better answer choice for that reason.

Passage V

61. **D** You have helping verbs changing in the answer choices, and recall the helping verbs need to agree with the subject, just like regular verbs. In this case, the subject of the sentence is *relationship*, which is singular, so eliminate (A), which is plural. (B) is an incorrect construction: It's "should have," not "should of." (C) makes the sentence seem to imply that the relationship was only complicated in the past, and isn't anymore, but there's no support for the latter in the passage. (D) is the best answer choice: The relationship *has always been complicated*.

62. **G** The answer choices are all similar-sounding, so your ear isn't going to help much on this question. Expand out (F)—it means "they are," which doesn't make sense here. You need a word that shows the buffalo was the favored animal of the tribes, and in this context, that's the possessive pronoun *their*, answer choice (G).

63. **A** The passage says the hunts were carried out *according to such strict rules… the hunt seemed more like a religious ritual*. When you use the word *such* in this context, you have to pair it with *that*, answer choice (A). If you chose (D), you may have misunderstood the relationship; the rules weren't strict as a result of the hunts seeming like a religious ritual—it's the other way around.

64. **J** You need to choose an answer choice that makes a *clear allusion* to a story later in the essay. The only answer choice that even mentions a story is (J): *folklore and stories relating to humans' relationship with animals*.

65. **C** You need to find the answer choice that is NOT a suitable replacement for the correctly-written underlined portion in the passage. (A), (B), and (D) all mean the same thing as the underlined word, *stories*. *Narrator* does NOT mean the same thing—it refers to someone who tells stories—so (C) is the correct choice.

66. **G** You have three answer choices with *regularly* and one with *regular*, so check that one first. You need an adverb to modify the verb *interact*, so eliminate (H). In both (A) and (C), the verb *interact* has no subject, so eliminate them—(G), which joins the two verbs *live* and *interact* with *and*, giving them both a subject, is correct.

67. **D** The answer choices all have Stop (comma + FANBOYS) and Go punctuation changing after the same word: *world*, so check for Complete/Incomplete on either side. *Human-rat coexistence may be common all around the world* is complete, and so is the part after the underlined portion: *different cultures respond to that closeness in different ways*. (A) has Go punctuation and adds *with*, which makes the second idea incomplete, but also doesn't make sense. (B) joins two complete ideas with a comma—eliminate it. (C) has the FANBOYS conjunction you're looking for, but like (A), adds *with*, which makes no sense. (D) is the best answer choice—it uses Stop punctuation to separate the two complete ideas.

68. **F** All four answer choices say the same thing in slightly different ways, and none contains a grammatical error. Therefore, pick the one that is the most concise: (F), NO CHANGE.

69. **B** The answer choices mostly have commas changing around, but one uses a colon, so start there. The colon follows a complete idea, *They don't*, which is proper, but what follows the colon is not a list, definition, or expansion of that idea (not to mention it's an extremely awkward construction), so eliminate (B). To choose the correct comma placement, remember your comma rules: *at least not directly* is unnecessary information, so you need to set it off with commas—the only answer choice that does that is (B).

70. **H** In the end of the sentence you have the statement *rats cause such a problem that a town has to hire a piper to call them all away* and you need to find the word to describe how rats have been portrayed that agrees with that most closely. (H), *negative*, agrees with the notion of the rats being a *problem* better than *different*, *mystical*, or *juvenile*.

71. **B** Aside from being the most concise, (B) avoids the problems found in the other choices. Remember, there's no slang on the ACT! (A) and (C) are too informal, besides being far too wordy. (D) might be tempting, but it's not concise as well as being a bit too strong; remember the author has already told you different cultures respond to that [human-rat] closeness in different ways, so an example of one of those ways shouldn't really shock you.

72. **F**   The correct answer choice has to provide a physical detail about rats, so (G) and (H) can be eliminated—neither of those is a physical detail. (J) certainly is a physical characteristic, but probably has less to do with the rat's association with teeth than a description of the rat's *very strong* teeth.

73. **A**   The underlined portion introduces a new paragraph and the sentence *attitude toward the rat can be seen in the Chinese zodiac.* (B) and (C) cause redundancy in the sentence: The phrase *Chinese zodiac* already tells you you're talking about mysticism in China. (D) is temptingly concise, but the pronoun *their* has no noun to refer to, so you can't use it. (A) is the best answer since it both makes sense in the sentence and acts as an effective transition to the new paragraph after the discussion of a different example of people's attitude toward rats in the previous paragraph.

74. **H**   Remember your comma rules here: This isn't a list, introductory idea, or unnecessary information, so there's really no reason to use a comma between any of the underlined words—eliminate (F), (G), and (J); the only choice you have is (H).

75. **C**   If you want to divide the last paragraph into two based on a non-cultural frame of reference, you'll need to begin after the rat's description based on the Chinese zodiac—eliminate (A) and (B). The most logical place to begin the new paragraph, then, is (C), which begins talking about the rat's *cleverness*.

Chapter 7
English
Practice Test 3

ACT ENGLISH TEST
45 Minutes—75 Questions

DIRECTIONS: In the five passages that follow, certain words and phrases are underlined and numbered. In the right-hand column, you will find alternatives for each underlined part. In most cases, you are to choose the one that best expresses the idea, makes the statement appropriate for standard written English, or is worded most consistently with the style and tone of the passage as a whole. If you think the original version is best, choose "NO CHANGE." In some cases, you will find in the right-hand column a question about the underlined part. You are to choose the best answer to the question.

You will also find questions about a section of the passage or the passage as a whole. These questions do not refer to an underlined portion of the passage but rather are identified by a number or numbers in a box.

For each question, choose the alternative you consider best and blacken the corresponding oval on your answer document. Read each passage through once before you begin to answer the questions that accompany it. For many of the questions, you must read several sentences beyond the question to determine the answer. Be sure that you have read far enough ahead each time you choose an alternative.

PASSAGE I

Cheeseburgers and Cats That Can Make You "lol"

Everyone knows that cats love to chase mice, but who knew they also love to eat cheeseburgers? [A] It's a very special kind of cat that does: a *lolcat*. The concept is simple: take a funny photograph of a cat and written a humorous caption over it. [B] The name is a compound word combining *cat* and *lol*, the slangy Internet abbreviation for "laughing out loud." [C] In some ways, the phenomenon of the lolcat is nothing new. [D] In the 1870s, Brighton-based photographer, Henry Pointer took a series of images of his pet cats. The images were intended to form the backgrounds for *cartes de visite*, having at times been called "visiting cards." To enhance a photo's appeal, Henry Pointer would often add a humorous caption.

Pointer's first photographs, those without captions, did not sell well initially, though they have recently been better appreciated. Pointer made a good deal of money from his photos because photography equipment was still

1. If the writer were to delete the underlined portion (changing the comma after *mice* to a period), the sentence would primarily lose:
   A. a description of one of the things that make lolcats unique.
   B. a scientific fact describing a well-known species.
   C. a concise statement of the essay's main idea.
   D. nothing at all, because it strays from the topic unnecessarily.

2. F. NO CHANGE
   G. is writing
   H. wrote
   J. write

3. A. NO CHANGE
   B. photographer Henry Pointer
   C. photographer, Henry Pointer,
   D. photographer; Henry Pointer

4. F. NO CHANGE
   G. a French term meaning
   H. being things called
   J. and naming them

5. Given that all the choices are true, which one best conveys the idea that captions contributed to the humor of Pointer's photographs?
   A. NO CHANGE
   B. Pointer would occasionally reuse captions when the picture could communicate most of what he wanted it to.
   C. In fact, he soon understood that the humorous caption could make even the most mundane cat pictures charming or funny.
   D. Pointer took so many pictures and wrote so many captions that neither required much effort of him.

relatively rare and expensive for his day. He likely never knew,
₆
however, that his pictures would be the basis for a hugely

popular movement over a century later. ⁷

Today, though, anyone with a camera and a computer can
₈
create a lolcat image. The only requirement is a basic fluency
in the language of *lolspeak*, a grammatically-incorrect, often
misspelled form of English. The most famous

phrase known widely in all of lolspeak is "I can has
₉
cheezburger?", or "Can I have a cheeseburger?"

Additional phrases and the language are fairly easy to
₁₀
learn, and lolcats have become some of the trendiest images on
the Internet.

As a result of their popularity, lolcats have attracted all
₁₁
kinds of new press in recent years. *Time* magazine covered
lolcats in a July 2007 issue. Even the American Dialect Society

has named "lolcat" one of the mainly creative coinages of the
₁₂
decade. There have been financial gains as well: in 2007, the
"I Can Has Cheezburger?" website was purchased by a group
of investors for $2 million and has spawned many spinoffs.
It would seem, then, that the lolcat is here to stay, and that

6. F. NO CHANGE
G. with
H. in
J. of

7. If the writer were to divide this paragraph into two, the most logical place to begin the new paragraph would be at Point:
A. A.
B. B.
C. C.
D. D.

8. Which of the following alternatives to the underlined portion would NOT be acceptable?
F. in fact,
G. however,
H. by contrast,
J. on the other hand,

9. A. NO CHANGE
B. phrase
C. phrase that many people know
D. phrase that is pretty popular

10. F. NO CHANGE
G. is being
H. is
J. were

11. A. NO CHANGE
B. Now earning lots of money,
C. With their cameras in hand,
D. Promoting them on the Internet,

12. F. NO CHANGE
G. more
H. most
J. a lot

cheeseburger-flavored cat food can't be far off. 13

13. If the writer were to delete the phrase "cheeseburger-flavored" in the preceding sentence and replace it with "another line of," the paragraph would primarily lose:

   A. a particular detail that ends the essay on a humorous note.
   B. a more detailed discussion of the different types of cats discussed in the essay.
   C. a resolution to a difficult problem posed earlier in the essay.
   D. an open question that is left to the reader to decide.

Question 14 asks about the preceding passage as a whole.

14. Suppose the writer's goal had been to write a brief essay describing a new generation's interest in animal photography. Would this essay accomplish that goal?

   F. Yes, because it shows how important lolcats have been to a broader interest in photography.
   G. Yes, because it narrates the simultaneous rise of digital photography and Internet usage.
   H. No, because it details the different types of animal photography popular on the Internet.
   J. No, because it focuses on lolcats and their history, not on photography more generally.

PASSAGE II

My Summer as a Teacher . . . or as a Student?

I was there only for a summer, but the memories I have of teaching English in Mexico have stayed with me. The experience didn't start well. I was assigned to a small village— located a few hours west of Monterrey; in the central north part of the country, in the state of Durango. The most direct route was to fly into the large city of Monterrey and then take a seven-hour bus ride. Once we got out of the city, the ride was bumpy, and the bus's air conditioning was no match for the heat of the desert sun burning overhead.

Mexico's climate is warmer than that of the United States because Mexico is closer to the equator. The adults in the village, many of whom did not even know I was coming,

welcomed me when they got around to it. More than that, my host family had reserved a room in their house exclusively for me, so I could have some privacy when I needed it. Even though I was in a new place, I already felt like I was at home.

The language situation was more difficult than I expected. I learned very quickly that the good grades I had received in my Spanish classes would not necessarily translate to success here

where people spoke the Spanish language and no other. Still, my host family and others in the village were very patient

15. **A.** NO CHANGE
    B. Monterrey. In
    C. Monterrey in
    D. Monterrey—in

16. **F.** NO CHANGE
    G. burning.
    H. scorching.
    J. DELETE the underlined portion and end the sentence with a period.

17. Given that all the choices are true, which provides material most relevant to what follows in this paragraph?

    A. NO CHANGE
    B. I had only been to Mexico one time before, when I went with my parents to the beach.
    C. Once I got there, though, I didn't have any of the problems that I had worried about in advance.
    D. The heat from the sun was nothing compared to the heat of the spicy food my family liked to cook.

18. Which choice most effectively expresses that the narrator's host family was extremely welcoming?

    F. NO CHANGE
    G. as if I had lived there my whole life.
    H. and asked how long I would be staying.
    J. to their town.

19. Which of the following alternatives to the underlined portion would NOT be acceptable?

    A. no language other than Spanish.
    B. Spanish language others or no.
    C. Spanish and no other language.
    D. no other language.

with me. Before long, we had held all of our conversations in
                        ——————
                          20
Spanish.

The family I was hosting in Mexico asked me about my family
    ——————————
         21
and encouraged my school interests. They told me about their

lives and some of their childrens' previous English teachers. In
                        ——————
                          22
particular, my host father became a very close friend, and I still

correspond with him today.

    I had been sent to this town to teach English to some of

the children and their parents, but I soon realized that I was

learning all about Mexican food and culture. I was learning
        ——————————————————————
                  23

in circumstances not only how to speak everyday Spanish, but
——————————
    24

also how to coexist with people who lived unlike my own. [25]

    On my last day of class. I noticed a map of North America
                        ————
                          26
on the wall. I realized then what I had sensed all along.

20. **F.** NO CHANGE
    G. hold
    H. have held
    J. held

21. **A.** NO CHANGE
    B. family that hosted me
    C. family I hosted
    D. family, which hosted me,

22. **F.** NO CHANGE
    G. childrens's
    H. childrens
    J. children's

23. Which choice most logically contrasts with the first part of this sentence?
    A. NO CHANGE
    B. my way around the town.
    C. more than I could ever teach.
    D. about the lives of those in my host family.

24. The best placement for the underlined portion would be:
    F. where it is now.
    G. after the word *speak*.
    H. after the word *Spanish*.
    J. after the word *lived*.

25. At this point, the writer is considering adding the following true statement:

    In Spanish, the word for "coexistence" sounds just like ours: *coexistencia.*

    Should the writer make this addition here?
    A. Yes, because it clarifies the narrator's earlier discussion of how welcome he felt with his host family.
    B. Yes, because it supports the paragraph's main idea by translating a word into Spanish.
    C. No, because it digresses from the main topic of the paragraph.
    D. No, because it shows that the narrator's Spanish was not as proficient as he claimed.

26. **F.** NO CHANGE
    G. class, I
    H. class but I
    J. class; I

In one sense, I was farther away from home than I'd ever was.

However, in another sense, I had simply found a new place that

I could call home. Remembering the details of my trip, I'm

more and more convinced that the river that separates

Mexico and the United States is actually very small next to all

of the wonderful things that bring us together. 29

27. A. NO CHANGE
    B. had been.
    C. been.
    D. being.

28. F. NO CHANGE
    G. Identified as one of the borderlands,
    H. Showing all the mountains and rivers,
    J. Becoming a new place for me,

29. Which of the following sentences, if added here, would most effectively express one of the main ideas of the essay?

    A. To be honest, though, I was really glad to get home when it was all over.
    B. The main thing I miss about the trip is the opportunity to practice my Spanish.
    C. Ever since that time, I've often thought how alike my two homes really are.
    D. That was my initial reaction, but I don't think I really want to go back.

PASSAGE III

"Haunted" Authors

[1]

In 1915, Maurice E. <u>McLoughlin, a well-known tennis player</u>
published an instructional autobiography called *Tennis as*
I Play It. Two years earlier, McLoughlin had become the first
American finalist at the Wimbledon tournament in England,
and tennis fans were excited to uncover the <u>tricks</u> of his
success. Anticipation for McLoughlin's story grew even more

in 1914. He was <u>winning</u> a number of major tournaments that
year, he was declared the Number 1 tennis player in the world.
When *Tennis as I Play It* finally did come out in 1915, no
one had any reason to suspect that it might have been written
<u>by</u> someone else. However, the author of *Tennis as I Play It*
was not McLoughlin at all, but the as-yet unknown novelist
Sinclair Lewis, his ghostwriter. Why, then, is *Tennis as I Play It*
considered <u>the tennis player's</u> book?

[2]

A ghostwriter is an author who writes a text that is officially
credited to another author, and the history of such practices
<u>are lasting</u>

longer than we might expect. [36]

30. F. NO CHANGE
   G. McLoughlin a well-known tennis player
   H. McLoughlin, a well-known tennis player,
   J. McLoughlin a well-known tennis player,

31. A. NO CHANGE
   B. skills
   C. secrets
   D. abilities

32. F. NO CHANGE
   G. Won
   H. He won
   J. Winning

33. A. NO CHANGE
   B. for
   C. about
   D. DELETE the underlined portion.

34. F. NO CHANGE
   G. the athletes'
   H. the tennis players
   J. the athletes

35. A. NO CHANGE
   B. were
   C. are
   D. is

36. At this point, the writer is thinking about adding the following true statement:

> Some suggest that ghostwriting is as old as authorship itself.

Should the writer make this addition here?

   F. Yes, because it provides a transition from the previous paragraph to this one.
   G. Yes, because it expands upon a point made in the preceding sentence.
   H. No, because it does not apply to the main subject discussed in this paragraph.
   J. No, because it suggests that most historical texts are ghostwritten.

In other words, *Tennis as I Play It* was not, the first famous ghostwritten book, and it won't be the last. Ghostwriting can

happen for a number of reasons, and although it's merits are debatable, it remains an acceptable practice in the publishing world.

[3]

Today, ghostwriting can take a number of different forms. It is perhaps most prominent in the autobiographies and memoirs of celebrities. How does a celebrity decide to ask a ghostwriter to write his or her book? No, ghostwriting is equally prominent in lesser-known spheres as well. Political speeches, for example, are often credited to the politician who

delivers them, and then that politician just reads the speech from a teleprompter. In addition, many popular songs claim a

popular singer or performer as songwriter, although they have been shaped more by a producer than by any of the credited songwriters.

[4]

Ghostwriting—whether we approve of it or not—is here to stay. Sometimes, as in the case of Sinclair Lewis, the ghostwriters will eventually become famous authors in

37. **A.** NO CHANGE
B. was not the first,
C. was not the first
D. was, not the first,

38. **F.** NO CHANGE
G. its
H. her
J. their

39. Which choice provides the most logical and effective transition to the rest of the paragraph?
A. NO CHANGE
B. Is the practice restricted to celebrity autobiographies and memoirs?
C. Why would celebrities want other people to tell their stories?
D. What makes celebrities think ghostwriters know all the details of their lives?

40. Given that all he choices are true, which one provides the best support for the statement in an earlier part of this sentence?
F. NO CHANGE
G. but the speeches are usually written by a team of speechwriters.
H. but very few politicians have the oratorical skills of politicians from last century.
J. although many politicians like to speak from notes rather than fully written speeches.

41. Which of the following alternatives to the underlined portion would NOT be acceptable?
A. songwriter, yet
B. songwriter; therefore,
C. songwriter, but
D. songwriter; however,

42. **F.** NO CHANGE
G. not
H. not,
J. not;

their own right. [43] Much more often, though,

since we are moved by the writing of authors whose names we
‾‾
44
will never learn.

---

43. The writer is thinking about deleting the preceding sentence. Should this sentence be kept or deleted?

- **A.** Kept, because it shows the importance of ghostwriting to Sinclair Lewis's career.
- **B.** Kept, because it provides a contrast to the fact stated in the next sentence.
- **C.** Deleted, because it discusses a famous novelist in a paragraph about ghostwriters.
- **D.** Deleted, because Sinclair Lewis is already mentioned in the first paragraph.

44. F. NO CHANGE
   G. because
   H. yet
   J. DELETE the underlined portion.

Question 45 asks about the preceding passage as a whole.

---

45. While reviewing his research for this essay, the writer discovers a statistic and composes the following sentence:

> Some in the industry suggest that as many as half of non-fiction books are written with help from ghostwriters.

If the writer were to include this sentence in the essay, the most logical place would be after the last sentence in Paragraph:

- **A.** 1.
- **B.** 2.
- **C.** 3.
- **D.** 4.

PASSAGE IV

From Broadcasts to Podcasts

In the first half of the twentieth century, Americans couldn't spend their evenings in front of the TV. The television didn't become a regular feature of the American home until well into the 1960s. Instead, the major form of mass entertainment in this period was provided by the radio. The radio had begun its rise to prominence in the 1930s. It was especially popular in the 1940s, when most American households, as many as 91%, had a radio. 46 The residents of many small towns and rural

areas in non-urban parts of the country didn't have access
to the newest movies or books, but those residents did have
radios.

[1] Throughout the 1930s and 1940s, Americans turned to radio for all that. [2] During World War II, listeners could get more frequent information from their radios than they could from

the newspapers. [3] In 1932, U.S. President Franklin Roosevelt, began his series of "fireside chats" over the radio. [4] For those

looking for lighter fare, the radio had plenty of mystery programs, comedy and variety shows, westerns, and quiz programs. [5] These chats were intended to be as informal as a chat between friends and family members by the fireside, but they tackled some of the most complex political issues

46. The writer is considering deleting the phrase "as many as 91%" from the preceding sentence (adjusting the punctuation accordingly). Should this phrase be kept or deleted?

F. Kept, because it supports the idea that radio was on the decline after the 1930s.
G. Kept, because it gives specific evidence of radio's popularity in the 1940s.
H. Deleted, because it discusses American households in a passage about radio listening.
J. Deleted, because it doesn't describe the households that had radios.

47. A. NO CHANGE
B. in parts of the country outside cities
C. despite their possession of radios
D. DELETE the underlined portion

48. F. NO CHANGE
G. their wants and other things that might be perceived as needs, but were more likely wants.
H. the things they needed to listen to, such as comedy, news, sports, and drama, or other kinds of programs sometimes.
J. their listening needs.

49. A. NO CHANGE
B. U.S. President Franklin Roosevelt
C. U.S. President, Franklin Roosevelt
D. U.S. President, Franklin Roosevelt,

50. Which of the following alternatives to the underlined portion would NOT be acceptable?

F. scouring
G. desiring
H. wanting
J. seeking

of the day:
51

war, depression, and international affairs. 52

By the 1950s, however, radio was losing its dominant position. The main reason for radio's decline was the advent of television. As television's continuing success has shown, Americans would rather *see* their favorite stars mere than *hear*
53

them. Listening (to anything other than music) to appear with
54
a thing of the past.

55 This portable device could hold more music than any record, tape, or CD ever could before. The iPod also brought back forms other than music. New *podcasts* hearkened back to

old-time radio programs called *broadcasts*. Whether funny or
56

serious, whether they're mainstream or they're underground,
57
these podcasts might never reach the heights of old-time radio

broadcasts, but there basically bringing non-musical listening
58
to a whole new generation. These days, when it can seem like everyone wants *more* visual culture—IMAX screens, 3D movies—along comes the podcast to provide a welcome but not altogether unfamiliar alternative.

---

51. A. NO CHANGE
  B. day, these included
  C. day,
  D. day having been

52. For the sake of the logic and coherence of this paragraph, Sentence 5 should be placed:

  F. where it is now.
  G. before Sentence 1.
  H. after Sentence 2.
  J. after Sentence 3.

53. A. NO CHANGE
  B. merely then
  C. mere then
  D. than merely

54. F. NO CHANGE
  G. was apparently
  H. to appearance was
  J. appeared as

55. Given that all the following statements are true, which one, if added here, would most clearly and effectively introduce the main subject of this paragraph?

  A. Radio's most popular programs, such as *Gunsmoke*, became popular television hits.
  B. At least it seemed like a thing of the past until the iPod came along in 2001.
  C. One of the last popular programs, *The Zero Hour*, was on in the early 1970s.
  D. The presidential radio address has become a custom ever since Roosevelt's early broadcasts.

56. F. NO CHANGE
  G. radio broadcasts.
  H. radio broadcasts'.
  J. radio broadcast's.

57. A. NO CHANGE
  B. being mainstream in the underground,
  C. mainstream or underground,
  D. if they're so underground they're actually mainstream,

58. F. NO CHANGE
  G. they're
  H. it's essentially
  J. their

Question 59 asks about the preceding passage as a whole

59. Suppose the writer's goal had been to write a brief essay focusing on how contemporary broadcasters have been influenced by earlier broadcasters. Would this essay fulfill that goal?

   A. Yes, because it makes clear that the podcast would not be likely to exist without old-time radio.
   B. Yes, because it implies that the podcast has encouraged listeners to go back to earlier recordings.
   C. No, because it does not offer a contemporary equivalent for Roosevelt's fireside chats.
   D. No, because it is more focused on sketching the rise in popularity of the podcast.

PASSAGE V

Vladimir Nabokov, Books, and Butterflies

Vladimir Nabokov (1899-1977) is best known as a novelist. His first novels <u>were written</u> in Russia in the 1920s.

60. **F.** NO CHANGE
 G. was written
 H. were wrote
 J. was wrote

However, his <u>novels and books that people seem to like the most</u> were published in the United States and England in the 1940s and 1950s. The most notorious of all was *Lolita* (1955), a novel praised for its skillful construction and beautiful style but often banned for its lurid descriptions and shocking plot. [62]

61. **A.** NO CHANGE
 B. most famous works
 C. works that are the most popular among readers
 D. books that are very popular among critics and general readers alike

62. The writer is considering deleting the parenthetical information (and the parentheses) from the preceding sentence. If the writer were to make this deletion, the paragraph would primarily lose:

 F. a detail that helps to place *Lolita* chronologically in Nabokov's literary career.
 G. the time during which Nabokov stopped writing to conduct his entomological research.
 H. a detail needed to understand the historical and literary significance of *Lolita*.
 J. the number of years that Nabokov spent writing *Lolita*.

<u>Nabokov left Russia to escape persecution from the newly formed Soviet government.</u>

63. Given that all the choices are true, which one most effectively leads the reader from this paragraph into the remainder of the essay?

 A. NO CHANGE
 B. Nabokov's other novels include *Pnin*, *Pale Fire*, and the highly experimental *Ada*.
 C. However, Nabokov was not exclusively a novelist and a man of letters.
 D. *Lolita* is now considered an American classic, despite its original reception.

In fact, he made significant contributions to <u>entomology;</u>

64. **F.** NO CHANGE
 G. entomology being
 H. entomology of
 J. entomology,

the study of insects. Nabokov's work in charting the <u>structure,</u> and migration patterns of butterflies was a major contribution to science.

65. **A.** NO CHANGE
 B. structure of
 C. structure
 D. structure;

Moreover, at what might have seemed a high point in his literary

career Nabokov accepted a research fellowship from Harvard
<u>66</u>
University's Museum of Comparative Zoology.

Then, he used this fellowship to conduct his fieldwork and to
<u>67</u>
curate the museum's butterfly collection at a time when

he could <u>just as well, of</u> been earning a fellowship to work
<u>68</u>
exclusively on writing.

Although <u>Nabokov's work by the scientific community</u>
<u>69</u>
was occasionally dismissed as the ideas of an amateur, recent

findings have supported some of his hypotheses. For example,

Nabokov was <u>the primary one in a long list of scientists</u> to
<u>70</u>
suggest that the *Polyammatus blue* species of butterfly came to

North America from Asia in five waves over the Bering Strait.

Moreover, Nabokov was <u>mainly interested in the study of</u>
<u>71</u>
<u>moths and butterflies, but studied some plants.</u> In belated
<u>71</u>
recognition of his contributions, a genus of butterfly was

renamed. *Nabokovia* in his honor.
<u>72</u>

We can't know whether Nabokov's fiction or his scientific

work was more important, <u>than which</u> pursuit Nabokov found
<u>73</u>

more enriching. Nabokov the famous novelist <u>could of been</u>
<u>74</u>
Nabokov the famous entomologist. Who can say? What we

can say is that Nabokov's story is a reminder of the vastness of

human potential. One might say that Nabokov was just

66. F. NO CHANGE
    G. career;
    H. career.
    J. career,

67. A. NO CHANGE
    B. He
    C. Finally, he
    D. Consequently, he

68. F. NO CHANGE
    G. could just as well, have
    H. could, just as well of
    J. could just as well have

69. The best placement for the underlined portion would be:
    A. where it is now.
    B. after the word *dismissed*.
    C. after the word *ideas*.
    D. after the word *supported*.

70. F. NO CHANGE
    G. the first
    H. the one before anyone else
    J. the scientist that was before others in the field

71. Given that all the choices are true, which one most effectively concludes the sentence by giving a specific example of Nabokov's contribution to the study of moths and butterflies?
    A. NO CHANGE
    B. aided in his scientific researches by his wife, Vera, who drove Vladimir to his research sites.
    C. the first to describe some species of moth and butterfly, including the Karner blue.
    D. working on his novels at the same time that he made his scientific discoveries.

72. F. NO CHANGE
    G. renamed, *Nabokovia*
    H. renamed *Nabokovia*
    J. renamed; *Nabokovia*

73. A. NO CHANGE
    B. for example
    C. nor
    D. DELETE the underlined portion.

74. F. NO CHANGE
    G. could have
    H. has
    J. have

an exceptional person, but isn't it equally possible that these
$\overline{}$
75
alternate personalities exist inside of all of us?

75. **A.** NO CHANGE
    B. an exception to
    C. exceptionally a
    D. an exceptionally

Chapter 8
English Practice
Test 3
Answers and
Explanations

ENGLISH PRACTICE TEST 3 ANSWERS

1.	A	39.	B	
2.	J	40.	G	
3.	B	41.	B	
4.	G	42.	F	
5.	C	43.	B	
6.	H	44.	J	
7.	C	45.	B	
8.	F	46.	G	
9.	B	47.	D	
10.	F	48.	J	
11.	A	49.	B	
12.	H	50.	F	
13.	A	51.	A	
14.	J	52.	J	
15.	D	53.	D	
16.	J	54.	G	
17.	C	55.	B	
18.	G	56.	G	
19.	B	57.	C	
20.	J	58.	G	
21.	B	59.	D	
22.	J	60.	F	
23.	C	61.	B	
24.	J	62.	F	
25.	C	63.	C	
26.	G	64.	J	
27.	C	65.	C	
28.	F	66.	J	
29.	C	67.	B	
30.	H	68.	J	
31.	C	69.	B	
32.	J	70.	G	
33.	A	71.	C	
34.	F	72.	H	
35.	D	73.	C	
36.	G	74.	G	
37.	C	75.	A	
38.	G			

SCORE YOUR PRACTICE TEST

Step A
Count the number of correct answers: _____. This is your *raw score*.

Step B
Use the score conversion table below to look up your raw score. The number to the left is your *scale score*: _____ .

English Scale Conversion Table

Scale Score	Raw Score	Scale Score	Raw Score	Scale Score	Raw Score
36	75	27	62	18	41–42
35	73–74	26	60–61	17	39–40
34	71–72	25	58–59	16	36–38
33	70	24	56–57	15	33–35
32	69	23	54–55	14	30–32
31	67–68	22	52–53	13	28–29
30	66	21	49–51	12	26–27
29	65	20	46–48	11	24–25
28	63–64	19	43–45	10	22–23

ENGLISH PRACTICE TEST 3 EXPLANATIONS

Passage I

1. **A**   The question *but who knew they also love to eat cheeseburgers?* introduces a unique feature of the cats described in this passage. *Lolcats* are not an actual species, eliminating choice (B). The essay deals with *lolcats* themselves, not their love of cheeseburgers, eliminating (C). However, their love of cheeseburgers *is* unique, which means that this detail is important, eliminating choice (D). Only choice (A) remains.

2. **J**   The verb in this sentence will need to agree with the other verb in the sentence, *take*, which is in the present tense. Of the choices, only choices (G) and (J) are in the present tense, eliminating choices (F) and (H). Of choices (G) and (J), choice (J) is better because choice (G) introduces a participle unnecessarily. Note: Be careful of verbs ending in "-ing." They can often make sentences unnecessarily wordy!

3. **B**   This sentence would be incomplete if the photographer's name were removed. In other words, *In the 1870s, Brighton-based photographer took a series. . .* would be incomplete. Therefore, the photographer's name should not be set off by commas as it is in choices (A) and (C), nor should it be set off by a semi-colon as in choice (D). Only choice (B) correctly indicates that *Henry Pointer* is essential to the meaning of the sentence.

4. **G**   Only choice (G) contains specific information that is not redundant. Choice (J) cannot work because it does not indicate who is doing the *naming*, and choices (F) and (H) do not make sense in the given context.

5. **C**   The question asks for an option that shows that *the caption was an essential part of the humor of Pointer's photographs*. Therefore, we will need a choice that suggests the importance of captions. Choices (B) and (D) suggest that captions were not important, so they can be eliminated. Choice (A) does not address the importance of captions, so it, too, can be eliminated. Only choice (C) remains, and it works because it shows that captions could often be used to enliven otherwise dull pictures.

6. **H**   The idiom *in his day* must be kept intact here, making choice (H) the best choice. Choices (F) and (J) create a meaning different from the intended one, and choice (G) creates the phrase *with his day*, which is not used, thus eliminating these choices.

7. **C**   Sentences A and B offer a general description of the *lolcat*. Sentence C changes the focus of the paragraph to the *lolcat*'s historical roots. Therefore, because it changes the focus of the paragraph, Sentence C offers a good place to start a new paragraph. Sentence D continues the historical discussion and should therefore be in the same paragraph with Sentence C.

8. **F** Each answer choice offers a word or phrase of transition. Choices (G), (H), and (J) offer transitions that suggest a contrast, matching the contrasting word *though* in the passage. Choice (F) offers a transition that suggests a continuation. Therefore, choice (F) is the answer that does NOT work in the given context, meaning that it is the correct answer.

9. **B** The non-underlined portion of this sentence contains the words *most famous*. These make the words in the following redundant: *known widely* in choice (A), *that many people know* in choice (C), and *that is pretty popular* in choice (D). Only choice (B) contains no redundant phrasing, and choice (B) is therefore the correct answer.

10. **F** The subjects of the underlined verb are *phrases* and *language*. Therefore, the verb will need to agree with a plural subject, eliminating choices (G) and (H). The passage is talking about phrases and language in the present tense, eliminating choice (J). Only choice (F) offers a verb that agrees in number and tense.

11. **A** The noun being modified by the underlined portion is *lolcats*. Choice (B) cannot work because the *lolcats* are not *earning lots of money*. Choice (C) cannot work because *lolcats* do not have *cameras in hand*, nor can choice (D) work because *lolcats* are not *promoting*. Only choice (A) provides an appropriate modifier for the word *lolcats*.

12. **H** Of all the *creative coinages* of the decade, the *lolcat* has been called one of the *most creative*. Choice (G) cannot work because more than two coinages are being compared. Choices (F) and (J) cannot work because they do not offer comparative words in a sentence that requires them. Only choice (H) can work in the given context.

13. **A** Choice (B) cannot work because the *cheeseburger* refers only to one type of cat. Choice (C) cannot work because *cheeseburger-flavored* does not solve any problem posed in the essay. Choice (D) cannot work because no question is being posed. Only choice (A) can work, suggesting that *cheeseburger-flavored* is more detailed than *another line*, and that it is intended for humorous effect.

14. **J** The passage as a whole discusses the past, present, and future of the *lolcat*. Though it touches on photography, Internet usage, and types of animals, none of these can be described as the passage's main idea. Only choice (J) reflects the passage's main idea accurately, while suggesting that the writer has *not* succeeded in writing a passage that discusses *animal photography* more generally.

Passage II

15. **D** Note the dash in the non-underlined part of the sentence. The answer will need to contain another dash to keep this notation consistent and to set off the unnecessary phrase *located a few hours west of Monterrey*. Only choice (D) contains a dash. Choice (A) contains a semi-colon, which can only be used when separating two complete ideas.

16. **J** The words *burning* and *scorching* mean similar things, and when they are paired with the word *heat* in the non-underlined portion, they become redundant. Therefore, in order to remove this redundant construction, it is best to remove these words—eliminating choices (F), (G), and (H)—and to delete the underlined portion. Note: Always give "DELETE" or "OMIT" special consideration. They are often correct!

17. **C** The first paragraph discusses the author's difficult trip to the small town in Mexico, but the second paragraph switches to the pleasant time he had there with his host family. The discussion of the weather does not continue, which eliminates choice (A). The paragraph does not discuss Mexican cuisine, which eliminates choice (D). The paragraph does not discuss the author's earlier trip with his parents, which eliminates choice (B). Only choice (C) offers the appropriate transition into the new paragraph.

18. **G** Read the question carefully. It asks for an option that shows that the narrator's host family was *extremely welcoming*. Choices (F), (H), and (J) do not contain any indication that the family was welcoming. Choice (G), however, suggests that the family was as welcoming as they would have been if the narrator had *lived there* [his] *whole life*. Choice (G) is therefore the best answer.

19. **B** This question asks for the alternative that would NOT be acceptable. Choices (A), (C), and (D) rearrange the words, but they are not grammatically or idiomatically incorrect. Choice (B) is unclear, though, in that it makes *Spanish language* modify the word *others*, whereas the sentence requires that *Spanish language* and *others* be separate nouns. Choice (B), therefore, would NOT be acceptable and is the correct answer.

20. **J** Note the other verbs in this paragraph: *were, asked, told, became*. The verb in this sentence must be consistent with these verbs. Therefore, only choice (J), *held*, is consistent with the simple past tense. Choices (F) and (H) change the type of past tense and the meaning of the sentence, and choice (G) switches to the present.

21. **B** The sentence as written cannot work, because the narrator does not host the family; rather, the family hosts the narrator. Choice (C) makes the same mistake. Then, the words *that/which hosted me* are necessary to the meaning of the sentence: They clarify which *family* the narrator is referring to. Therefore, because this information is necessary, the information should not be set off by commas and should contain the word *that*, as in choice (B).

22. **J** The sentence describes the *previous English teachers* of the *children* and therefore requires that *children* be made possessive. Choice (H) contains no apostrophe and can therefore be eliminated. Choice (F) and (G) make the word *children* possessive in incorrect ways. Only choice (J) offers the correct possessive form of *children*. Note: What comes before the apostrophe must be a word. In other words, *childrens'*, as in choice (F), is incorrect because *childrens* is not a word. The same is true for choice (G).

23. **C** The first part of the sentence discusses the narrator teaching English. Therefore, in order to contrast with the first part of the sentence, we will need some indication that he is *not* teaching English, or that he is not exclusively teaching English. Choices (A), (B), and (D) are not related to English, nor do they contrast with the idea that the narrator is a teacher. Only choice (C) offers the appropriate contrast: While the narrator is a teacher, he is also *learning more than [he] could ever teach*.

24. **J** The current placement of the underlined portion cannot work because it does not clarify what the *circumstances* are, eliminating choice (F). The same is true for choices (G) and (H). Only choice (J) clarifies: *circumstances unlike my own*; therefore, choice (J) is the best answer.

25. **C** When you are asked whether to add a sentence to the given passage, make sure you have a very good reason to do so. In this particular case, the proposed sentence does not contribute meaningfully to the main idea or development of the paragraph or passage, so it should not be added, eliminating choices (A) and (B). Choice (D) can be eliminated because the passage does not give adequate grounds to assess the narrator's proficiency in Spanish. Only choice (C) works.

26. **G** The sentence as written cannot work because the phrase *On my last day of class* does not offer a complete idea, meaning that choices (F) and (J) can be eliminated. Then, the word *but* suggests a contrast where none is present, eliminating choice (H). Only choice (G) works, setting *On my last day of class* off as an introductory idea.

27. **C** Separate the contraction *I'd* into its component parts: *I had*. This makes choice (B) clearly redundant. This also eliminates choices (A) and (D), which use *had* again incorrectly. Only choice (C) works in the context created by the non-underlined portion.

28. **F** The word after the underlined portion is *I'm*; therefore, the underlined portion must modify the word *I*. The sentence works as written because *Remembering the details of my trip* refers appropriately to the *I* it is modifying. Choice (G) can be eliminated because *Identified as one of the borderlands* refers to some part of Mexico or the United States. *Showing all the mountains and rivers* refers to the *map*, eliminating choice (H). Choice (H) can also be eliminated because *Becoming a new place for me* refers to the village.

29. **C** The essay details the author's trip to Mexico, where he goes to teach English and also learns a good deal about the people and himself. The first paragraph suggests that the start was difficult but that the narrator quickly feels at home. There is no indication that choices (A) and (D) will work in the context because both suggest that the narrator did not enjoy his trip. Choice (B) foregrounds the importance of Spanish, but it does so too much. Only choice (C) can work in the context of the paragraph and the essay as a whole.

Passage III

30. **H**   This sentence conveys the information that McLoughlin published a book. The phrase *a well-known tennis player* is not essential to conveying this meaning, and therefore that information is not essential to the meaning of the sentence. Because the information is not essential, it must be set off by commas as in choice (H). Note: On questions that test restrictive and non-restrictive information, the correct answer will typically have two commas or none, so if you're unsure, eliminate answers with only one comma.

31. **C**   Pay close attention to the non-underlined portion of the sentence. The word *uncover* indicates which word will be needed in the underlined portion. One does not uncover *tricks*, *skills*, or *abilities*, eliminating choices (A), (B), and (D). One does, however, uncover *secrets*, as in choice (C).

32. **J**   The sentence as written creates a comma splice because *He was winning a number of major tennis tournaments that year* and *he was declared the Number 1 tennis player in the world* are both complete ideas. We can't change the comma, so this eliminates choices (F) and (H). Choice (G) does not make sense in the given context. Only choice (J) correctly makes the first part of the sentence incomplete by turning it into the modifying phrase *Winning a number of major tournaments that year.*

33. **A**   A variety of prepositions can come after the word *written*, but each has a different meaning. *Written for* suggests that the book was written as a gift for someone, or that it was dedicated to that person. This can't work with the *someone else* in this sentence because there is no indication that the book was written *for* anyone in particular. Eliminate choice (B). The book is *about* McLoughlin, but there is no indication that the book was written *about* someone else, eliminating choice (C). We cannot delete the underlined portion because *written someone else* does not make sense. Only choice (A) remains: The book was not written *by* McLoughlin but *by* a ghostwriter.

34. **F**   This sentence refers to the *book* belonging to *the tennis player*; therefore, there should be an apostrophe to indicate possession. This eliminates choices (H) and (J). Choice (G) makes the word *athletes* into a plural possessive when there is only one athlete involved, eliminating choice (G). Choice (F) gives the correct singular punctuation of *the tennis player*. Note: If you were not sure whether to choose *the tennis player* or *the athlete*, you could still have solved this question by looking at apostrophes and using process of elimination.

35. **D**   The subject of the underlined verb is *history*, not the prepositional object *practices*. Therefore, the verb in the underlined portion should be singular, eliminating choices (A), (B), and (C). Only choice (D) offers a present-tense verb that agrees with a singular subject and has no redundant information.

36. **G**   The previous sentence concludes with the idea that *the history of such practices is longer than we might expect*. This suggests the following sentence should make some historical claim or give some

historical detail. The proposed addition does this, so it should be added, eliminating choices (H) and (J). It cannot, however, provide a transition from the previous paragraph because it is not the first sentence of this paragraph, eliminating choice (F). Only choice (G) correctly states that this sentence should be added and that it expands upon a point made in the preceding sentence.

37. **C**   The answer choices offer different opportunities to insert pauses in the phrase *was not the first*. In the given sentence, though, no pause is necessary, so no commas are necessary, eliminating choices (A), (B), and (D). Choice (C) gives the best option because it contains no unnecessary commas.

38. **G**   The sentence describes the *merits* of *ghostwriting*: in other words, *ghostwriting's merits* or *its* merits. Choice (F), *it's*, is the contraction of *it is*, not a possessive pronoun. Ghostwriting is not a person, so choice (H) can be eliminated, nor is it a plural, so choice (J) can be eliminated. Only choice (G) offers the correct possessive pronoun.

39. **B**   The sentence that follows reads, *No, ghostwriting is equally prominent in lesser-known spheres as well.* Therefore, the sentence in this problem should offer some question to which the next sentence could answer *No*, particularly one that deals with ghostwriting in *well-known spheres*. The preceding sentence says that ghostwriting is *most prominent in the autobiographies and memoirs of celebrities*. Only choice (B) expands upon this idea and sets up the appropriate contrast with the following sentence. Choices (A), (C), and (D) deal exclusively with the details of celebrity ghostwriting.

40. **G**   The passage as a whole discusses ghostwriting, and the sentence preceding this one reads *No, ghostwriting is equally prominent in lesser-known spheres as well.* Therefore, the sentence in the underlined portion should address ghostwriting somehow. The sentence will not be concerned with styles of reading, *oratorical skills*, or speech notes, eliminating choices (F), (H), and (J). Only choice (G) sets up the contrast that speeches *are often credited to the politician who delivers them* but actually are *written by a team of speechwriters*.

41. **B**   The question asks for the punctuation and transition that would NOT be acceptable. The ideas surrounding this punctuation-transition combination are as follows: *In addition, many popular songs claim a popular singer or performer as songwriter* and *they have been shaped more by a producer than by any of the credited songwriters*. As the original sentence shows with the word *although*, these ideas should contrast. Therefore, choices (A), (C), and (D) WOULD be acceptable and can be eliminated. Only choice (B) removes this contrast and therefore would NOT be acceptable.

42. **F**   Note the dash in the first part of this sentence, which sets off the non-essential phrase *whether we approve of it or not*. The answer will need to include another dash in order to keep this punctuation consistent. The sentence must be correct as written because only choice (F) contains that dash.

43. **B**   The sentence following this one begins with the words *Much more often, though*. If we remove this sentence, we are left with the question *Much more often* than what? Therefore, the sentence should be kept, offering as it does a description of what happens *sometimes*. Eliminate choices (C) and

(D). Then, eliminate choice (A) because it does not show the importance of ghostwriting to Sinclair Lewis's career: In fact, the sentence suggests that Lewis became a well-known novelist *even though* he was initially a ghostwriter. Only choice (B) addresses the fact that this sentence gives the first part of a contrast completed in the next sentence.

44. **J** As written, this sentence is actually a sentence fragment. The subordinating conjunction *since* makes the sentence incomplete, so eliminate choice (F). Eliminate choice (G) for the same reason. The word *yet* in choice (H) is a coordinating conjunction, but it does not fix the problem. The only viable solution to the problem is to remove the conjunction entirely, as in choice (J). Note: Give serious consideration to "DELETE" and "OMIT" when you see them. They are often correct!

45. **B** The proposed sentence addresses the prevalence of ghostwriting, suggesting as it does that ghostwriting is a much more common practice than we might suspect. This sentence does not belong in Paragraph 1, which discusses a particular example of ghostwriting. The sentence does not belong in Paragraph 3, which gives some of the places where ghostwriting is used. The sentence does not belong in Paragraph 4, which offers some concluding ideas on ghostwriting. The only possible place for the sentence would be in Paragraph 2, which discusses ghostwriting and its historical importance and prevalence.

Passage IV

46. **G** The phrase in question appears in the sentence *It was especially popular in the 1940s when most American households, as many as 91%, had a radio*. In this instance, the *91%* statistic gives a specific number of how many *American households* had radios. Therefore, because the information serves a specific purpose in the sentence, it should be kept. Eliminate choices (H) and (J). Then, eliminate choice (F) because the statistic does not indicate that radio was on the decline.

47. **D** The sentence as written is redundant because the non-underlined portion already contains the words *of many small towns and rural areas*. This eliminates choice (A), and choice (B) can be eliminated for the same reason. Choice (C) is redundant with a later part of the sentence, *those residents did have radios*. The only viable alternative is to delete the underlined portion entirely, as in choice (D). Note: Give serious consideration to "DELETE" and "OMIT" when you see them. They are often correct!

48. **J** The sentence as written does not contain adequate information because it is unclear what *that* refers to. Eliminate choice (F). Choices (G) and (H), however, go to the opposite extreme by giving way too much information, so eliminate them as well. Choice (J) strikes a happy medium: It is not too long and not too ambiguous.

49. **B** In order to determine whether the name *Franklin Roosevelt* is essential to the meaning of the sentence, see if the sentence works without it. Without the name, the sentence would read *In 1932, U.S. President began his series of "fireside chats" over the radio*. There's something missing from this

sentence, which means that the name *Franklin Roosevelt* is essential to the sentence's meaning. Therefore, the information should not be set off by any commas, and only choice (B) can work.

50. **F**   The sentence as written is correct: One can be *looking for lighter fare*. This question is asking for an alternative that would NOT be acceptable. One can be *desiring lighter fare*, *wanting lighter fare*, or *seeking lighter fare*, eliminating choices (G), (H), and (J). One cannot be *scouring lighter fare*, however, which means that choice (F) would NOT be an acceptable alternative to the underlined portion.

51. **A**   *War, depression, and international affairs* are some examples of the *complex political issues* mentioned in the first part of the sentence. The word *day* is not part of this list, eliminating choice (C). Choice (D) creates an awkward construction, and choice (B) creates a comma splice by making the second half of the sentence into a complete idea. Only choice (A) can work: A complete idea comes before the colon, and a list comes after it.

52. **J**   The first words of Sentence 5 are *These chats*, which suggest that the sentence that precedes Sentence 5 will clarify what the *chats* are. Only Sentence 3 has any mention of *chats*, in its discussion of Roosevelt's *fireside chats*. Therefore, Sentence 5 must come directly after Sentence 3, as in choice (J).

53. **D**   There are two main parts to this answer. First, the sentence offers a comparison between *seeing* and *hearing*, suggesting that the sentence will need the comparative word *than*, not the time word *then*. Eliminate choices (B) and (C). Second, the remaining word will modify the verb *hear*. Because the word will modify a verb, the word must be the adverb *merely*, making choice (D) the best choice.

54. **G**   The sentence does not make sense as written, because one cannot *appear with a thing of the past*. Eliminate choice (F). The same can be said of choice (H). Choice (J) creates a different meaning from the intended meaning, so it can be eliminated. Only choice (G) offers an alternative that turns the sentence into the clear expression of an idea.

55. **B**   This paragraph discusses the rise to prominence of the iPod, and the attendant rise of podcasting. It does not continue the discussion of specific radio programs, eliminating choices (A) and (C), nor does it address political speechmaking on the radio, eliminating choice (D). Only choice (B) can work because it is the only choice that addresses either podcasting or the iPod.

56. **G**   The *broadcasts* mentioned in the sentence are not in possession of anything; therefore, an apostrophe is unnecessary, eliminating choices (H) and (J). The two remaining choices have essentially the same meaning, but choice (G) is more concise, which means it is the better answer.

57. **C**   The underlined portion is part of a list that includes *funny or serious*. All items in a list must be parallel, and only choice (C) gives a parallel construction. The other choices break this parallelism and add unnecessary words, so eliminate choices (A), (B), and (D).

58. **G**   The sentence may *sound* correct, but this could be said for a number of the choices. Moreover, the adverb *there* does not apply here because no place or location is being indicated. Eliminate choice (F). Choice (H) cannot work because the singular *it's* does not agree with its plural antecedent, *podcasts*. We don't need a possessive pronoun in this portion of the sentence, which eliminates choice (J). Only choice (G), *they're*, the contraction of the words *they are*, makes this sentence clear and complete.

59. **D**   The main idea of the passage is that new *podcasts* are similar to old-time radio *broadcasts*. It does not create a direct line of influence between *contemporary broadcasters* and *earlier broadcasters*. If it had been the writer's goal to discuss this line of influence, then this essay would not fulfill that goal, eliminating choices (A) and (B). It is true that the essay does not offer a contemporary equivalent for Roosevelt's fireside chats, but the essay is not primarily concerned with these chats. Instead, choice (D) offers the best reason that the essay has not fulfilled the writer's goal. The essay is more concerned with *podcasts* than with *contemporary broadcasting* generally.

Passage V

60. **F**   This answer will have two main parts. First, the verb must agree with the plural subject *novels*, which only choice (F) and (H) do. Then, we will need the form of the verb that goes with the helping verb *were*. Because *wrote* needs no helping verb, it can't work as *were wrote*, eliminating choice (H). Only choice (F) remains.

61. **B**   Since all the options have essentially the same meaning and are grammatically correct, choose the option that is the most concise. This is clearly choice (B), which is much shorter than the other choices and does not contain any excessive words.

62. **F**   Most sentences of this first paragraph contain a year or some piece of the chronology of Nabokov's career. Therefore, the parenthetical portion of this sentence, containing the year of publication of the novel *Lolita*, continues to situate Nabokov's life and work historically. The mere mention of a year cannot give *historical and literary significance*, eliminating choice (H). It would be unreasonable for Nabokov to have spent 1,955 years writing this novel, eliminating choice (J). Also, because this is the date of publication of a novel, we can't assume that Nabokov stopped writing at this point, eliminating choice (G). Only (F) makes the appropriately modest claim that the year gives historical context.

63. **C**   The first paragraph discusses Nabokov's fame as a novelist, but the remainder of the essay discusses his significant contributions to entomology. Therefore, a transitional sentence should somehow signify that the remainder of the essay will be about something other than Nabokov's career as a novelist. This eliminates choices (B) and (D). The essay does not turn to Nabokov's political beliefs, eliminating choice (A). Only choice (C) indicates that the remainder of the essay will be about something other than Nabokov's career as a novelist.

64. **J**   Choice (F) can be eliminated because semi-colons separate only complete ideas, and *the study of insects* is not a complete idea. Choice (G) introduces the awkward construction of the participle *being*, so it can also be eliminated. *Entomology* is the *study of insects*; therefore, it would not make sense to do the *entomology of entomology*, eliminating choice (H). Choice (J) indicates appropriately that *the study of insects* is meant as an appositive defining the word *entomology*.

65. **C**   This sentence describes the way that Nabokov charts the *structure and migration patterns of butterflies*. There is no reason to set the word *structure* off from the rest of this phrase, eliminating choices (A) and (D). The word *of* in choice (B) is redundant because the word *of* is already contained in the non-underlined portion of the sentence. Therefore, the best answer is choice (C) because it includes no unnecessary pauses.

66. **J**   The words *In fact, at what might have seemed a high point in his literary career* do not create a complete idea or a sentence that can stand on its own. Therefore, these words should not end with a period or a semi-colon, eliminating choices (G) and (H). However, they do offer an introductory idea that will lead into the rest of the sentence, so the words should be set off with a comma, eliminating choice (F) and making choice (J) the best answer.

67. **B**   Choices (A), (C), and (D) all introduce transition words where no transition word is necessary. Choice (B) is the best choice because it is the most concise while preserving the meaning of the sentence.

68. **J**   Although the two forms may sound identical, the correct verb form is *could have*, not *could of*, eliminating choices (F) and (H). Then, because the words *could have* are part of a single verb, they should not be separated by a comma, as in choice (G). Therefore, the correct verb form with the correct lack of unnecessary pauses is shown in choice (J).

69. **B**   The sentence as written is idiomatically incorrect. If the underlined portion were to go where it is now, it would need to read *in, with,* or *for the scientific community*. Eliminate choice (A). Choice (C) and choice (D) insert the underlined phrase awkwardly. Only choice (B) provides a viable placement for the underlined portion, suggesting that Nabokov's work was *dismissed by the scientific community*.

70. **G**   All four answer choices have the same basic meaning, and all are grammatically correct. When this is the case, choose the most concise of the answer choices. In this case, the most concise choice is choice (G).

71. **C**   Read the question carefully. The correct answer must contain a *specific example of Nabokov's contribution to the study of moths and butterflies*. Choice (A) speaks of his work too generally. Choice (B) discusses Nabokov's wife. Choice (D) returns to a discussion of his novels. None of these gives a *specific example of Nabokov's contribution*. Only choice (C) does that in giving the name of one of the butterfly species he discovered.

72. **H** The phrase Nabokovia *in his honor* cannot stand on its own, so it cannot be punctuated with either a semi-colon or a period, eliminating choices (F) and (J). Then, choice (G) adds an unnecessary pause before the word *Nabokovia*, so it can be eliminated. Only choice (H) remains, and it correctly omits unnecessary punctuation.

73. **C** The sentence begins *We can't know*, and the second part of the sentence should continue in this vein, as if to suggest *nor can we know*, making choice (C) the best answer. The word *than* suggests a comparison where none is present, eliminating choice (A). The words *for example* are not followed by an example, eliminating choice (B). Then, deleting the underlined portion suggests that the phrase *which pursuit Nabokov found more enriching* modifies *more important*, which it does not, eliminating choice (D).

74. **G** The first paragraph of the passage suggests that Nabokov is most famous as a novelist, but the rest of the passage suggests that he *could have* been a famous entomologist instead. It would not make sense to say that Nabokov *has* an entomologist, eliminating choice (H) and choice (J), which offers an incorrect verb in any case. Only choice (G) works because the similar-sounding words *could of* are not used.

75. **A** Nabokov was a person, but to say that he was *exceptionally a person* doesn't make sense, eliminating choices (C) and (D). The same is true of calling Nabokov *an exception to a person*, eliminating choice (B). Only (A) gives the correct form: The noun *person* is modified by the adjective *exceptional*.

Part III
Reading

Chapter 9
The ACT
Reading Test

Even students with superior reading skills find this test to be tough. To crack the Reading test, you have to learn a strategic approach of *how* to work the passages in an order that makes sense for you. In this chapter, you'll learn how to order the passages and apply a basic approach.

FUN FACTS ABOUT THE READING TEST

The Reading test consists of 4 passages, 10 questions each, for a total of 40 questions that you must answer in 35 minutes. There are many factors about the structure of this test that make it difficult. For one thing, the particular passages will obviously vary from test to test, so you can't predict whether you'll like the topic or find the passage more readable than not. Moreover, the questions are in neither order of difficulty nor chronological order. And while line references in the questions can make finding answers easier, it's not unusual to have passages with few line reference questions.

There are, however, several consistent factors on each test. The passages are all roughly the same length, and they always come in the same order: Prose Fiction, Social Science, Humanities, and Natural Science. But just because that's ACT's order doesn't mean it has to be yours.

PERSONAL ORDER OF DIFFICULTY (POOD)

To get your best score on the Reading test, you have to pick your own order of the passages, and on each passage, your own order of the questions. When time is your enemy, as it is on the ACT, find and work up front what's easier for you. Leave for last, or never, what's difficult for you.

The Passages

You can't risk doing the passages in the order ACT provides *just* because they're in that order. What if the Natural Science passage turned out to be the easiest and you ran out of time before you could get to it?

Every time you take the ACT, for practice and for real, pick the order of the passages that makes sense for you. There are four issues to consider when picking your order. In practice, you may build up a track record to determine a typical order. But pay attention to the particulars of each test and be willing to adapt your order.

1. Your POOD

Use your own POOD to identify the genres and topics you like best. For example, do you rarely read fiction outside of school? Then the Prose Fiction is unlikely to be a smart choice to do first. The topics, however, may change your mind. Read the blurbs to see if that day's Social Science, for example, is a topic you know more about than, say the topic of the Humanities.

2. Paragraphs

The passages are all roughly the same length, but how they're arranged in paragraphs will differ. It's much easier to find answers on a passage with more, smaller paragraphs than on a passage with just a few huge paragraphs. Look for passages with six to eight decent-sized paragraphs.

3. Questions

ACT can be pretty cheap with line references, so the more questions with line references the better. Glance at the questions: Do you see many with numbers? That's a great sign.

4. Answers

Difficult questions tend to need longer answers. So look for many questions with short answers. Just like with line references, the more the better.

Be Flexible and Ruthless

Picking your order isn't a long, deliberative process. Use the practice tests in Chapters 10, 12, 14, and 16 to determine a typical order, but always be prepared to adapt. Take 10 seconds at the start of every ACT to look at the topics, paragraphs, questions, and answers to confirm or adapt your order.

Need More Practice?
1,296 ACT Practice Questions provides 6 tests' worth of Reading passages. That's 24 passages and 240 questions.

The Questions

Same song, different verse. You can't do the questions in the order ACT provides. They're not in order of difficulty, and they're not in chronological order. Instead, think of *Now, Later, Never.* Do Now any question that is either easy to answer OR for which the answer is easy to *find*. Do Later, or perhaps Never, questions that are both difficult to answer AND for which the answers are difficult to find.

1. Easy to Answer

ACT describes the questions in two categories: those that ask you to *refer* to what is directly stated, and those that require you to *reason* an implied meaning. In other words, reference questions ask what does the author *say*, while the reasoning questions ask what does the author *mean*. It's easier to answer "what does the author say?" than to answer "what is the author *really* saying?"

2. Easy to Find the Answer

A question easy to answer may do you no good if you can't find the answer in the passage. On the other hand, a reasoning question with a line reference tells you exactly where you can find the answer. Even if it's a tougher question to answer, do it Now if you know where to find the answer.

In a perfect world, we'd give you an exact order to follow every time. The ACT is not a perfect world. Instead, you have to consider the particulars of each test and know how to make an order that works on that test.

PACING

With just 35 minutes to do 4 passages and 40 questions, you don't have even 9 minutes for every passage. But should you do all 4 passages? Think about the pacing chart we discussed in Chapter 1. You may hit your scoring goals if you take more time and if you do fewer passages. On the other hand, you may decide that you can't get all of the questions right no matter how much time you spend. In that case, you're better off getting to as many Now questions as you can.

$35 \div 4 \neq 36$

Whichever pacing strategy works for you, don't treat all the passages you work equally. That is, even if you work all 4, you shouldn't spend 8.75 minutes on each. Spend more time on your best passages and spend less on your worst. For example, spend 12 minutes on your first passage, 10 minutes on your second, 8 minutes on your third, and 5 minutes on your last. This is just an example: practice, practice, and practice to figure out a pacing strategy that will reach your target score.

POE

Many students destroy their pacing with one particular bad habit on the Reading test: They keep rereading and rereading part of the passage, trying to understand the answer to a tough question. But you're ignoring the one advantage of a multiple-choice test: The correct answer is right on the page. Use POE to eliminate three wrong answers to find the correct answer. It's not always easy to answer these questions, but you will likely be able to spot at least one wrong answer. In fact, using POE is a crucial step of our 4-step Basic Approach.

Now that you know how to pick your order of the passages, it's time to learn the Basic Approach.

THE BASIC APPROACH

The Reading test is an open-book test. You wouldn't read a whole book and answer all the questions from memory, so you shouldn't do that on the ACT. Instead, you need a smart, effective strategy.

Step 1: Preview

This step involves two parts.

First, check the blurb to see if there is additional information other than the title, author, and copyright. There usually isn't, but occasionally there is. You have to check each time to see if this one time is the exception.

> **HUMANITIES:** This passage is taken from The Century by Peter Jennings (© 1998 by ABC Television Network Group).

Second, map the questions. Put a star next to each line or paragraph reference, and underline the lead words. By lead words we mean words you'll actually find in the passage. Don't underline generic words like "main idea" or "how the author would characterize."

Here are ten mapped questions.

21. One of the main points the author formulates is that:

☆ 22. The author mentions a "photographic motion study" (line 36) in order to emphasize what quality of Duchamp's *Nude*?

☆ 23. The first paragraph states that certain early <u>critics of modern art</u>:

☆ 24. It can be inferred from the author's reference to "an explosion" and "an earthquake" (lines 38–40) that <u>Duchamp's *Nude*</u>:

☆ 25. As it is used in line 42, the word *abhorrent* most nearly means:

26. It can be reasonably concluded from the passage that the most important characteristic of <u>"modern" art</u> was that it was:

27. Which of the following best describes <u>Roosevelt's reaction to modern art</u>?

☆ 28. It can reasonably be inferred that the use of the words "Ellis Island" (line 17) indicated that:

☆ 29. It can be inferred from the last paragraph that the <u>organizers of the Armory Show</u>:

30. Which of the following is NOT answered by the passage?

Spend no more than 30 seconds mapping the questions. Do not read the questions thoroughly for comprehension at this stage. Just spot the line and paragraph references to star and the lead words to underline.

Do look at the lead words you've underlined, however. They telegraph the main idea before you've read one word of the passage: This passage is about modern art.

Step 2: Work the Passage

In this next step, spend no more than 3 minutes on the passage. Look for and underline your lead words. If you struggle with time, read only the first sentence of each paragraph. You'll read what you need to answer specific questions.

Here are the first sentences of each paragraph to our passage, with the lead words from some questions found and underlined.

> The show was grandly titled "The International Exhibition of <u>Modern Art</u>," but the dynamite, as *The New Yorker* later commented, was in the word <u>"modern."</u>

> The star image of the exhibition was most certainly <u>Duchamp's *Nude Descending a Staircase*</u> (or, as <u>Roosevelt</u> called it, "a naked man going downstairs"), a painting so abstract it defied its own title, which, of course, was the point.

> <u>Roosevelt said Duchamp's *Nude*</u> reminded him of a Navaho rug he stood upon while shaving each morning in his bathroom.

> Anticipating a reluctant audience, the <u>organizers of the Armory Show</u> had included an editorial in the exhibition catalog urging viewers to greet the new art with an open mind.

Between the stars and the lead words you found in the first sentences of the paragraphs, you have a lot of questions whose answers are easy to find, and you're ready to move on to the next step.

Step 3: Work the Questions

Work the questions in an order that makes sense: Do Now the questions that are easy to answer or whose answers are easy to find. Look at all the stars on questions 22, 23, 24, 25, 28, and 29. You know where to read to find those answers. But when you worked the passage, you found the locations for questions 26 and 27.

Do Later, or Never, questions that are both difficult to answer and whose answers are difficult to find. Questions 21 and 30 are both good Later/Never questions.

As you make your way through the Now questions, read a window of five to ten lines to find the answer.

Here's an example.

---○---

22. The author mentions a "photographic motion study" (line 36) in order to emphasize what quality of Duchamp's *Nude*?

Now read lines 27–37 to find the answer.

> The star image of the exhibition was most certainly Duchamp's *Nude Descending a Staircase* (or, as Roosevelt called it, "a naked man going downstairs"), a painting so
> 30 abstract it defied its own title, which, of course, was the point. As critic Robert Hughes has pointed out, the nude had a long and distinguished history with painting, where she (and, more rarely, he) was usually portrayed in a blissful state of recline; by contrast, Duchamp's *Nude*, to the degree that it looked at
> 35 all like what it was supposed to be, was a nude on the move (indeed, the painting had the quality of a photographic motion study), a metaphor for the change that it heralded.

Never answer specific questions from memory. Always read a window of five to ten lines to find the answer to each question, using the line references and lead words as a guide.

You may feel you've spotted the exact line with the answer, but don't worry if you haven't. Move to the last step, and Work the Answers with POE.

Step 4: Work the Answers

If you can answer the question in your own words, go through the answers and look for a match. If you can't answer it, don't worry. Review each answer, and eliminate the ones you're confident are wrong.

    F. The different interpretations of the painting
    G. The painting's photographic realism
    H. The painting's inappropriate subject matter
    J. The movement implied in the painting

Here's How to Crack It

Lines 35–37 describe the painting as *a nude on the move*, which choice (J) paraphrases well. Alternatively, use POE to get rid of choice (F), because there is only one interpretation of the painting, and choice (H), because there is no proof that the author disapproves of the subject matter. Choice (G) may tempt you because of *to the degree that it looked at all like what it was supposed to be* in lines 34–35, but those lines actually argue against photographic realism.

---○---

Repeat

Steps 3 and 4 repeat: Make your way through the rest of the questions, reading what you need for each. Use POE to find the answers. Continue to make smart choices about the order of your questions, doing Now every question that is easy to answer or whose answer is easy to find.

Save for Last

The toughest reasoning questions should be done last (if at all—your pacing strategy may mark them as Never). After you've worked all the specific questions on the passage, you understand the main theme better. Questions 21 and 30 for this passage are both smart choices to do last.

Now move to Chapter 10 to practice picking your order and applying the Basic Approach.

Summary

o   Pick your order of the passages.

o   Use your POOD to identify the genres and topics you like best.

o   Pay attention to your track record in practice.

o   Examine the particulars of each test and be pre-pared to confirm or change your order each time.

o   Look for passages with many, small paragraphs.

o   Look for passages with many line reference questions.

o   Look for passages with many short answers.

o   Use the 4-step Basic Approach.
   1.   Preview
   2.   Work the Passage
   3.   Work the Questions
   4.   Work the Answers

Chapter 10
Reading Practice
Test 1

READING TEST

35 Minutes—40 Questions

DIRECTIONS: There are four passages in this test. Each passage is followed by several questions. After reading each passage, choose the best answer to each question and blacken the corresponding oval on your answer document. You may refer to the passages as often as necessary.

Passage I

PROSE FICTION: The following passage is adapted from the short story "Between Two Homes" by Herbert Malloy (© 1993 by Herbert Malloy).

The fact that air travel allows me to fall asleep on the west coast and wake up on the east coast is bittersweet magic. On a red-eye flight, the continent passes stealthily underneath like an ugly secret we prefer not to acknowledge. Passengers drift
5 in and out of an unsteady slumber, reluctantly awakening to the realization that they are still stuck on an airplane. Sometimes I open my eyes wide enough to gaze out the window at the twinkling lights of the towns and cities below.

I try to decipher which city glimmers below from the size
10 of its grid of light, as well as my perception of how long I have been flying. Could that be Denver? Have I already napped a third of the flight? I look around the cabin to see how many other people are having trouble sleeping and become instantly jealous of the families and couples who have the luxury of
15 leaning on each other.

The aura of cool sunlight begins to infiltrate the cabin as we near Dulles, Virginia. We see flocks of birds sharing the sky with us. By the time we arrive, we will have flown through three time zones, compressing a normal night by removing three of
20 its sacred hours. We are not only cheating space by crossing a continent in the course of a long nap, but also cheating time by turning back our watches and rushing prematurely toward the sunrise.

My hometown is still a car ride away, but the vicinity of
25 the airport is close enough to be a tonic to my nostalgic yearnings. As soon as I see the dense stands of oak and hickory blanketing the hills, I know I am back home. There's no trace of palm trees, no unrelenting flat stretches of compacted and perpendicular city streets. Left behind in our plane's exhaust,
30 Southern California is still fast asleep.

*   *   *   *   *   *

My dad has driven to the airport to pick me up, but I very nearly miss him—I'd forgotten he now drives a different car. I'm sure I've heard him speak of his new blue Toyota, but I always expect him to be driving the brown Lexus he owned
35 when I moved away. Happily, the smell inside the car remains the same: stretched leather, cologne, and the faint hint of a cigarette that was meant to go undetected. I covertly scan the

side of his face while he drives, hoping to see the same face I remember. Instead I see new wrinkles, new spots on his face,
40 new folds of skin on his neck.

We pass by familiar landmarks as we near our house, as well as some not-so-familiar ones. The performance stage in the town center that was merely a proposal when I left is now up-and-running, according to the marquee listing its upcoming
45 shows. The Olde Towne Tavern is apparently now called Summit Station. The old dance studio above the apartment buildings on West Deer Park seems to have finally closed — I always wondered how it stayed in business. The cluster of shops that famously burned to the ground near the high school has open
50 doors and cars gliding in and out of the parking lot.

We've arrived at the house, and as soon as I walk through the door, I am flooded with further reminders of my absence — trinkets on the wall I don't recognize, rearranged furniture in the kitchen and living room, sugary cereals and snacks strangely
55 absent from the top of the fridge. What was once my home has become someone else's house — my parents' house.

I suddenly see the mundane routines of my parents cast in a tragic light: my mother's agitation at the grackles that scare the goldfinches away from the bird-feeders, my father's habit
60 of pretending to read the newspaper on the porch (just an opportunity to keep an eye on the neighborhood), the uninspired television they watch at night, often in separate rooms, and, most depressingly, the way they often fall asleep in front of the television, mouths gaping.

*   *   *   *   *   *

65 The in-flight movie on the way back to California portrays the story of a physicist who awakens after spending ten years in a coma. His initial joy gradually subsides and ultimately leads to confusion and sadness as he attempts to reintegrate into a world that has moved on without him. Even science, that rock
70 of immutable truths, has changed in his absence. He finds the entire body of research he had been working on prior to his coma now obsolete—years of advances in his field had furnished the answers he was pursuing.

As a physicist, he knew that time is a relative phenomenon,
75 a concept that only has meaning in relation to an individual's succession of experiences and ordering of memories. Clearly, though, his world, like mine, had continued to age, changing despite his lack of participation in it. Years are passing whether you're there to observe them or not.

1. It can reasonably be inferred from the passage that the narrator thinks air travel is:

   A. the most enjoyable way to travel.
   B. an ordinary part of the world.
   C. more uncomfortable than convenient.
   D. somewhat unnatural in what it makes possible.

2. The first three paragraphs (lines 1–23) establish all of the following about the narrator EXCEPT that he is:

   F. onboard an airplane
   G. traveling east.
   H. departing from Denver.
   J. noticing sights below.

3. The point of view from which the passage is told is best described as that of:

   A. a young adult returning from a vacation to Southern California.
   B. an adult relating his reactions to visiting to his hometown.
   C. a young adult awakening from a long coma.
   D. an adult who prefers Southern California to his new home.

4. According to the narrator, which of the following things is relatively new to his parents' house?

   F. Certain trinkets on the wall.
   G. The fridge.
   H. His father's brown Lexus.
   J. The bird-feeders.

5. The passage contains recurring references to all of the following EXCEPT:

   A. difficulty sleeping.
   B. birds.
   C. grids of light.
   D. dancing.

6. The narrator indicates that the most upsetting habit of his parents is:

   F. buying new cars.
   G. how and where they fall asleep.
   H. what they watch on television.
   J. how many trinkets they buy.

7. According to the passage, the coma victim has a sense of time as a relative phenomenon because:

   A. ten years had gone by quickly.
   B. he was a physicist.
   C. it was a side effect of his medical treatments.
   D. it was the focus of his research before his coma.

8. Based on the narrator's account, all of the following are part of the present, rather than the past, in his hometown EXCEPT:

   F. the closed dance studio.
   G. the upcoming show marquee.
   H. Summit Station.
   J. the burnt remains of a shopping center.

9. Details in the passage most strongly suggest that one characteristic of the narrator's hometown is:

   A. flat stretches.
   B. palm trees.
   C. oak trees.
   D. perpendicular streets.

10. When the narrator refers to science as "that rock of immutable truths" (lines 69–70), he is most likely directly referring to:

    F. the unchanging nature believed to be characteristic of scientific knowledge.
    G. the physicist's inability to understand the recent advances in science.
    H. the body of research conducted in the physicist's field during his coma.
    J. the ten years' worth of scientific advances that the narrator had missed.

Passage II

SOCIAL SCIENCE: The following passage is adapted from the 2002 article "Indigenous Goes Global" by Sally Mayfield.

MayaWorks is a nonprofit organization that attempts to promote fair trade practices with Mayan artisans who would otherwise have little commercial outlet for their talents. In a broader sense, the organization aims to help traditionally
5 marginalized Guatemalan women attain the literacy, advanced skills, business acumen, and confidence they need to contribute to the economic well-being of their families.

"Buried deep in the Guatemalan mountains are these amazing pockets of Mayan communities," begins Dennis Ho-
10 gan, a chief program administrator for Berhorst Partners for Development. Communities such as Agua Caliente, Xetonox, and Tzanjuyu are often as small as 50–100 people. They speak their own ancient Mayan dialects and rarely interact with the Spanish-speaking majority of Guatemala. "They have a rich
15 lineage of religious, linguistic, and artistic traditions that get passed down from generation to generation. However, they are deeply threatened by extreme poverty and lack of potable water. We want to find a way for these women to grow with the times, despite rigidly-defined gender roles that relegate women to food
20 preparation and child care, but also to help them utilize and preserve the cultural traditions that make them so irreplaceable."

When representatives from MayaWorks first reached out to women in Agua Caliente in 1994, the men of the village were deeply suspicious. The women were extremely shy, avoiding
25 almost all eye contact with the strangers. Ultimately, though, the women of the village agreed to the idea of forming a weaving cooperative and came up with an initial product order they felt they could fill. Each of eight women was to weave a dozen brightly colored wall hangings that spelled the word "peace"
30 in a number of languages. Weeks later, with great pride, the women delivered their order, using local material for the hanging rods and the finest yarn they could find, dyed and then washed to prevent staining.

"When we returned to pick up the finished products and
35 pay them, there was a remarkable change in the way we were received by the villagers," Hogan reflects with deep satisfaction. "The women were beaming with self-confidence, and the children even thanked us in their native tongue for helping give their mothers work."

40 The variety of wares created by MayaWorks artisans has greatly expanded over time. Corn husks are used to make decorative angels. Yarn is woven into brightly-colored placemats, napkins, pouches, Beanies, and footbags. Some groups even make religious items, such as stoles for Christian priests
45 and yarmulkes, or kippahs, for Jewish observers. Making the kippahs was initially an engineering challenge for the villagers, as the small head-coverings frequently came out either too flat or too round. Given a mannequin, however, the villagers were soon able to master the correct shape. Once told that the kippah

50 was a symbol for the wearer's reverence to God, the villagers became even more devoted and loving in their craft.

The capacity of these artisans for learning, adapting, and innovating has delighted the founders of MayaWorks. As relationships develop between MayaWorks and individual groups of
55 artisans, new equipment and training is introduced to broaden their design capacity. 36-inch treadle-foot looms now allow members of Xetonox to create fabrics that can be sold by the yard side-by-side with mass-manufactured textiles.

In addition to broadening the range of products these vil-
60 lagers can create, MayaWorks hopes to expand the knowledge base of the women and help provide infrastructure to enable a better life for them and future generations. Leslie Buchanan heads up the Literacy Initiative for MayaWorks and explains, "Part of the challenge these communities face is their cultural
65 isolation from other Guatemalans. They avoid going to marketplaces in nearby cities because they don't speak Spanish. That makes it difficult for them to navigate the buses and other transportation. And it makes it hard to negotiate with Spanish-speaking merchants. In an economy where the first price you
70 hear is never supposed to be the final price, the inability to haggle makes you unfit to make purchases."

Although literacy programs provided by outsiders are typically met with resistance by Mayan communities, MayaWorks has achieved considerable success in motivating Mayan villag-
75 ers to learn Spanish. This success where others have failed has more to do with the economic initiatives of MayaWorks than its literacy campaigns: once the villagers have the opportunity and means to expand their economic base, the desire to learn Spanish comes naturally, from within, as a tool to help them
80 achieve even greater success. Rather than appearing as a threat to their traditions, the Spanish language now appears as a means of preserving the well-being of their traditional communities.

Another component of MayaWorks is coordinating and encouraging the financing of microcredit loans, small loans
85 offered to impoverished people who have no collateral or credit history (and thus could never qualify for a traditional banking loan). By providing these Mayan villagers with much-needed capital, MayaWorks helps them to upgrade their weaving equipment, install water pumps (which greatly reduces the
90 health problems associated with meager and contaminated water sources), and buy crops such as blackberries, potatoes, and strawberries. These measures both increase the sustainability of the community and encourage entrepreneurship. So far, MayaWorks reports, 100% of their microcredit loans have
95 been paid back in full and on time.

11. In the context of the passage, the statement "the men of the village were deeply suspicious" (lines 23–24) most nearly suggests that Mayan men:

   A. felt uneasy about the potential interest in employing their village's women.
   B. didn't believe that MayaWorks representatives were who they said they were.
   C. rarely were visited by people who could speak Spanish.
   D. were skeptical that the women of the village had artistic talents.

12. The main purpose of the second paragraph (lines 8–21) is to:

   F. lend support to the notion that women in Guatemala deserve stronger legal rights.
   G. point out the small number of people who live in Amazon villages.
   H. establish the value that programs such as MayaWorks could provide.
   J. explain how Berhorst Partners for Development became based in Guatemala.

13. The passage indicates all of the following as problems initially faced by the fledgling Mayan artisans EXCEPT that:

   A. they lacked a mannequin to facilitate designing head-wear.
   B. they could not communicate well in Spanish-speaking marketplaces.
   C. they did not have looms capable of making yard-width fabrics.
   D. they were unable to find material for the hanging rods in their wall hangings.

14. It can most reasonably be inferred from the passage that regarding MayaWorks, the author feels:

   F. appreciative of the organization's methods and intentions.
   G. convinced that mountain villagers in other countries will join MayaWorks.
   H. doubtful about the quality of the artisans' wares.
   J. confused by the organization's conflicting priorities.

15. Which of the following assumptions would be most critical for a reader to accept in order to agree with the author's claims in the passage?

   A. Mayan communities should fully assimilate into their surrounding Spanish-speaking communities.
   B. One's self-esteem can be improved by performing productive work in exchange for money.
   C. Mayan artisans have much difficulty in adapting to design specifications of items that are not traditionally Mayan.
   D. Most major banks would consider the Mayan artist cooperatives to be appealing candidates for loans.

16. The passage indicates that approximately how many wall hangings were part of the initial order filled by the Agua Caliente village?

   F. Eight
   G. A Dozen
   H. One hundred
   J. One thousand

17. According to the passage, when villagers were told of the religious function of a kippah, they became even more:

   A. confused about its shape.
   B. appreciative of their mannequin.
   C. intrigued about Judaism.
   D. dedicated to their work.

18. The passage states that each of the following is among the products made by MayaWorks artists EXCEPT:

   F. yarmulkes.
   G. wall hangings.
   H. mass-manufactured textiles.
   J. placemats.

19. The main function of the last paragraph (lines 83–95) is to:

   A. discuss the specific terms and requirements of several types of loans.
   B. describe some important ways that outside investment has helped strengthen Mayan communities.
   C. itemize some of the ways Mayan artisans have reinvested their earnings.
   D. demonstrate that Mayan villagers are as trustworthy in business as they are skilled in art.

20. The passage indicates that the efforts of MayaWorks to increase the Spanish literacy of the Mayan community may succeed because they:

   F. have instilled in the Mayan women an economic incentive to learn Spanish.
   G. have familiarized Mayan women with the bartering rules of Guatemalan marketplaces.
   H. convinced Mayan women that their traditions will be better preserved in Spanish.
   J. designed a more innovative and thoughtful literacy campaign than had previous initiatives.

Passage III

HUMANITIES: This passage is adapted from the article "Life in the Pits" by Bob Gullberg (© 2003 by Hennen Press).

Mozart and Handel refer to Wolfgang Amadeus Mozart (1756-91), Classical-era composer, and George Frideric Handel (1685-1759), Baroque-era composer.

Looking back over a twenty-year career of playing, composing, and now conducting orchestra music, I often feel a sense of wonder—not at what I have accomplished, but how someone with my agrarian, rather workaday upbringing should
5 have chosen such a path at all. It would have been easy for me to stay on the family farm, eventually to become part-owner, as my brother did quite successfully. However, rewarding as this existence was, it was somehow unfulfilling; my youthful imagination, much to my parents' dismay, often cast about for
10 other, greater pursuits to occupy it. Still, growing up as I did in a household where the radio dispensed milk prices instead of Mozart and hog futures instead of Handel, the thought of embarking on a career in classical music went beyond even my wildest imagination.

15 Perhaps what started me down this unforeseen path was my fascination with other languages. At church services I would hear snippets of Latin and Greek; I was learning Spanish at school; I was instantly drawn to the German, Italian, and Yiddish words and phrases I heard in movies and on T.V.
20 Surrounded as I was by the fairly common language of farm and field, these "glamorous" expressions seemed to fill a void in me, and I collected them with the energy of a lepidopterist netting butterflies. As my interest in other languages grew, so did my awareness that music is itself a language, just as capable
25 of expressing and inspiring emotion or thought as the spoken word—sometimes even more so. Take The Tempest, the piece I'm currently rehearsing with my orchestra. It begins in a major key, with just the stringed instruments playing lightly, evoking a sense of peace and contentment—a calm, sunny summer's
30 day. In the second movement, the key diminishes; the mood darkens—clouds and apprehension are building. As the piece progresses, wind instruments, as if blown by the storm, begin to howl, horns blare and shout, overwhelming the senses, thrilling and frightening at once. As the "storm" reaches its height,
35 timpani-roll thunder echoes, and cymbal-clash lightning bolts crash relentlessly, until, when it becomes almost unbearable, the music eases, hope and reason are restored, and soothing notes help the listener forget the chaos and fear he or she felt only moments ago. I've read many accounts of severe weather,
40 even seen them in movies and on TV, but few of them, if any, have been able to replicate not only the sensory experience of a thunderstorm, but also the emotional one the way this piece of music can.

I believe it was music's emotive influence—particularly
45 powerful in my impressionable youth—that ultimately led me to pursue a career in music. Once I began to experience music on an emotional level, I remember having the feeling that others just didn't "get it" like I did, as if somehow music were meant just for musicians. It was only later that I became
50 aware of music's true value—it is a universal language, able to speak to all people, regardless of the linguistic differences that may exist between them. Eventually, of course, music began to eclipse the numerous other "passions" I had throughout my adolescence. Years before I began to pursue music in earnest,
55 I had developed quite an interest in all things motorized. I've always had a mechanical bent (which has served me well in later life, allowing me to turn my hand to almost any musical instrument), and being around farm equipment from an early age certainly gave me an outlet to exercise my abilities. How-
60 ever, my real focus was on cars—I virtually never set down *Automobile Monthly*, a magazine for auto enthusiasts, and I eagerly devoured articles describing which models had the highest horsepower or quickest times in the quarter-mile, and effortlessly committing that information to memory. Eventu-
65 ally, though, like my previous infatuations with archery, and before that dinosaurs, my fixation on cars was to take a "back seat" to a new, greater, and this time lasting, passion for music.

So what made the difference? What made my passion for music continue to burn where other passions had fizzled out?
70 Maturity, perhaps—I know I'd like to think that's the case—or maybe it was just a process of compare-and-contrast; trying different things until I found the one that "fit." If I'm honest with myself, however, I'm forced to admit the answer isn't a "what" or "when", but a "who." For me, like many who find
75 themselves adrift on a sea of uncertainty, it took a mentor to help me find my way to dry land. In my case, that mentor was the conductor of my high-school orchestra, Ms. Fenchurch. A woman of boundless energy and enthusiasm, and with an all-consuming love for music, it was she who first taught me the
80 joy of composition and creation, and helped me to realize that making music is more than just playing notes in a particular order, no matter how well it's done—it's about expression, and perhaps more important, communication. Just like a language.

---

21. The author mentions *Automobile Monthly* and his mechanical bent primarily to suggest that his:

    A. infatuation with cars was at one time as intense as his passion for music.

    B. interest in and love of all things motorized has remained unchanged throughout his life.

    C. experience with motorized things accounts for his mechanical style of playing music.

    D. obsession with automotive knowledge distracted him from focusing on music.

22. In the first paragraph, the author most nearly characterizes his upbringing as:

- **F.** easy and usually spent working with his brother.
- **G.** frustrating yet able to translate easily into music.
- **G.** somewhat satisfying yet ultimately unable to captivate.
- **J.** unfulfilling and invariably resulting in his parents' approval.

23. Based on the passage, which of the following was most likely the first to engage the author's passionate interest?

- **A.** Automobiles
- **B.** Archery
- **C.** Dinosaurs
- **D.** Music

24. Viewed in the context of the passage, the statement in lines 39–43 is most likely intended to suggest that:

- **F.** music more vividly conveys some experiences than do visual or written accounts.
- **G.** movies can provide a misleading experience of what a thunderstorm is like.
- **H.** news reports should more accurately reflect emotional experiences.
- **J.** thunderstorms are among the hardest experiences to accurately replicate.

25. The passage suggests that the lepidopterist netting butterflies represents:

- **A.** the author as a child, relishing learning foreign expressions.
- **B.** the author presently, enjoying his most recent passion.
- **C.** Ms. Fenchurch, with her boundless energy.
- **D.** the opening movement of The Tempest.

26. In the context of the passage, lines 34–39 are best described as presenting images of:

- **F.** jealously, mercy, and resentment.
- **G.** hate, fear, and disbelief.
- **H.** conflict, optimism, and love.
- **J.** chaos, resolution, and relaxation.

27. The author discusses "playing notes in a particular order" (lines 81–82) as part of Ms. Fenchurch's argument that:

- **A.** the order of notes matters less than the speed at which they are played.
- **B.** all music consists of the same parts but rearranged in creative ways.
- **C.** while one aims to be skilled at performing notes, one should also aim to convey their meaning.
- **D.** although communication is important, there is more joy to be found in composition itself.

28. Which of the following does NOT reasonably describe a transition presented by the author in lines 27–34?

- **F.** Lightness to darkness
- **G.** Calm to thrilling
- **H.** Apprehension to fright
- **J.** Overwhelmed to peaceful

29. The main purpose of the last paragraph is to:

- **A.** describe the lasting influence of Ms. Fenchurch's encouragement.
- **B.** present an anecdote that conveys Ms. Fenchurch's unique conducting style.
- **C.** provide detailed background information about Ms. Fenchurch.
- **D.** illustrate the effect music has on teachers such as Ms. Fenchurch.

30. The passage is best described as being told from the point of view of a musician who is:

- **F.** telling a linear story that connects momentous events from the beginning of his career to some from the end.
- **G.** describing how modern works of music such as The Tempest have advanced the vision of classical composers such as Mozart and Handel.
- **H.** suggesting that people who have an interest in universal languages would be well served in studying music.
- **J.** marveling at his eventual choice of career and considering the people and interests that contributed to it.

Passage IV

NATURAL SCIENCE: This passage is adapted from the article "Debunking the Seahorse" by Clark Millingham (© 2002 by Halcyon Press).

Scientists and laymen alike have long been fascinated by fish known colloquially as seahorses, due to the species' remarkable appearance, unusual mating habits, and incredibly rare reversal of male and female parental roles. The scientific
5 name for the genus is Hippocampus, which combines the Greek word for "horse," *hippos*, with the Greek word for "sea monster," *kampos*. Its distinctive equine head and tapered body shape are a great disadvantage when it comes to the seahorse's swimming ability. It manages to maneuver about by fluttering
10 its dorsal fin up to 35 times a second, but it lacks the caudal, or "tail" fin, which provides the powerful forward thrust for most fish. Instead of swimming to find food, the seahorse coils its signature prehensile tail around stationary objects while using its long snout like a straw to suck in vast numbers of
15 tiny larvae, plankton, and algae. Because the seahorse lacks teeth and a stomach, food passes quickly through its digestive tract, resulting in the need for nearly incessant consumption of food (a typical seahorse can ingest more than 3,000 brine shrimp per day).

20 The peculiar physical features of the seahorse are intriguing, but its mating and reproductive habits are most often the subject of scientists' fascination and debate. Seahorses' courtship rituals often involve a male and a female coordinating their movements, swimming side by side with tails intertwined or coiling around
25 the same strand of sea grass and spinning around it together. They even "dress up" for these rituals, turning a whole array of vivid colors—a sharp contrast to the dull browns and grays with which they typically camouflage themselves among the sea grasses. Courtship typically lasts about two weeks, during
30 which the female and her potential mate will meet once a day, while other males continue to compete for the female's attention, snapping their heads at each other and tail-wrestling.

By the end of the courtship, the female has become engorged with a clutch of around 1,000 eggs, equivalent in mass to one-
35 third her body weight. It is the male, however, who possesses the incubating organ for the eggs, a brood pouch located on his ventral (front) side. The male forces sea water through the pouch to open it up, signifying his readiness to receive the eggs. Uncoiling their tail-grips, the two attach to each other and begin
40 a spiraling ascent towards the surface. The female inserts her ovipositor, a specialized biological apparatus for conducting the eggs into the male's pouch, and the eggs are transferred over the course of eight or nine hours. After that, the male stays put while the female ventures off, only to check in briefly once a
45 day for the next few weeks.

Inside the male's brood pouch, the eggs are fertilized and receive prolactin, the same hormone mammals use for milk production. The pouch delivers oxygen to the eggs via a network of capillaries and regulates a low-salinity environment. As the
50 gestation continues, the eggs hatch and the pouch becomes increasingly saline to help acclimate the young seahorses to the salt water that is waiting outside. The male typically gives birth at night, expelling anywhere from 100 to 1,500 live fry from its pouch. By morning, he once again has an empty pouch
55 to offer his partner if she is ready to mate again.

Because male parenting is such a rarity in the animal kingdom, and male gestation almost unheard-of, scientists often speculate on why male seahorses assume birthing duties. Since giving birth is so energy-intensive and physically limiting,
60 it greatly increases one's risk of death and therefore needs an explanation in terms of evolutionary cost. Bateman's principle holds that whichever sex expends less energy in the reproductive process should be the sex that spends more energy competing for a mate. Only with seahorses do we see the males both
65 compete for mates and give birth. A study conducted by Pierre Robinson at the University of Tallahassee argued that, contrary to appearances, the total energy investment of the mother in growing the clutch of eggs inside of her still outweighed the energy investment of the male in the incubation and birthing
70 process. Male oxygen intake rates go up by 33% during their parental involvement, while the female spends twice as much energy when generating eggs.

In addition to male pregnancy, seahorses also have the distinction of being one of a very small number of monoga-
75 mous species. Scientists believe this is due to the tremendous investment of time and energy that goes into each clutch of eggs a female produces. If her eggs are ready to be incubated and the female does not have a trustworthy male partner ready to receive them, they will be expelled into the ocean and months
80 will have been lost. Additionally, by transferring incubation and birthing duties to the male, a stable monogamous couple can develop an efficient birthing cycle in which he incubates one clutch of eggs while the female begins generating the next.

31. The passage notes that the courtship rituals of seahorses include:

   A. males snapping their heads at females.
   B. camouflaging their body coloring.
   C. allowing sea water to open the brood pouch.
   D. daily meetings for two weeks.

32. The passage states that the seahorse's swimming ability is hindered by its:

   F. tapered body shape.
   G. weak caudal fin.
   H. fluttering dorsal fin.
   J. lack of teeth.

33. Which of the following pieces of information does the most to resolve scientists' confusion as to why male seahorses both compete for mates and give birth?

   A. The fact that the female seahorse possesses an ovipositor.
   B. Pierre Robinson's research on the total energy investment of each sex.
   C. The habit of seahorses to mate with only one partner.
   D. The length of time male seahorses devote to courtship rituals.

34. One of the main ideas established by the passage is that:

   F. seahorses are actually quite capable swimmers, despite their unusual appearance.
   G. scientists cannot come up with any coherent explanation for why male seahorses have the evolutionary burden of gestation.
   H. the brood pouch of the male is located on its ventral side.
   J. it is not customary in the animal kingdom for animals to keep the same mating partner for life.

35. As it is used in line 13, the word *signature* most nearly means:

   A. distinctive-looking.
   B. very useful.
   C. autograph.
   D. legally obligated.

36. The main purpose of the fourth paragraph (lines 46–55) is to describe the:

   F. process linking fertilization to hatching.
   G. intricacies of the seahorse's capillary network.
   H. quantity of fry to which males give birth.
   J. amount of salinity seahorse eggs can tolerate.

37. The passage most strongly emphasizes that the monogamy of seahorse mates is most advantageous for the transition from:

   A. low-salinity to high-salinity.
   B. one birthing cycle to the next.
   C. fertilization to incubation.
   D. courtship to mating.

38. As it is used in line 80, the word *lost* most nearly means:

   F. mislaid.
   G. disoriented.
   H. squandered.
   J. defeated.

39. According to the passage, which of the following aspects of a male seahorse's pregnancy provides the best evidence that the seahorse species conforms to the idea behind Bateman's Principle?

   A. Brood pouch
   B. Ovipositor
   C. Prolactin
   D. Oxygen intake

40. The passage indicates that the brood pouch becomes increasingly saline because seahorse eggs:

   F. would otherwise run the risk of prematurely hatching.
   G. begin gestation in a low salinity environment but ultimately get released into the surrounding water.
   H. have salt extracted from them by the capillary network that delivers oxygen to the brood pouch.
   J. receive the hormone prolactin but do not have the exposure to salt that other mammals do.

END OF TEST 3
STOP! DO NOT TURN THE PAGE UNTIL TOLD TO DO SO.
DO NOT RETURN TO A PREVIOUS TEST.

Chapter 11
Reading Practice
Test 1
Answers and
Explanations

READING PRACTICE TEST 1 ANSWERS

1.	D
2.	H
3.	B
4.	F
5.	D
6.	G
7.	B
8.	J
9.	C
10.	F
11.	A
12.	H
13.	D
14.	F
15.	B
16.	H
17.	D
18.	H
19.	B
20.	F

21.	A
22.	H
23.	C
24.	F
25.	A
26.	J
27.	C
28.	J
29.	A
30.	J
31.	D
32.	F
33.	B
34.	J
35.	A
36.	F
37.	B
38.	H
39.	D
40.	G

SCORE YOUR PRACTICE TEST

Step A
Count the number of correct answers: _____. This is your **raw score**.

Step B
Use the score conversion table below to look up your raw score. The number to the left is your **scale score**: _____.

Step
A

Step
B

Reading Scale Conversion Table

Scale Score	Raw Score	Scale Score	Raw Score	Scale Score	Raw Score
36	40	27	30	18	18
35	39	26	29	17	16–17
34	38	25	27–28	16	15
33	37	24	26	15	14
32	36	23	24–25	14	12–13
31	35	22	23	13	11
30	34	21	22	12	9–10
29	32–33	20	20–21	11	8
28	31	19	19	10	6–7

READING PRACTICE TEST 1 EXPLANATIONS

Passage I

1. **D** By saying that air travel is *bittersweet magic* (line 2) and that it is *cheating time*, the author is describing it as unnatural. Choice (A) is incorrect because no comparison is being made, and the author mentions some uncomfortable aspects of his flight. Choice (B) is incorrect since the author describes air travel as *magic*. Choice (C) is incorrect because, while the author does mention uncomfortable aspects of flying, he is still taking the flight for the convenience of getting from the west coast to the east coast in the course of a *long nap*.

2. **H** The narrator is looking for Denver when he thinks the flight is a third of the way through, which means he did not depart from Denver. Choices (F) and (G) are revealed in the very first sentence. Choice (J) is supported by numerous references to estimating city size by the grid of light seen from above.

3. **B** The passage involves the experiences of someone who has moved out of his parents' house, returns to visit them, and becomes a bit depressed by the changes that have taken place. Choice (A) is incorrect since the passage never mentions a vacation and suggests the narrator has been absent for some time (he doesn't remember what car his father drives). Choice (C) is incorrect because the coma was only involved in an in-flight movie the narrator watches. Choice (D) is incorrect—the narrator's new home is in Southern California.

4. **F** In line 54 the author states he doesn't recognize the trinkets on the wall—they have been added during his absence. (G), (H), and (J) can all be eliminated: Although the *fridge* (line 55), the *brown Lexus* (line 34), and the *bird-feeders* (line 59), are all mentioned, they are not described as "new."

5. **D** Although a dance studio is mentioned, there is no mention of dancing. Choices (A) and (C) are both mentioned once in the first and once in the second paragraph. Choice (B) is mentioned in the third and eighth paragraph.

6. **G** The narrator uses the phrase *most depressingly* to describe the way his parents *often fall asleep in front of the television, mouths gaping* (lines 63–64). Choice (F) is incorrect because, though a new car is mentioned, no habit of buying new cars is ever described. Choice (H) is incorrect because it is not described as the *most* depressing habit. Choice (J) is never discussed as a habit that upsets the narrator.

7. **B** The passage states that *as a physicist*, the coma victim *knew that time is a relative phenomenon* (line 74), implying a connection between the two ideas. Choices (A), (C), and (D) are not supported by any details in the passage.

8. **J**   The narrator explains that a *cluster of shops famously burned to the ground* (lines 48–49), in the past, but that presently it is back up and running with customers filtering in and out. Choices (F), (G), and (H) are all mentioned in the sixth paragraph as present-day changes to his hometown that the narrator notices.

9. **C**   The narrator says that as soon as he sees *dense stands of oak*, he knows he's home. Choices (A), (B), and (D) are details which describe Southern California, which is not the author's hometown.

10. **F**   The narrator refers to science as *that rock of immutable truths* as a way to emphasize the physicist's sense of bewilderment—before his coma he had believed scientific truth to be unchanging, but awoke to find his life's work obsolete. Choice (G) is incorrect because there is no support for the physicist's inability to comprehend the scientific advances, Choices (H) and (J) can be eliminated since both refer to the time he spent in a coma, not before.

Passage II

11. **A**   The men felt suspicious because, as stated in the previous paragraph, the traditional roles for women in these villages were food preparation and child care. Choice (B) is incorrect because no mention is made of how the representatives introduced themselves or why the men would doubt such an introduction. Choice (C) is incorrect because the passage does not suggest that the strangeness of the MayaWorks representatives was due to their language, but more that it was due to their intention of partnering with the village women. Choice (D) is unsupported by anything in the passage relating to men's estimation of the women's artistic abilities.

12. **H**   The content of the second paragraph depicts the problems facing Mayan villagers as well as the *irreplaceable* nature of their heritage, foreshadowing the way in which MayaWorks hopes to modernize and sustain these communities. Choice (F) is unsupported since *legal rights* are never mentioned in the passage. Choice (G) is incorrect because, although the size of Mayan villages is mentioned in this paragraph, it is too narrow a fact to be considered the purpose of the paragraph in relation to the rest of the passage. Choice (J) is incorrect because the passage does not indicate that Berhorst is based in Guatemala, nor is Berhorst an important part of the paragraph in relation to how it functions in the passage.

13. **D**   In the third paragraph, it says that the artisans used local materials for the hanging rods. Choice (A) is supported by information in the fifth paragraph as the artisans worked on kippahs. Choice (B) is supported by information in the seventh paragraph about the complications of not speaking Spanish in a Spanish-speaking marketplace. Choice (C) is supported by information in the sixth paragraph about a 36-inch treadle loom that allowed the artisans to now sell fabric by the yard.

14. **F**   While the author writes in a relatively neutral voice, she provides nothing but positive affirmations of what MayaWorks intends to do and what its partnerships have accomplished. Choice (G) is unsupported because the author doesn't discuss whether people in other countries will join

MayaWorks. Choice (H) is unsupported because the author never questions the quality of the Mayan commodities. In fact, she mentions at one point that the artisans use the finest yarn they can find. Choice (J) is incorrect because, although MayaWorks has several objectives in mind, they are never indicated to be in conflict with each other.

15. **B**   The fourth paragraph describes the more confident demeanor shown by the Mayan artisans when they were through with their work and getting paid for it. More generally, the author discusses the positive effects these art partnerships have had on the morale and self-sufficiency of the Mayan communities. Choice (A) is incorrect because, although the author points out the advantages of having some Spanish literacy, the author portrays the efforts of MayaWorks as being directed at helping the women grow with the times while retaining their invaluable heritage. She would not want *full* assimilation. Choice (C) is incorrect because the author mentions the success of the Mayan women learning to make Jewish kippahs. Choice (D) is incorrect because the final paragraph indicates that Mayan villagers would be typically excluded from *traditional banks*, hence the need for innovative micro-loans.

16. **H**   The passage states that *each of eight women was to weave a dozen* (line 28). Eight times twelve is 96, leaving (H) as the only possible answer choice—the others are far too big or small.

17. **D**   The last sentence of the fifth paragraph says the effect of being told of the kippah's symbolic meaning was becoming *even more devoted and loving in their craft* (line 51). Choice (A) is incorrect because the confusion regarding the shape had no relation to the kippah's religious significance. Choices (B) and (C) are unsupported by anything in the passage.

18. **H**   Although the passage indicates that MayaWorks artists make fabrics that are sold side-by-side with mass-manufactured textiles, it does not imply that the Mayan artists are mass-manufacturing textiles. Choices (F) and (J) are supported in the fifth paragraph. Choice (G) is supported by the third paragraph.

19. **B**   The paragraph relates another way that MayaWorks seeks to improve these communities, via coordinating loans that allow Mayans to improve their quality of living and sustainability. Choice (A) is incorrect because the terms of the loans are not explicitly discussed or focused upon. Choice (C) is incorrect because the money in the final paragraph comes from loans, not from money the artisans have earned selling their wares. Choice (D) is incorrect because the function of this paragraph is not to convince the reader that Mayans are trustworthy, but rather inform the reader of another way in which MayaWorks provides a benefit to these communities.

20. **F**   The passage states that the success of MayaWorks *has more to do with the economic initiatives…than its literacy campaigns* (lines 76–77); eliminate choice (J). While the rules of the marketplace are certainly mentioned, there is no indication that the Guatemalan women had to learn them from the people at MayaWorks—eliminate choice (G). Choice (H) is unsupported and goes against the goal of helping the Mayans preserve their culture.

Passage III

21. **A**   The discussion of the author's infatuation with cars is prefaced by the explanation that it came before his interest in music. The end of the discussion (lines 59–67) of cars states that *Eventually, my fixation on cars was to take a "back seat" to a new, greater, and this time lasting, passion*, (music). Choice (B) is incorrect because the author indicates that his infatuation with cars was ultimately overtaken by his interest in music. Choice (C) is incorrect because the passage never describes the author's playing style, so there is no support for calling it "mechanical." Choice (D) is incorrect because the author explains his love of cars came before his love of music; this answer makes it seem as though they were in competition and his love of cars was winning.

22. **H**   The author says *rewarding as this existence was* (lines 7–8) it did not fulfill him; he needed *greater pursuits to occupy* (line 10) his imagination. Choice (F) is wrong because the passage does not support that the author usually worked with his brother. Choice (G) is incorrect because the passage makes it seem like the author's upbringing made *the thought of embarking on a music career* beyond his *wildest imagination*. Choice (J) is incorrect because the passage does not support invariably resulting in parental approval. It even contains the phrase *much to my parents' dismay* (line 9).

23. **C**   The third paragraph (lines 44–67) explains the author's previous obsession (*years before I began to pursue music*) with cars. The end of that paragraph refers to his *previous infatuations* (before cars) of *archery, and before that dinosaurs*. This means that dinosaurs is the earliest. Choices (A), (B), and (D) are incorrect because the passage clearly indicates that some other passion predated each of them.

24. **F**   The context of the statement is the author summarizing his impressed delight with how effectively the music replicates the sensory and emotional experience of a thunderstorm. Choice (G) is incorrect because the passage does not suggest movies mislead the audience, only that they often do not replicate the experience of the thunderstorm as well as this music does. Choice (H) is incorrect because the author is not concerned with changing the character of news reports. He is only pointing out how well music can communicate. Choice (J) is incorrect because the author does not comment on whether thunderstorms are "among the hardest." Though it is suggested that it is not easy to replicate a thunderstorm, since *few, if any*, movies or television programs can do it, the context of this statement is not trying to make a point about thunderstorms but rather a point about music's ability to convey a rich experience.

25. **A**   In the second paragraph, the author is recounting the early experiences in his youth that led him to have an interest in music. He describes the thrill he took in learning Latin, Greek, Yiddish, German, Spanish, and Italian and compares the eagerness with which he learned them to *the energy of a lepidopterist netting butterflies* (lines 22–23). Eliminate both (B) and (D) because the comparison being made is between collecting butterflies and learning foreign phrases, not anything music-related. Choice (C) is incorrect because Ms. Fenchurch does not have anything to do with this paragraph or what it is describing.

26. **J** There is chaos described in the thunder and lightning stage, resolution when *the music eases, hope and reason are restored* (line 37), and relaxation in *soothing notes*. Choice (F) is incorrect because jealousy and resentment do not match up with anything. Although there is a violent thunderstorm described, violence is different from jealousy and resentment. Choice (G) is incorrect because "hate" and "disbelief" do not match up very well with the storm being described. Although storms are sometimes described as "angry," they are not described as "hateful." Also, *disbelief* is not a strong match for anything in the sentence. Choice (H) is incorrect because love is not a strong match for anything described in the sentence.

27. **C** The lesson Ms. Fenchurch imparts to the author is that music is more than just the notes on the page, *it's about expression, and perhaps more important, communication* (lines 82–83). Since language involves conveying meaning, choice (C) is supportable. Choice (A) is incorrect because the speed of notes is not discussed. Choice (B) is incorrect because it does not provide an accurate summary of the "argument" being made by Ms. Fenchurch in the last paragraph. Choice (D) is incorrect because Ms. Fenchurch places greater emphasis on communication.

28. **J** These two lines portray a calm lightness darkening into a cloudy apprehension and ultimately becoming a howling, thrilling, and frightening sensory overload. Choice (J) describes the transition in reverse. Choices (F), (G), and (H) all match up with something in these two sentences and are in correct chronological order.

29. **A** The last paragraph begins with the author's rhetorical question *So what made the difference?* The author reveals that what made his love for music *continue to burn where other passions had fizzled* (line 69) was a "who," Ms. Fenchurch. Choice (B) is incorrect because an anecdote means a specific story, which the author does not provide, and there are no details relating to Ms. Fenchurch's "conducting style." Choice (C) is incorrect because, although there are some character traits mentioned about Ms. Fenchurch, there is little "detailed background information," and even if there were, the purpose of the paragraph is to explain how influential Ms. Fenchurch was on the author's musical development. Choice (D) is incorrect because the paragraph does not mention the effect music has on Ms. Fenchurch. Rather, the paragraph mentions the influence Ms. Fenchurch had on the author's love of music.

30. **J** Phrases such as *sense of wonder* and *unforeseen path*, support that the author is surprised by his career choice, and several paragraphs deal with people, events, and subject matter that influenced the author's interest in music. Choice (F) is incorrect because the passage is not linear. It moves back and forth in time. Also, the passage does not list momentous events in the author's career, but more momentous influences on why the author has such a career. Choice (G) is incorrect because the passage does not delve into any specifics regarding Mozart and Handel, and the description of *The Tempest* is presented without comparison to any other piece of music. Choice (H) is incorrect because the passage as a whole is not persuasive in nature. The author is relating personal reflections, not advocating a certain course of action.

Passage IV

31. D   The end of the second paragraph (lines 29–30) indicates that *courtship typically lasts about two weeks, during which the female and her potential mate will meet once a day*. Choice (A) is incorrect because the males snap their heads at other males to try gain the attention of females. Choice (B) is incorrect because during courtship, the seahorses *dress up* their body coloring, whereas it is normally camouflaged. Choice (C) is incorrect because it relates to mating/birth, not courtship.

32. F   The third sentence of the first paragraph (lines 7–9) states that the seahorse's *tapered body shape is a great disadvantage* when it comes to *swimming ability*. Choice (G) is incorrect because the seahorse *lacks* a caudal fin. Choice (H) is incorrect because the dorsal fin is what gives the seahorse what little swimming ability it has. Choice (J) is incorrect because the passage does not link the seahorse's lack of teeth to swimming ability.

33. B   The confusion relates to Bateman's principle, which holds that whichever sex expends less energy in the reproductive process should be the sex that spends more energy competing for a mate. It may then seem confusing to scientists that males both compete for mates and give birth. However, Robinson's research shows that females do in fact expend more energy in the reproductive process than do males, which means that males should be the ones competing for mates after all. Choice (A) is incorrect because, although it is a detail involved in the mechanics of males giving birth, it does not resolve the confusion surrounding why the males also compete for mates. Choice (C) is incorrect because it provides no illumination as to why males give birth yet compete for mates. The monogamy of seahorses is explained by efficient birthing cycles, but it does not itself explain anything. Choice (D) is incorrect because the length of time spent competing for mates still does not explain why males, who give birth, are the ones who compete for mates.

34. J   The very first sentence of the passage foreshadows that the seahorse's *unusual mating habits* will be addressed. The last paragraph also begins by explaining that seahorses *have the distinction of being one of a very small number of monogamous species* (lines 73–75). Choice (F) is contradicted by information in the first paragraph. Although the passage explains that the seahorse manages some mobility, it still portrays the seahorse as a poor swimmer. Choice (G) is contradicted by information provided in the second to last paragraph. Pierre Robinson's research would potentially provide a coherent explanation for why male seahorses are responsible for birth. Choice (H) is incorrect because, although true, it can hardly be said to be a main idea of the passage.

35. A   The first paragraph mentions the seahorse's *remarkable appearance* and *distinctive equine head*. This mention of its *signature* prehensile tail is another indication that this feature is associated primarily with seahorses. Choice (B) is incorrect because, although the tail is useful, that is not what *signature* conveys. Choice (C) is a trap answer based on the equivalent meanings of "autograph" and "signature." Choice (D) is incorrect because it makes no sense to call a seahorse's tail legally obligated. This choice is also tempting because of the association to one's signature.

36. **F**   Because the paragraph begins with fertilization, ends with hatching, and contains sequential details in between those two events, choice (F) is well supported. Choices (G) and (H) may be eliminated since both capillaries and the number of fry are only mentioned in passing. Choice (J) is incorrect since the amount of tolerable salinity is never specified. Also, salinity does not relate to the whole paragraph, which means this could not be the main purpose of the paragraph.

37. **B**   The last paragraph explains that *a stable monogamous couple can develop an efficient birthing cycle in which* (lines 81–82) the male is incubating eggs at the same time that the female is generating eggs. Therefore, when the males give birth to one clutch of eggs, the females are almost ready with the next clutch. Choices (A) and (C) are incorrect because the transition from low to high salinity and the transition from fertilization to incubation both take place in and only relate to the gestation stage within the male's brood pouch. Choice (D) is incorrect because the initial transition from courtship to mating is when a female would actually select her mate. Monogamy only has meaning once a mate has been selected.

38. **H**   If the female can't find a male to receive her eggs, she expels them into the ocean, which is essentially throwing them away. The months she spent growing the eggs are wasted, or *squandered*. Choices (F), (G), and (J) are synonyms for *lost*, but none make sense in the context of the passage.

39. **D**   The second to last paragraph (lines 56–72) explains the paradox scientists see in the seahorse species, which is that males both give birth and compete for mates. According to Bateman's Principle, the sex that expends more energy in the reproductive process should NOT be the sex that competes for mates. Pierre Robinson found that male seahorses' increased oxygen intake during pregnancy does not qualify males as the sex that expends more energy in the reproductive process. Hence, seahorses conform to Bateman's Principle. Choices (A), (B), and (C) are incorrect because, although they refer to aspects of the seahorse's reproductive process, they do not relate to Bateman's Principle, which focuses on energy expenditure.

40. **G**   The fourth paragraph (lines 46–55) states that the brood pouch regulates a low-salinity environment initially, but the salinity increases *to help acclimate* the eggs to the salt water of the ocean that awaits them. Choice (F) is incorrect because nothing suggests or supports the idea of premature hatching. Choice (H) is incorrect because nothing suggests that the capillary network extracts salt. Choice (J) is incorrect because the passage does not suggest other mammals have exposure to salt.

Chapter 12
Reading Practice
Test 2

READING TEST

35 Minutes—40 Questions

DIRECTIONS: There are four passages in this test. Each passage is followed by several questions. After reading each passage, choose the best answer to each question and blacken the corresponding oval on your answer document. You may refer to the passages as often as necessary.

Passage I

PROSE FICTION: This passage is adapted from the novel *The Smell of Fresh Muffins* by Woody Jessup (©1985 by Woody Jessup).

The narrator is going to help his grandfather paint a room in the narrator's house. Garth is a friend of the narrator's grandfather.

Garth should be here any minute. I'm kind of glad, actually, that Grandpa sent his buddy to pick us up. Daddy always runs late because he tries to squeeze in one extra thing at the last minute, and Grandpa tends to misjudge how slowly he drives
5 nowadays. Garth has only picked us up a couple times before, but each time he was here at 2:17 on the nose.

Garth seems to see his schedule as various-sized blocks of activities that must be inserted into the correct-sized slot of time. Grandpa says that since Garth's wife died, Garth has
10 married his schedule. He says people use a routine to distract themselves from their life. Grandpa seems to know human nature pretty well, so I believe him.

We see Garth's tan Oldsmobile pull slowly into the parking lot. His car is a good match for his personality: boring but reli-
15 able. Garth doesn't joke too much with people besides Grandpa. He was in the Marines for many years in the fifties. His posture and his way of speaking to people are both perfectly upright.

"Hey, kids. How was school?" Garth asks as we start pil-ing into the back seat. "You know, one of you can sit up front."

20 Sis and I exchange a look with each other, hiding our feel-ings of reluctance. I remind her, with my eyes, that last time I rode up front, and she silently accepts her fate.

We start to drive off towards our house, where my Grandpa is currently re-painting our living room.

25 "You two ever done any painting?" Garth asks. We shake our heads. "It's like icing a cupcake. Does your mom ever let you do that? I mean, did she?"

"Sometimes." Clara chimes in. "She normally gave us one or two to play with, but she knew we couldn't make 'em as
30 pretty as she could, with that little swirl thing on top."

"Ah, of course." Garth grins. "Well, that swirl is what paint-ing is all about. If you start with too little icing, you smear it

out thin to cover the whole top of the cupcake, but you can still see the cake peeking through, right?"

35 We nod. He continues, "But if you start with a good dollop, more than you really need, you can swoosh it around with one clever twist of your wrist. The extra stuff just comes off onto your knife ... or your paintbrush if you're painting."

"Maybe I need smarter wrists," Clara sighs skeptically.

40 We park a block down from our house so that Daddy won't see Garth's car when he gets home from work. Grandpa wanted the painted room to be a surprise.

As soon as we step in our kitchen door, we can smell the paint from the living room. Grandpa is wearing paint-covered
45 overalls, but the paint stains are dry, and none of them are the bright sky color that Clara picked for the living room.

"Hey, Sam. Hey, Clara. Grab yourself a brush and a smock before I steal all the good spots for myself!" Grandpa chuckles. We assume he will not let us up on a ladder, so he must be
50 counting on us to work on the bottom three feet of the wall.

Sis and I grab two new brushes that Grandpa must have just bought at the store. It seems a crime to dip them into the paint the first time and forever ruin their purity.

"Don't be afraid to give it some elbow grease, now." Grandpa
55 encourages, letting us watch him as he applies thick strokes of paint to the wall.

We begin working in our own areas, creating splotchy islands of blue.

Grandpa pauses from his work to watch our technique. He
60 grins. "Fun, isn't it?"

"What if Daddy's disappointed he didn't get to do this himself?" I ask.

"Disappointed I did him a favor? If I know Arthur, he'll be happy to have avoided the manual labor. He'll just be dis-
65 appointed he didn't get to see his kids finally covering up the awful beige wall that came with the house."

Grandpa resumes painting and adds, "Maybe when we're done, we can cover up the awful beige on Garth's car." He starts laughing.

70　Garth seems not to mind or notice. He is concentrating on painting the corner without getting any stray streaks on the ceiling.

Grandpa notices Garth's serious expression and says, "He even paints like a Marine." Another chuckle. Garth does not 75 look away from his corner but adds, "and your Grandpa likes talking more than working—just like a civilian." Sis and I are accustomed to their jovial back-and-forth.

I feel sad to hear Grandpa say we will cover up the wall that came with the house. That is the color we grew up with. 80 That is the color of the living room with Mom still in it. I don't want to cover up our memories, even though they make us sad now. But covering up is different from removing. We will put a layer of sky blue on the surface so that we feel invigorated, but we will know that Mom's layer is always protected underneath.

1. Which of the following statements regarding the idea for painting the room is best supported by the passage?

A. While Clara was reluctant to do it, Grandpa ultimately convinced her it was okay.
B. Garth suggested the idea to Grandpa, who then told the narrator and her sister.
C. Clara envisioned the idea, and Garth helped provide some of the supplies.
D. Although Grandpa planned the activity, Clara was involved in the decision making.

2. As presented in the passage, the exchange between the narrator and his sister when Garth comes to pick them up can best be described as:

F. an expression of frustration due to the curiosity the narrator and his sister felt regarding Garth's unusual tardiness.
G. a situation that is initially confusing to the narrator until his sister reminds him about the project to repaint the living room.
H. a favorite game that the narrator plays with his sister to determine which person gets the honor of sitting in front.
J. a nonverbal conversation that allows the narrator and his sister to determine which of them receives an unfavorable consequence.

3. Based on the passage, Garth and Grandpa can be reasonably said to share all of the following characteristics EXCEPT:

A. painting experience.
B. good posture.
C. the ability to drive.
D. willingness to poke fun.

4. Clara's reference to having smarter wrists (line 39) primarily serves to suggest her:

F. remaining doubt about equaling her mother's skills.
G. growing excitement regarding learning how to paint.
H. deepening confusion about how painting relates to cupcakes.
J. increasing concern that people see her as intelligent.

5. Viewed in the context of the passage, Grandpa's grin (lines 59–60) most nearly reflects a feeling of:

A. irony.
B. intense relaxation.
C. mild satisfaction.
D. harsh disapproval.

6. The narrator's statement "His car is a good match for his personality" (line 14), most nearly means that in the narrator's opinion, Garth is:

F. too conservative in his choice of cars.
G. highly dependable, but not very flashy.
H. more upright than many Oldsmobile drivers.
J. too concerned with how others see him.

7. Garth clearly recommends that the children apply both paint and icing in which of the following ways?

A. Gently
B. Respectfully
C. Conservatively
D. Confidently

8. In the second paragraph, the main conclusion the narrator reaches is that:

F. Garth considers tardiness a character flaw.
G. Garth is extremely talented at organizing his schedule.
H. people can use a routine to avoid focusing on something painful.
J. Grandpa is a very keen observer of human behavior.

9. In terms of the development of the narrator as a character, the last paragraph primarily serves to:

A. add to the reader's understanding of his guilt.
B. explain his relationship to his mother.
C. describe his underlying emotional conflict.
D. portray the strained relationship he has with Grandpa.

10. It can most reasonably be inferred that Arthur is the name of:

F. Garth and Grandpa's friend.
G. the narrator.
H. the narrator's father.
J. the neighbor who lent them the ladder.

Passage II

SOCIAL SCIENCE: The following is an excerpt from the article "Electric Cars Face Power Outage" by Justin Sabo (© 2010 by Justin Sabo).

Many people look forward to the day when an American automobile company will mass-produce an emissions-free vehicle. Those people may be surprised to learn that day actually came to pass almost fifteen years ago.

5 So why are there hardly any purely electric vehicles on the road today? In 1996, General Motors released the EV1, the first fully electric vehicle designed and released by a major auto manufacturer. GM entered this unfamiliar territory bravely but reluctantly, motivated by emissions-control legislation enacted
10 by the California Air Resources Board (CARB). CARB felt automakers were dragging their feet in developing lower emissions vehicles, so it mandated that American car companies make a certain percentage of their cars available for sale in California to be electric vehicles.

15 This could not possibly have been good news for American automakers. Many believed that electric vehicles were not commercially viable. It would be very expensive to research, develop, and market a new type of car, and with consumer demand for such cars a big unknown, the companies feared stiff
20 economic losses would result from the new regulations. GM was pessimistic its EV1 could be a viable commodity, but it felt that the best way to force CARB to undo the mandate was to play ball: they would bring an electric car to the market and let everyone watch it fail.

25 Previous electric vehicle prototypes from major automakers had consisted of converting existing gasoline models, a process neither elegant nor inexpensive. The EV1, however, was designed from the start as an electric car, and lightness and efficiency were incorporated throughout the design. Engineers
30 selected aluminum for the EV's body, which, unlike the steel typically used in car frames, is a relatively light metal. The wheels were made with a magnesium alloy, which was another lightweight but sturdy replacement. The EV1's unusual, futuristic body shape is a consequence of aiming for a low drag
35 coefficient and reference area.

Early versions of the EV1 used a lead-acid based battery, replaced by nickel metal hydride in second generation models. Owners could charge their cars in their garages overnight or at power stations situated around the cities where they were
40 leased. A full charge would last 70 to 100 miles. The cars were only available to be leased, because GM wanted to be able to reclaim them if necessary. This also allowed GM to avoid having to comply with a law that requires car companies to maintain service and repair infrastructure for fifteen years following the
45 sale of any model of car (something GM thought would surely become a moot point since they didn't expect production of EV1's to get past the initial trial stage).

The public reaction to the EV1 is a source of ongoing debate to this day. The initial fleet of 288 EV1's that GM released was
50 not enough to meet consumer demand, as waiting lists began growing with customers who wanted their chance to lease an EV1. At a suggested retail price of $34,000, the cars were leased at a rate between $400–550/month. This high monthly payment skewed demand toward a more affluent customer
55 base, which included many famous and wealthy celebrities, politicians, and executives. However, the auto industry used the lessees' fame to portray the car as something beyond the limits of the average consumer (despite the fact that GM had hand-picked the lessees).

60 Ultimately, GM reclaimed all the EV1's it had leased, intending to destroy them. EV1 owners were livid that their prized possessions were going to become scrap metal. They offered GM "no-risk" purchasing terms, essentially begging GM to let them buy the car while exempting GM from being accountable
65 for any future maintenance or repair issues. They were denied.

Why? Skepticism brewed regarding GM's deeper motives for canceling the EV1 program. Alleged pressure from the oil industry helped coax CARB into repealing their electric-car mandate. Others pointed to the fiscal losses GM would suffer
70 if electric cars became popular: GM was currently making billions per year in the spare parts market, selling the types of mufflers, brake pads, air filters, and the like that would no longer be required with electric car technology.

While the passion and protest surrounding the recall of
75 the EV1 suggest a burning desire for electric vehicles, other researchers portrayed a different story. Dr. Kenneth Train of UC Berkeley presented a study which claimed Americans would only be interested in buying an electric car if it were priced at least $28,000 less than a comparable gasoline-fueled car.
80 This study was frequently touted by automakers who hoped to prove that the electric car was not a financially viable product. Meanwhile, similar studies conducted by the California Electric Transportation Coalition (CETC) disagreed, finding that consumer demand for electric vehicles would represent
85 12–18% of the market for light-duty new cars.

Whether the electric car can transcend consumers' distrust of the unfamiliar and the auto and oil industries' reluctance to change is unknown. What is certain is the fact that a new technology poses challenges that go well beyond mechanical
90 engineering. Technological hurdles can often come in the form of political, economic, and social obstacles.

11. The author implies that for an electric car to be more appealing to most car buyers, the most important factor would be changing which of the following?

   A. Body shape
   B. Distance per charge
   C. Aluminum frame
   D. Price

12. The statement in lines 16–17 most likely represents the view of all of the following groups EXCEPT:

   F. the executives at GM who commissioned the design of the EV1.
   G. the members of the California Air Resources Board who issued the mandate.
   H. the other American automakers at the time the CARB mandate was issued.
   J. Dr. Kenneth Train and his research team at UC Berkeley.

13. According to the passage, the number of drivers who first leased an EV1 was around:

   A. 70–100.
   B. 288.
   C. 400–550.
   D. 12–18% of the light duty market.

14. The author most nearly portrays the efforts of GM to design an electric car as:

   F. resulting from overconfidence in estimating consumer enthusiasm for electric vehicles.
   G. directed more at perfecting the marketing than at perfecting the science.
   H. intended to showcase GM's superiority over its competitors.
   J. motivated in part by a desire to fail.

15. According to information presented in the fourth paragraph (lines 25–35), which of the following comparisons between previous electric vehicle prototypes and the EV1 would the author make?

   A. The EV1s were more deliberately and insightfully designed.
   B. The EV1s were just converted from previous gasoline prototypes.
   C. The previous electric prototypes were basically the same as the EV1.
   D. The previous electric prototypes were made out of cheaper, lighter materials.

16. Based on information presented in the sixth paragraph (lines 48–59), it can reasonably be inferred that which of the following determinations would have the biggest effect on the potential marketability of electric vehicles?

   F. The strength of affiliation that most car buyers have for environmental organizations
   G. Whether most car buyers would consider buying an automobile that costs more than one powered by gasoline
   H. How many other states might enact regulations similar to that of CARB's in California
   J. The extent to which most car buyers identify with wealthy politicians and celebrities

17. According to the passage, aluminum's role in the EV1 was:

   A. a lightweight wheel.
   B. to lower drag coefficient.
   C. an alternative to steel.
   D. magnesium alloy substitute.

18. The author most likely intends his answer to the question posed in line 67 to be:

   F. definitive; he believes the real reasons are plain to see.
   G. incomplete; he is convinced that CARB had some unknown involvement.
   H. genuine; he is unsure about GM's motives for the denial.
   J. speculative; he thinks that plausible explanations have been put forth.

19. The author indicates that one cause behind GM reclaiming EV1's from their owners may have been:

   A. the unwillingness of owners to renew their leases.
   B. CARB's decision to change the terms of its original low-emissions mandate.
   C. a financial disincentive GM would face should the EV1 become popular.
   D. customers' sticker shock at the $28,000 price tag.

20. It can reasonably be inferred from the last paragraph that the author thinks that any forthcoming electric vehicle will:

   F. have to solve non-technological problems.
   G. be embraced by most automakers.
   H. overcome the skepticism of consumers.
   J. succeed if sold at a lower price.

Passage III

HUMANITIES: The following passage is adapted from the essay "The Torres Revolution" by Greg Spearman (©2001 by Greg Spearman).

The question of who invented the guitar may forever remain a mystery. However, the father of the modern classical guitar is generally regarded as Antonio Torres Jurado, a carpenter from Sevilla, Spain, who began making guitars as a hobby in
5 the 1850's and ultimately created the design that practically all classical guitar makers use to the present day. By refining the craft of guitar-making, Torres expanded the dynamic and tonal range of the instrument, allowing the guitar to go beyond its traditional, supporting role and into the spotlight as a featured
10 concert solo instrument.

Early guitars had four pairs of strings—the word "guitar" itself being a translation from a Persian word meaning "four strings." During the Renaissance, instruments resembling the modern guitar had begun to appear throughout Europe. One
15 of these, the lute, became the standard stringed instrument across most of Europe, but in Spain there was more variation in developing forms of the guitar. A plucked version called the *vihuela* was popular in aristocratic society, while a strummed instrument referred to as the *guitarra latina* was used by com-
20 moners. Once a fifth string was ultimately added to the latter, the *guitarra latina* became the national preference and rendered the *vihuela* obsolete.

As the 17th century progressed, Spanish guitars, widely adored by monarchs, noblemen, and common folk alike, spread
25 throughout the rest of Europe and began to displace the once-popular lute. Along the way a sixth string was added to the design. The 18th century saw the more "prestigious" music of harpsichords, pianos, and violins come to the fore, while the guitar was relegated back to the informal gatherings of com-
30 mon folk. Eventually, however, the virtuosity of such Spanish guitarists as Ferdinand Sor rekindled the public's respect and admiration for guitar music. Esteemed composers such as Haydn and Schubert began writing guitar music, but while the performances of the Spanish guitar masters were wildly popular,
35 the acoustic and structural limitations of the guitar continued to present a problem when playing in large concert halls—a problem that Andres Torres meant to solve.

One of the guitar's chief limitations that Andres Torres tackled was its feeble sound output. Torres enlarged the body
40 of the guitar, particularly the "bouts" (rounded parts) in the soundbox, significantly increasing its volume and giving the guitar its familiar hourglass shape. Because the guitar also had to compete with the impressive polyphony (the number of notes that can be played at one time) of the piano, Torres also
45 reduced the width of the fretboard, making it easier for guitar-ists to reach many notes at once and allowing them to perform music with a complexity comparable to that of pieces played on keyboard instruments.

The genius of Torres's design, however, was the way he
50 re-engineered the internal structure of the instrument. Because the strings on a guitar must be wound tightly to produce enough tension to vibrate at the correct pitch, they constantly pull on the neck of the guitar, essentially trying to snap it in two. The arch of the neck counters some of this force, but the majority
55 is absorbed by wooden braces inside the instrument. Torres did not invent the idea of fan-bracing, which refers to pieces of wood laid out diagonally inside the body to distribute both tension and sound waves, but he did perfect it. He increased the number of braces from three to seven, and organized them
60 in a symmetric pattern allowing the vibrations of the guitar to be evenly distributed within the soundbox.

The effectiveness and elegance of Torres's design was immediately apparent in the improved tone and volume of the instrument, and ultimately revealed by the fact that his design
65 has remained virtually unchanged in over 150 years. Torres guitars were extremely rare and highly-sought by musicians in the 19th century. One aspiring guitarist of the time, Francisco Tarrega, traveled to Sevilla in the hopes of buying one of Torres's famous guitars. Although Torres initially intended to sell Tarrega
70 one of the stock guitars he had available, he reconsidered once he heard Tarrega play. Deeply impressed, Torres instead gave Tarrega a guitar he had made for himself several years before.

Just as Torres revolutionized the design of classical guitars, so would Tarrega eventually become recognized as the singular
75 authority on classical guitar playing techniques. Tarrega had grown up playing both guitar and piano, the latter being rec-ognized as the more useful compositional tool, while the guitar was regarded as merely a functional accompaniment to a singer or a larger ensemble. Once Tarrega beheld the beauty and range
80 of expression of the Torres guitar, he committed himself fully to exploring its compositional palette.

Tarrega, who studied at the Madrid Conservatory, rose to great prominence, not only playing original pieces but also translating the great piano works of such composers as Beethoven
85 and Chopin for guitar. He became a global ambassador for the guitar, introducing and refining many of the techniques that classical guitarists worldwide now consider essential, including how to position the guitar on one's knee and optimal fingering and plucking techniques for the left and right hand.

21. Based on the passage, the author would most likely agree that both Torres and Tarrega were:

A. not fully appreciated for their musical genius until after their deaths.
B. local sensations whose reputation never reached the global fame of other composers.
C. extremely influential contributors to the evolution of classical guitar playing.
D. very talented instrument makers who gained much fame for their talents.

22. As it is used in lines 49–50, the phrase *the genius of Torres's design* most nearly refers to the:

F. innovative idea that classical guitars could be the centerpiece of a performance, rather than merely an accompaniment.
G. improved tonal quality and volume resulting from the number and positioning of wooden braces within the soundbox.
H. invention of an arched neck, which counters the effects of the tension caused by the tightly wound strings.
J. expansion of the width of the guitar, in order to accommodate a sixth string and allow for more polyphony.

23. Which of the following statements best describes how the second paragraph (lines 11–23) relates to the first paragraph?

A. It provides supporting details concerning Torres's innovative idea to use a fifth string.
B. It compares the modern guitar to its earlier relatives, such as the lute and *vihuela*.
C. It moves the discussion to a period that predates the innovator described in the first paragraph.
D. It counterbalances the argument in the first paragraph by providing details that suggest early guitars were superior in many ways to later guitars.

24. As it is used in line 81, the phrase *compositional palette* most nearly means:

F. artistic potential.
G. colorful components.
H. volume output.
J. physical features.

25. For purposes of the passage, the significance of Spanish guitarists such as Ferdinand Sor is that they:

A. were reluctant to accept modifications to the traditional design of the guitar.
B. gave Torres suggestions about his design.
C. were among the most talented lute players in Europe at the time.
D. helped develop and sustain interest in the guitar as a reputable instrument.

26. Which of the following questions is NOT answered by the passage?

F. What is the meaning of an instrument's polyphony?
G. When was the beginning and the ending of the Renaissance?
H. Who is the father of the modern guitar?
J. What were some of the earlier forms of the guitar?

27. According to the passage, the *vihuela* was a Renaissance version of the guitar that:

A. was ultimately overtaken in national popularity by another type of guitar.
B. became the Spanish aristocrats' version of the lute.
C. initially came to fame through the notoriety of Ferdinand Sor.
D. one of Torres's earlier models before he perfected his fan-bracing design.

28. According to the passage, the Torres guitar was better suited than previous versions of the guitar to:

F. Beethoven's works.
G. being a featured instrument.
H. five strings.
J. folk music.

29. According to the passage, the popularity of Spanish-style guitars during the 18th century was:

A. increasing due to the simultaneous decline in popularity of the lute.
B. aided by the growing popularity of other instruments that complemented the guitar's sound.
C. hindered by common folk's inability to master fingering and plucking techniques.
D. diminished by the perception that it was not as refined as other contemporary instruments.

30. It can most reasonably be inferred that which of the following was a direct expression of respect for Tarrega's playing abilities?

F. The manner in which Torres determined which guitar he would sell to Tarrega.
G. The translation of Beethoven's and Chopin's works from piano to guitar.
H. The eventual end to the popularity of the *guitarra latina*.
J. The way Haydn and Schubert began composing music specifically for guitar.

Passage IV

NATURAL SCIENCE: The following passage is adapted from the article "Heavyweights of the Sea" by Carmen Grandola (©2001 by Carmen Grandola).

The earth's oceans possess an incredible variety of life, ranging from nearly microscopic plankton to the blue whale, the largest animal on the planet. In the world of fish, the mola sunfish and the whale shark are the two biggest varieties. The
5 mola is the biggest bony fish, whereas the whale shark, which is a cartilaginous fish, is simply the biggest fish there is. While most ocean-dwellers spend their days balancing their position on the food chain as both predators and prey, these titanic swimmers have little to worry about from predators. Instead, they must
10 focus on finding enough food to sustain the massive amounts of nutrients needed to support their bulky bodies.

Truly one of the most unusual-looking products of evolution's creative hand, the mola sunfish resembles a giant fish head with a tail. Most fish have long bodies, with fins in the
15 middle roughly dividing their length in two. Rather than having a caudal (tail) fin, like most fish, the mola looks like a fish that has been chopped just past the halfway point, with a rounded clavus joining its dorsal (top) and anal (bottom) fins. The mola uses its clavus to steer its rather awkwardly-shaped body
20 through the water. Its body has a very narrow cross-section—it is basically a flattened oval with a head at the front, and very high dorsal and anal fins at the back. In fact, the mola's height is often equal to its length, which is unusual in fish, which are typically elongated. Mola means "millstone" in Latin, and these
25 fish live up to their name, growing to 10–20 ft. in length and height and weighing in at an average of 2,000 lbs.

The mola's diet is extremely varied but nutrient-poor, consisting mainly of jellyfish, but also comb jellies, squid, and eel grasses. In order to consume enough daily nutrients, the mola
30 must be a voracious eater and be willing to travel through a wide range of oceanic depths—from surface to floor in some areas—in search of their food. After ascending from cooler waters, the mola will float on its side at the ocean's surface in order to warm itself through solar energy. Molas have a beaked
35 mouth that does not totally close, so they chew their food in several stages, breaking down each mouthful into smaller chunks before spitting them out and then going to work on the more bite-sized pieces.

The whale shark, another giant of the sea, grows to sizes
40 that dwarf the maximum size of a bony fish. Some have been measured at over 40 ft. in length and over 75,000 lbs. in weight. This leviathan, like the mola, mostly frequents tropical and warm-temperate waters. The whale shark possesses over 300 rows of teeth, but it does not use them in the same manner as
45 most other sharks. The whale shark is one of only a handful of filter-feeding sharks. This means rather than using powerful teeth and jaws to rip apart large prey, the whale shark eats tiny, nearly microscopic food such as zooplankton, krill, and macro-algae. The whale shark "hunts" by opening its mouth

50 and sucking in a huge mouthful of ocean water. It then closes its mouth and expels the water through its gills, at which point gill rakers act as sieves, separating the tiny, sometimes millimeter-wide, life forms from the water. Once all the water is expelled, the food is swallowed.

55 When you're one of the biggest species in your neighborhood, you probably don't have to worry about getting picked on much. This is certainly true of the whale shark, which has no natural predators and can easily live 70–100 years in the ocean. Its biggest health risk comes through exposure to
60 humans. The whale shark does much of its feeding near the surface of the water, where it has been known to accidentally bump into boats. Both animal and vessel can end up severely damaged in these exchanges. The other hazard humans create for whale sharks is pollution in the water. As the whale
65 shark filter feeds, it sometimes takes in garbage and nautical debris such as oars.

The mola, on the other hand, has a few challenges. Its thick skin is covered in a dense layer of mucus, which is host to a vast array of parasites. To try and rid itself of these uninvited
70 guests, the mola will often float on its side near the surface of the water, inviting gulls and other birds to feast on the parasites. Similarly, the mola will sometimes launch its considerable bulk up to ten feet out of the water before crashing back down in an effort to dislodge some of the parasites. With its habit of
75 floating near the surface, the mola, like the whale shark, often runs the risk of being hit by boats. Finally, smaller molas are sometimes subject to attack by sea lions.

31. The author's attitude regarding molas and whale sharks can best be described as one of:

A. conviction that human interference will ultimately jeopardize each species.

B. resentment towards their need to eat so much other marine life on a daily basis.

C. impartiality in considering the perils of their environment compared to other fish.

D. interest in how their grandiose size affects their habits and survival.

32. It can reasonably be concluded from the passage that the mola temporarily expels its food when eating due to the fact that it:

F. is a bony fish rather than a cartilaginous one.

G. possesses a mouth that cannot completely close.

H. hunts on the ocean floor but eats at the surface.

J. is normally floating on its side near the surface.

33. According to the passage, the most significant difference between the predatory threats facing the whale shark and the mola is that the whale shark:

    A. does not compete for the same food as its predators do, while the mola competes for the same food its predators do.

    B. is unaffected by its proximity to humans while the mola is sometimes endangered by humans.

    C. faces few genuine environmental threats but must contend with the nuisance of parasites.

    D. is less likely to be attacked by another ocean-dwelling species than is the mola.

34. It can most reasonably be inferred from the passage that nautical vessels pose a threat to both the mola and the whale shark primarily because these vessels:

    F. can sometimes unsuspectingly collide with fish.

    G. stir up a violent wake that disrupts the ocean currents.

    H. jettison large debris overboard which can land on fish.

    J. deplete the fish's supply of prey through overfishing.

35. The passage indicates that the quantity of food a fish must eat is primarily determined by the:

    A. mass of the fish's body.

    B. depth at which the fish hunts.

    C. type of gill rakers it has.

    D. number of its teeth and size of its mouth.

36. The passage supports the idea that all of the following are included in the diet of the mola EXCEPT:

    F. comb jellies.

    G. zooplankton.

    H. eel grasses.

    J. squid.

37. The main purpose of the last two paragraphs is to:

    A. provide additional support for the earlier claim that the mola and the whale shark are two of the biggest creatures inhabiting the ocean.

    B. convey to the reader to the ironic fact that such large species of fish can be vulnerable to miniature threats such as parasites.

    C. summarize the types of threats, or lack thereof, present in the environments of the mola and whale shark.

    D. demonstrate the fact that even the biggest fish in the sea have to worry about being preyed upon by something.

38. According to the passage, the gill rakers a whale shark has are primarily intended to:

    F. spit out partially chewed food.

    G. rip apart the whale shark's large prey.

    H. bridge together its 300 rows of teeth.

    J. filter out food from a mouthful of water.

39. According to the passage, the Latin-derived name for the mola refers to the:

    A. atypical rounded clavus of the mola.

    B. mola's distinctive half-fish shape.

    C. voracious eating the mola's diet requires.

    D. mola's enormous size and weight.

40. The main purpose of the passage is to:

    F. offer support for the notion that the mola is pound-for-pound a better hunter than is the whale shark.

    G. provide a general overview of the habitats, eating habits, and survival challenges relating to two of the biggest species of fish.

    H. increase awareness for the fragile status of mola and whale shark populations and encourage conservationists to intervene.

    J. suggest that the unlikely traits possessed by the mola and the whale shark do not have clear evolutionary answers.

END OF TEST 3
STOP! DO NOT TURN THE PAGE UNTIL TOLD TO DO SO.
DO NOT RETURN TO A PREVIOUS TEST.

Chapter 13
Reading Practice
Test 2
Answers and
Explanations

READING PRACTICE TEST 2 ANSWERS

1. D		21. C	
2. J		22. G	
3. B		23. C	
4. F		24. F	
5. C		25. D	
6. G		26. G	
7. D		27. A	
8. H		28. G	
9. C		29. D	
10. H		30. F	
11. D		31. D	
12. G		32. G	
13. B		33. D	
14. J		34. F	
15. A		35. A	
16. G		36. G	
17. C		37. C	
18. J		38. J	
19. C		39. D	
20. F		40. G	

SCORE YOUR PRACTICE TEST

Step A
Count the number of correct answers: _____. This is your *raw score*.

Step B
Use the score conversion table below to look up your raw score. The number to the left is your *scale score*: _____.

Reading Scale Conversion Table

Scale Score	Raw Score	Scale Score	Raw Score	Scale Score	Raw Score
36	40	27	30	18	18
35	39	26	29	17	16–17
34	38	25	27–28	16	15
33	37	24	26	15	14
32	36	23	24–25	14	12–13
31	35	22	23	13	11
30	34	21	22	12	9–10
29	32 33	20	20–21	11	8
28	31	19	19	10	6–7

READING PRACTICE TEST 2 EXPLANATIONS

Passage I

1. **D** The passage states that the bright sky color was something *Clara picked*, and it suggests that Grandpa *wanted to do* the narrator's father *a favor* and *wanted the painted room to be a surprise*. There is no support for Clara's reluctance, which eliminates choice (A). There is no support for Garth coming up with the idea, which eliminates choice (B). There is no support for Garth providing any of the supplies, which eliminates choice (C).

2. **J** The passage explains that the narrator and his sister feel *reluctance* about sitting up front. The narrator reminds her with his *eyes* that it is her turn to accept that *fate*. Choice (F) is unsupported by the passage because nothing ever suggests that Garth shows up late. Choice (G) is unsupported because the narrator does not suggest confusion, and their exchange is purely about who is riding in front. Choice (H) is off the mark because the context does not portray the front seat as an *honor*, nor is their taking turns much of a *game*.

3. **B** Posture is only mentioned while describing Garth. Since Garth offers painting advice (lines 31–38), and Grandpa wears *paint-covered overalls* (lines 44–45), (A) is supported. Because they have both picked up the narrator and his sister before, (C) is supported. Because the passage mentions their *jovial back-and-forth*, (D) is supported.

4. **F** The context leading up to this quote involves Clara mentioning a talent her mother had for swirling icing that Clara does not possess. Once Garth explains how to achieve that effect, Clara remains skeptical about her own ability to perform the feat. Choice (G) lacks support because Clara's sigh and her skepticism do not indicate "excitement." Choice (H) is incorrect because there is no context to indicate Clara's confusion. Choice (J) is incorrect because Clara is not self-conscious of her intelligence. Her use of the adjective *smarter* applies only to her wrists and is in response to Garth's phrase *clever twist*.

5. **C** Since the context is Grandpa watching the kids getting started painting, and his following comment is making sure they're having fun, we can infer that he is feeling good about the situation. There is nothing in the context to support "intense" relaxation, as choice (B) implies. There is also nothing in the context to support "irony" or "disapproval" as choices (A) and (D) imply.

6. **G** The narrator describes both the car and Garth's personality as *boring but reliable* (lines 14–15). This agrees with choice (B). The narrator is not critiquing Garth's choice in cars as choice (A) indicates, rather the narrator says Garth's car is a very fitting choice. There is no comparison between Garth and other Oldsmobile drivers in the passage to support choice (C). There is no also no support for choice (D), that Garth is concerned about how he is seen by others.

7. **D** Garth's painting and icing advice consists of starting with a large dollop and then *cleverly* swooshing it on. Because the context emphasizes applying a healthy quantity of paint in a single motion, choice (D) is supported. Choices (A), (B), and (C) seems to go against the idea of large dollop of paint and one swift but effective motion. They all suggest a more tentative process.

8. **H** The paragraph describes Garth's habitual planning and Grandpa's assessment of the motivation for Garth's behavior. When he says *I believe him* (line 12), the narrator concludes that Grandpa is correct about the idea that Garth uses his routine to distract himself from his wife's death. Choices (F) and (G) mention traits resembling the paragraph's description of Garth, but neither are the main conclusion the narrator reaches. Similarly, choice (J) says something that the narrator believes seems to be true about Grandpa, but it is not the main conclusion he reaches in the paragraph. He only mentions Grandpa's ability to judge human nature as part of his analysis of Garth's behavior, which is the real point of the paragraph.

9. **C** In the last paragraph (lines 78–84), the passage implies that the narrator's mom has died and reveals the reluctance the narrator feels to move on without her. Although the narrator's sadness about painting over the old color of wall may imply some degree of guilt, choice (A) is incorrect because the paragraph is not focused solely on that one negative emotion and the answer implies that the last paragraph *adds* to the portrayal of the narrator's guilt, when such an emotion is never discussed before this paragraph. Choice (B) is close, but the paragraph does not provide any details explaining their relationship. It provides details about the narrator's reaction to covering up a memory of his mother. Choice (D) is unsupported because there is no context in the passage that portrays a strained relationship between the narrator and Grandpa.

10. **H** Since in lines 61–62 the narrator asks about his father, it makes sense to think that Grandpa's response is referring to the narrator's father by name. There is no context to suggest it's Grandpa's friend as choice (F) states. Grandpa is responding to the narrator about a third person, so there is no context for choice (G). And there is no discussion of the ladder belonging to a neighbor to support choice (J).

Passage II

11. **D** In the sixth paragraph, the author states that the monthly lease payment *skewed demand towards a more affluent customer base* (lines 54–55). Choice (A) is incorrect because, though unusual, the body shape is not mentioned as undesirable. Choices (B) and (C) are mentioned in the passage, but there is no indication of consumers' negative reactions to them.

12. **G** CARB would not have required automakers to offer electric vehicles if it thought that they would lose money in doing so. Choice (F) is incorrect because the passage indicates that the EV1 was designed with the expectation that it would fail. Choice (H) is incorrect because the passage suggests that automakers considered the CARB mandate to be bad news that would potentially be very costly. Choice (J) is incorrect because Dr. Train's study suggested that consumers would only buy electric vehicles if they cost much less than gas-powered cars.

13. **B** The sixth paragraph states the *initial fleet* (line 49) was 288 EV1s. Choice (A) refers to the distance in miles an EV1 got on one battery charge. Choice (C) refers to the average monthly payment of lease holders. Choice (D) refers to the CETC's estimate.

14. **J** At the end of the third paragraph, the author says that GM planned to show CARB an electric car was not viable by bringing one to the market and letting everyone *watch it fail*. Choice (F) is incorrect because GM was pessimistic about the market for electric cars. Choice (G) is incorrect because, if anything, GM was more concerned about building a working car and less concerned about helping it succeed in the marketplace. Choice (H) is incorrect because the passage never mentions a competitive motivation. Rather, it suggests the motivation was to demonstrate that CARB's mandate was ill-advised.

15. **A** The author states that the EV1 was *designed from the start as electric*, while the previous prototypes were just converted from gasoline models. He also mentions that *lightness and efficiency were incorporated into the design* (lines 28–29). Choice (B) is incorrect because the electric prototypes were converted, not the EV1. Choice (C) is incorrect because the author points out a distinct difference in the design process of EV1s and lists several details that resulted. Choice (D) is incorrect because the prototypes were described as expensive conversions and the light materials were only mentioned in relation to the EV1.

16. **G** The passage indicates that electric cars cost more than gasoline-powered cars, and the higher cost is cited in the passage as a potential concern for buyers. Choice (F) is incorrect because the study did not address environmental concerns of customers. Choice (H) is incorrect because the study did not address the motivation of car companies to comply with other states' regulations. Choice (J) is incorrect because the study did not address a psychological connection between car buyers and famous wealthy people.

17. **C** The passage explains that aluminum was used for the car's body unlike the typical choice of steel. Choice (A) is incorrect because that describes the role of the magnesium alloy. Choice (B) is incorrect because that describes the role of the body shape. Choice (D) is incorrect because the aluminum replaced what would have otherwise been steel.

18. **J** The author presents the two explanations offered in the eighth paragraph (lines 67–74) as *alleged* and something *others pointed to*. The author treats these theories with some degree of legitimacy but does not fully endorse either. Choice (F) is incorrect because the author does not use language supporting "definitive, real answers." Choice (G) is incorrect because the author does not mention an undiscovered influence from CARB. Choice (H) is incorrect because the author is not unsure about the motives—he goes on to talk about what they may have been.

19. **C** The passage states that *GM was currently making billions per year on the spare parts market* (lines 71–72) that would be threatened by an expanded electric vehicle market. Choice (A) is incorrect because the owners were willing to do anything to keep their vehicles, including renew their leases. Choice (B) is incorrect because the passage only mentions CARB repealing its mandate, not

changing its terms. Choice (D) is incorrect because the suggested retail price of the car was $34,000, not $28,000.

20. **F**   The last paragraph discusses the *political, economic, and social obstacles* new technologies face. None of these are technological problems. Choices (G) and (H) are incorrect because the author states that whether the electric car can transcend the obstacles of consumer skepticism and automaker reluctance is *unknown*. Choice (J) is incorrect because, even though the passage discusses the price of electric cars as a disincentive for consumers, the author never says anything strong enough to justify choice (J)'s prediction.

Passage III

21. **C**   The author credits Torres as *the father of the modern classical guitar* and Tarrega as the *singular authority on classical guitar playing techniques* (lines 74–75). Choice (A) is unsupported because there is nothing in the passage that relates to being appreciated more after death. Choice (B) is unsupported because there is nothing in the passage that restricts the influence of either man to a certain geographical area. Choice (D) is incorrect because Tarrega was famous for playing guitar, not making guitars.

22. **G**   The fifth paragraph (lines 49–61) describes the genius of Torres's design is the way he re-engineered the *internal structure* of the guitar. Choice (G) refers to the fan-bracing layout that Torres *perfected* (line 58). Choice (F) is incorrect because nothing in this paragraph relates to the idea of the guitar as a showcased instrument. That guitars became a more featured instrument is an effect of Torres's ingenious restructuring, but it isn't referring to Torres's design. The passage does not say that Torres invented the arched neck, nor does it say that he widened it to fit a sixth string—eliminate choices (H) and (J).

23. **C**   Although the first paragraph establishes that the passage will focus on how Torres paved the way for the modern guitar, the second paragraph (lines 11–22) begins providing background info on the emergence of early guitar forms. Choice (A) is unsupported because there is no mention that Torres was involved in adding a fifth string. Choice (B) is incorrect because the second paragraph does not mention the modern guitar and, thus, did not compare it to anything. Choice (D) is incorrect because there is nothing in the second paragraph that mentions or compares advantages of early guitars versus later ones.

24. **F**   Since Tarrega went from composing music on a piano, as did most people, to composing on guitar, he would be searching for the songwriting possibilities on the guitar. This agrees with (F). Choice (G) is too literal, and it is a trap answer based on similarity between colors and palettes. Volume output and structural limitations are mentioned as a consideration for performing music (lines 35–36 and 38–39), not composing it—eliminate choices (H) and (J).

25. **D**   The passage states that Spanish guitarists *rekindled the public's respect and admiration for guitar music* (lines 31–32). There is nothing supporting their reluctance to consider new designs as choice (A) says; in fact, the passage explains the limitations of the traditional design that frustrated them. There is no support for choice (B), that they had contact with Torres during his design process. They are guitar players, not lute players, as choice (C) suggests.

26. **G**   Specific dates for the Renaissance are never given. Choice (F) is answered in the fourth paragraph. Choice (H) is answered in the first paragraph. Choice (J) is answered in the second paragraph.

27. **A**   The passage states that the *guitarra latina became the national preference and rendered the vihuela obsolete* (lines 21–22). Choice (B) is incorrect because the passage does not indicate that the *vihuela* was intended to be a substitute for the lute. Choice (C) is incorrect because there is no mention that Ferdinand Sor played or popularized the *vihuela*. Choice (D) is incorrect because the passage never mentions Torres as having any involvement with the *vihuela*.

28. **G**   The first paragraph explains that Torres's innovations allowed the guitar to go from being a *supporting* instrument to a *featured solo* instrument. Choice (F) is unsupported because the passage never discusses the demands placed on a guitarist in playing Beethoven's works. Choice (H) is incorrect because Torres did not work with five string guitars. Choice (J) is incorrect because it is the opposite of what Torres guitars accomplished: They brought the guitar out of its folk context and into the spotlight of formal concerts.

29. **D**   The passage states that as more *"prestigious"* (line 27) instruments rose in popularity, the guitar was *relegated* (line 29) back to being a folk instrument. Choice (A) is incorrect because it describes what happened in the 17th century. Choice (B) is incorrect because the passage states that the growing popularity of other instruments hurt the guitar's popularity. Choice (C) is unsupported as the passage never discusses whether common folk could master playing techniques.

30. **F**   The passage indicates that Torres originally planned to sell Tarrega a stock guitar until Torres heard him play. *Deeply impressed* (line 71), Torres instead sold him a more sentimentally valuable guitar. Choice (G) is incorrect because this is something Tarrega did himself, not something someone did for Tarrega out of respect. Choice (H) is incorrect because the passage attributes this to the fifth string added to the *guitarra latina*. Choice (J) is incorrect because the passage attributes this to the popularity of Spanish guitarists such as Ferdinand Sor.

Passage IV

31. **D**   From the outset, the author introduces the fish as the two biggest of their kind, explains that their size puts them near the top of their local food chain, and goes on to describe their behaviors. Choice (A) is incorrect because, although the author mentions each species potentially being harmed by proximity to humans, these dangers are not described as species-threatening. Choice (B) is incorrect because nowhere is the author's tone or language resentful. Choice (C) is incorrect because the author

suggests in the first paragraph that the mola and whale shark have much less to worry about in terms of predators than do other fish.

32. **G** The passage states that *molas have a beaked mouth that does not totally close, so they chew their food in several stages* (lines 34–36). Choice (F) is unsupported, since the passage does not discuss eating habits as a function of being bony or cartilaginous. Choice (H) is unsupported since the passage does not indicate that the mola eats only at the surface. Choice (J) is unsupported since the passage indicates the mola floats on its side to warm up, not to eat.

33. **D** The passage indicates that the whale shark has *no natural predators* (line 58), while smaller molas are *sometimes subject to attack by sea lions* (line 76). Choice (A) is unsupported since neither species is subject to consistent predation, and there is no discussion of a predator's food source. Choice (B) is incorrect because the passage indicates that both species are sometimes adversely affected by contact with humans. Choice (C) is incorrect because the passage only speaks of molas being bothered by parasites.

34. **F** The passage states that the *mola, like the whale shark, often runs the risk of being hit by boats* (lines 74–75). Choices (G) and (J) are unsupported by any details in the passage. Choice (H) is incorrect because, although nautical debris is said to be a hazard for the whale shark's filter feeding, it is not identified as a threat to both species, and the threat is not from debris landing on the fish.

35. **A** The first paragraph states that molas and whale sharks *must focus on finding enough food to sustain the massive amounts of nutrients needed to support their bulky bodies* (lines 9–11). Choice (B) is incorrect because the passage never connects ocean depth and food requirements. Choice (C) is incorrect because this only relates to how the whale shark eats, not the quantity that any fish eats. Choice (D) is incorrect because the passage doesn't connect teeth or mouth size with dietary needs.

36. **G** Choices (F), (H), and (J) are all mentioned as part of the mola's diet in the third paragraph (lines 27–38). Zooplankton are specifically described as part of the whale shark's diet (line 47).

37. **C** The transition into the last two paragraphs begins with a mention of how these big fish are rarely picked on (lines 55–57). The paragraphs then go on to detail the types of dangers each fish faces, which are not very numerous or threatening in nature. Choice (A) is incorrect because, although some details in these paragraphs reinforce the large size of the two species, the purpose of the paragraphs is to discuss potential threats. Choice (B) is incorrect because it would only relate to the mola and conveying irony is not the main purpose of these paragraphs. Choice (D) is incorrect because the whale shark *has no natural predators*, so this answer couldn't apply to the second to last paragraph.

38. **J** The passage indicates that the gill rakers function by *separating the tiny* (line 52) bits of food from the mouthful of water. Choice (F) is incorrect because the mola, not the whale shark, spits out partially chewed food. Choice (G) is incorrect because the whale shark does not rip apart prey. Choice (H) is incorrect because the gill rakers are not mentioned in connection with the whale shark's teeth.

39. **D** The passage explains that *these fish live up to their name* (line 25) and proceeds to discuss the mola's impressive size. Choices (A), (B), and (C) are details mentioned about the mola but not connected to the explanation of the Latin name presented in the passage.

40. **G** The tone of the passage is mostly objective and informative. Choice (F) is incorrect because the two fish are rarely compared and never on the level of their hunting abilities. Choice (H) is incorrect because, though he does discuss what threats are present in their environment, the author does not specifically mention that either species is threatened. Choice (J) is incorrect because although the author refers to evolution in one passing remark, his discussion of the two fish is not based on how they evolved.

Chapter 14
Reading Practice
Test 3

READING TEST

35 Minutes—40 Questions

DIRECTIONS: There are four passages in this test. Each passage is followed by several questions. After reading each passage, choose the best answer to each question and blacken the corresponding oval on your answer document. You may refer to the passages as often as necessary.

Passage I

PROSE FICTION: This passage is an excerpt from the short story "Whimpering Wanderlust" by Gretchen Mueller (© 1955 by Gretchen Mueller).

Jacob Mathinson accepted, almost too early in his life, that he would never be a world-famous architect. His grandmother had instilled an indelible streak of humility in Jacob as a boy, telling him that he was special to her, but that the rest of the world
5 was under no obligation to feel the same way. He attended Mount St. Mary's College, not because it had a renowned architectural program, but because he was able to get a partial scholarship by playing on the school's tennis team. Jacob did not want to admit it, especially years later, but his decision may have also
10 been swayed by his desire to follow Erin Crawford, his high school crush, wherever she decided to go. Architecture was not his first calling, and, hence, his ambition towards ascending in the field extended only so far as his desire to walk through the streets of, say, Prague one day, a fetching girl on his arm,
15 commenting on the array of Baroque, Renaissance, and even Cubist masterpieces along the Old Town Square.

Growing up in Gettysburg, Pennsylvania, Jacob, an average though not exceptional student, was not exactly exposed to a climate of forward thinking. The local economy was a traditional,
20 if unimaginative, one. Most of the infrastructure had been built during the Reconstruction to support the railroad industry. In the summer of 1919, when Jacob was born, the town seemed frozen in the late 19th century, with bootblack, locksmith, and apothecary shops that seemed more at home in pre-industrial
25 times. This lack of innovation deepened Jacob's disinterest in personal or academic enterprise. His impression was that there was little of interest to be discovered outside of Gettysburg, save a patchwork of towns as predictable as the repeating pattern of black and white tiles on a checkerboard.

30 During his junior year in high school, Jacob worked as a tour guide on one of the double-decker buses that shuttled tourists, Civil War enthusiasts mostly, around the perimeter of Gettysburg. Fancying himself as cutting quite a figure in his clean, pressed uniform, it was his great hope that one day Erin
35 Crawford might take the tour and see him in action. He even went so far as to give her a voucher for a free ride, but as each tour began, he would heave a lonesome sigh, crestfallen that she with her sweet lilac fragrance had not whisked past him as the customers loaded on to the bus.

40 Nonetheless, Jacob enjoyed the job, partly because it was easy—it consisted of reading a script of noteworthy details about the Gettysburg Battlefield—but mostly because it allowed for personal embellishment, since the tour included some of the area's historic buildings as well. Jacob spent months explain-
45 ing to his customers that the sloping roof on the Dobbin House Tavern is a pristine example of Celtic style architecture, and that the Shriver House Museum is one of the oldest standing pre-colonial buildings in America. Although for months he described these buildings of architectural interest, it wasn't
50 until he left that job that he actually began to think about them, notice them, and allow the buildings to "speak" to him in an aesthetic conversation.

The following summer, Jacob worked with his uncle, a residential plumber. Jacob enjoyed seeing homes in the in-
55 termediate stages of construction, half-naked, their internal structure exposed. Jacob found great satisfaction in the task of finding the most efficient and cohesive way to intertwine the circulatory system of plumbing into the skeletal structure of each house's wooden framework. Again, he found a way to
60 incorporate visions of Erin into his work, imagining that Erin's parents would get a flooded basement, and he and his uncle would arrive heroically, save the day, and leave her parents thinking, "that Jacob is a great boy." (Jacob's fascination with the science and art of building blossomed in his freshman
65 year at Mount St. Mary's, as did his fascination with the many young women also attending the school. Perhaps their attentions provided much-needed distraction from the difficulties he was having in his pursuit of Erin.)

He had not accounted for Mount St. Mary's size relative
70 to his high school and the difficulty of "accidentally" running into someone in the halls. Throughout the first semester, Erin might as well have been a ghost to Jacob, who tried his very best to make her acquaintance, but to no avail. Many years later, already married to Martha, a seamstress from Gettysburg, Jacob
75 would daydream about the single time he and Erin had some-thing resembling a date. With a resigned sigh, he remembered his hands trembling, even while jammed into the pockets of his pressed Ogilvy's slacks; and the curious nature of her fragrance that seemed floral from a distance but minty up close; and the
80 musical sound her shoes made on the cobblestone road leading to the assembly hall; and the way she seemed to be fearlessly striding toward an unknown future while he was just trying to acclimate to the present.

1. The passage supports all of the following statements about Jacob's job as a tour guide EXCEPT that:

   A. he observed many buildings with their skeletal structure exposed.
   B. there were some prepared remarks that Jacob was to read.
   C. the tour catered to certain people with a common interest.
   D. he wore what he considered to be a flattering uniform.

2. One of the main ideas of the second paragraph (lines 17–29) is that:

   F. due to the nature of Gettysburg, Jacob did not have much desire to travel elsewhere.
   G. Jacob imagined a better architectural plan for the town's older buildings.
   H. it was hard for Jacob to find a job with mainly pre-industrial types of merchants.
   J. Jacob lacked motivation for his studies because he planned to work for the railroad.

3. The events in the passage are described primarily from the point of view of a narrator who presents the:

   A. actions and thoughts of both Jacob and Erin.
   B. the inner emotions and thoughts of only Jacob.
   C. actions and thoughts of all the characters discussed.
   D. dialogue of all the characters, which suggests their thoughts.

4. According to the passage, all of the following were aspects of Jacob's job with his uncle EXCEPT:

   F. seeing unfinished construction.
   G. impressing Erin's parents.
   H. daydreaming while he worked.
   J. finding efficient paths for plumbing.

5. According to the passage, Jacob's ambition toward becoming an architect included a desire to:

   A. point out interesting architecture to a girl.
   B. find a new way to utilize plumbing.
   C. redesign the Dobbin House roof.
   D. enroll at a renowned architectural school.

6. Which of the following questions is NOT answered by the passage?

   F. What factors influenced Jacob's choice to go to Mount St. Mary's College?
   G. Did Erin ever use her voucher for a free tour with Jacob?
   H. How many people went to Jacob's high school?
   J. What effect did the old infrastructure of Gettysburg have on Jacob?

7. The passage indicates that compared to when Jacob worked as a tour guide, after he stopped working there he found the buildings of Gettysburg:

   A. less fascinating.
   B. more fascinating.
   C. less historically noteworthy.
   D. more historically noteworthy.

8. The passage indicates that Jacob's primary response to the events described in the last paragraph is:

   F. remorse that he and Erin were largely disconnected.
   G. anger concerning the excessive size of Mount St. Mary's.
   H. gratitude for ultimately meeting and marrying Martha.
   J. contentment regarding the fact that he got to date Erin.

9. That Jacob had an indelible streak of humility was:

   A. a quality shared by most people who grew up in a working class community like that of Gettysburg.
   B. a consequence of accepting that he would probably never be a world-famous architect.
   C. an effect of Jacob's grandmother's words of caution regarding the unbiased impressions of the rest of the world.
   D. a character trait that evolved through years of pursuing but never obtaining Erin's affection.

10. In the passage, the statement that Erin was fearlessly striding toward an unknown future (lines 81–82) is best described as the opinion of:

    F. the author of the passage, but not the opinion of Jacob.
    G. Jacob as he struggled to "accidentally" run in to Erin at Mount St. Mary's.
    H. Erin, who has little interest in Jacob because he has no urge to leave Gettysburg.
    J. Jacob as he reflects on the one date he had with Erin.

Passage II

SOCIAL SCIENCE: This passage is excerpted from the article "The Irresistible Force" by Angela Suspak. (© 2008 by Luminary)

The author is reviewing the biographical book *The Long Walk Home* by Grace Jergensen.

During the summer of 1892, a reputable black store owner was lynched in Memphis, Tennessee. This outraged many local citizens, but Ida B. Wells felt compelled to take action and write a letter decrying the horrific act in the local press. However, as a
5 black woman, her race and identity posed formidable obstacles. The volatility of her message, combined with the pervasive chauvinism of the times, made her "a hushed voice in the race debate", according to Grace Jergensen, who writes a biography of Wells, entitled *The Long Walk Home*. Wells, taking matters
10 into her own hands, joined a fledgling black newspaper called "The Free Speech and Headlight" as co-owner and editor.

Writing under the pseudonym of "Iola," Wells lashed out against the intolerance and brutality of racially-motivated lynchings. She vilified the perpetrators of the crime, while also
15 chastising the white community at large for virtually condoning these actions by its inaction. With her incendiary rhetoric, Wells became a hero in the civil rights community and a potential target for violence. Jergensen details the difficulties Wells underwent shortly after her article was published. While at an
20 editing convention in New York, Wells learned that she had become a despised figure in Memphis, and the target of death threats. Considering the imminent danger she would face if she returned home, "Wells had to decide whether she would rather be a nomad or a martyr."

25 Wells was not used to backing down from a challenge, though. She was born just months before the Emancipation Proclamation declared an end to slavery. She grew up with the mindset of equal rights for all, despite being exposed to the deeply ingrained and intractable racial divisions in the South.
30 Her parents perished when she was only 18 during a bout of yellow fever that plagued her hometown of Holly Springs, Mississippi. Wells, the oldest of eight siblings, was thrust into the role of caretaker. Wells's Aunt Georgine recalls that "Ida saw herself now as the grown-up and wanted to be strong. She
35 did all her crying in private so the little ones wouldn't see her." Jergensen reflects that Wells learned early on "that she was in charge of protecting her brothers and sisters, and that feeling extended later in life to her figurative brothers and sisters in the struggle for racial and gender equality."

40 Wells went to Rust College to become a teacher, and her ability to mold the thought processes of others made her a persuasive orator and writer. Jergensen compares Wells's debating style to that of Socrates, who used shrewdly-worded questions and statements to lead his opponent from his original
45 sense of certainty into a state of doubt about the correctness of his convictions. Similarly, Wells frequently started her essays and speeches with general questions about morality, fairness,

and human rights, baiting her opposition into admitting certain core principles before challenging them to reconcile these
50 fundamental rights with the unfair and discriminatory laws and practices they endorsed.

After a public speaking tour of England, Wells made a home for herself in Chicago, where she met the man who would eventually become her husband, Ferdinand Barnett. Together, they
55 raised two sons and two daughters, though later in life, Wells would bemoan the fact that she felt as though the responsibility of raising and supporting the four children became her primary concern, while her husband became engrossed in a political bid to become a Circuit Court judge.

60 Domestic life didn't spell the end of Wells's struggle against inequality, however—during her time in Chicago, she founded the nation's first civic organization for black women. It was initially called the Women's Era Club, though it would later be renamed the Ida B. Wells Club. In 1895, her book
65 *A Red Record* was published, documenting the history of racially-motivated lynchings in America. Although the book succeeded in motivating an audience of progressive thinkers, race-related riots and violence continued virtually unabated into the early 20th century.

70 Jergensen conveys a clear appreciation for the deep reserves of patience on which Wells was repeatedly forced to draw in order to maintain her devotion to both family and society, despite often being castigated or ignored by both. By retracing Wells's "long walk home" from the grueling aftermath of her parents' death,
75 through her exile from Memphis, to her eventual involvement in creating the NAACP (National Association for the Advancement of Colored People), Jergensen leaves the reader feeling exhausted, expending such vast amounts of sympathy for the injustices Wells faces. As portrayed by Jergensen, Wells is a
80 protagonist who nobly walks a self-chosen path of monumental toil, with rewards few and far between. One such reward must have been the passage of women's suffrage in 1920 with the 19th Amendment which Wells, then a grandmother, was finally able to see first-hand.

11. In the statement in lines 36–39 Jergensen most strongly stresses:

   A. a consistent propensity Wells had to take care of those in need of help.
   B. the way Wells's family persuaded her to take part in the civil rights struggle.
   C. the lessons of equality that Wells learned by acting like a parent to her siblings.
   D. a powerful metaphor Wells would later use in many of her incendiary speeches.

12. As portrayed in the passage, the reaction of Wells to her parents dying from a bout a yellow fever is best described as:

F. sad and frightened.

G. mournful but resilient.

H. relieved and emboldened.

J. brave but hopeless.

13. The passage's author most strongly implies that Wells's relationship with her husband:

A. began a decline in her activism as she turned her focus to starting a family.

B. was the most lasting consequence of her public speaking tour in England.

C. did not halt her efforts in the struggle for equality.

D. was the main reason behind her starting the Ida B. Wells Club.

14. Lines 6–9 most nearly mean that Wells:

F. faced the problem of audiences reluctant to hear what she had to say.

G. spoke too softly for many people to take her ideas seriously.

H. did not believe that people would discredit her because of her race or gender.

J. had to create a pen name in order to have her newspaper articles be read by the mainstream.

15. According to the passage, who disapproved of the ideas described in lines 12–16?

A. Wells herself

B. Jergensen

C. Some people in Memphis

D. The civil rights community

16. Another reviewer of Jergensen's book sums up Wells in this way:

> A tireless and outspoken advocate of equality, Ida B. Wells did not shy away from making controversial demands of her audience ... sometimes jeopardizing her own safety, always reminding her listeners that equality was in accord with their fundamental sense of fairness.

How does this account of Wells compare to that of the passage's author?

F. This account portrays Wells's demands as fair, whereas the passage's author remains less convinced.

G. This account emphasizes the danger Wells put herself in, whereas the passage's author does not mention this.

H. Both provide a comparably unflattering portrayal of Wells's goals and tactics.

J. Both provide a comparably flattering portrayal of Wells's goals and tactics.

17. For the passage's author, lines 81–84 mainly support her earlier point that:

A. Wells did manage to see some of her goals realized in her lifetime.

B. family was an essential factor in motivating Wells's struggle.

C. significant changes happen in society with each new generation.

D. Wells became much wiser and more thankful in her old age.

18. According to the passage, Jergensen believes that Wells' had a style of debating similar to that of Socrates because Wells:

F. had a strong sense of certainty about her philosophical convictions.

G. did not advance her own agenda but only wanted to understand her opponent.

H. understood that clever oration can only do so much to further a cause.

J. used points of agreement to show her opponents problems with their points of view.

19. The passage's author characterizes the book *A Red Record* most nearly as:

A. a good effort that was troubled by philosophical inconsistencies.

B. unusually radical compared to other books from the same era.

C. impressively broad in the scope of social issues it tackled.

D. mainly effective at inspiring its like-minded readers.

20. The passage most strongly suggests that Wells approached her life as a:

F. bleak marathon.

G. determined struggle.

H. confusing journey.

J. constant triumph.

Passage III

HUMANITIES: This passage is adapted from the novel *Southern Charmed Life* by Robert Anderson (© 1978 by Robert Anderson).

B.B. King has been a popular singer and blues guitarist since the 1950s.

In the summer of 1953, Uncle Randy was particularly excited for our visit. Sis and I got to spend a couple weeks with him each summer, to escape the heat of our home in Thibadeux, Louisiana. He was choir director at St. Peter's church in Des
5　Moines, Iowa. Sometimes we went with him to visit the homes of the older parishioners, helping him clean up their yards, grocery shopping for them, or cleaning their gutters.

Uncle Randy told us his friend from Mississippi was coming through town, a man named Riley King, although people
10　called him 'B.B'. He spoke in hushed awe of his friend B.B., who was "King of the Blues." "I don't much like the Blues," Sis would say. "You can't dance to it."

Before we left for B.B.'s hotel, to take him over to Sunday mass, Uncle Randy cleaned his Chevrolet Deluxe like an infantry
15　man would his rifle. It was a humble man's car, but we got it shining like the President's limousine.

As we pulled into the parking lot of the Majestic Hotel, I saw a man waiting near the front doors, looking off into the distance. His guitar case stood vertically, parallel with his up-
20　right posture, his hands folded serenely on the top of the case, slightly rocking back and forth on his heels.

"Hey! Somebody! I need the world's best guitarist! It's an emergency!" yelled my Uncle, to get B.B.'s attention. B.B. recognized his voice immediately, but paused a half second to
25　finish his thought before smiling and turning to see us driving up.

"Well, then, let me get in the car and help you look for T-Bone Walker," B.B. said, leaning in through the passenger-side window. Seeing us, he added with a mischievous smile, "So these are the troublemakers?"

30　"Yup. Kathie Mae and Bobby. Kids, this is Mr. King." my uncle warmly, yet formally, announced.

"Aw, they don't gotta call me 'Mister'. I'm B.B." He offered each of us a handshake, which we timidly accepted. His hands were large and calloused, and he wore several gold rings
35　on his fingers.

Sis and I sat silently in the back, peering nervously at this strange new arrival who was filling the car with his large frame, his guitar, and his Sunday-best cologne. His pockmarked face was worn but jubilant. He seemed like a man who had seen
40　all the hardships of the road, but whose youthful, joyous spirit still remained.

My uncle was chatting with B.B., asking him about his recent performances, and about all the money he must be making, but B.B. seemed reluctant to boast. "Ah, you know. We just
45　make enough money to get to the next town and get a meal in us. Maybe sometimes a little extra to bring home."

My sister burst out, inquisitively, "Where's home?" B.B. was seated in front of Sis, but wanting to acknowledge her, he turned his head halfway and said, "Itta Bena." She asked back,
50　"Itta Whatta?" The adults laughed. Uncle Randy clarified that it was a town in Mississippi, near Indianola, where we had come to visit him before he moved to Iowa. Feeling particularly fearless for a ten year old, Sis asked B.B. why he likes playing sad music. B.B. gave a rich chuckle and decided he had to look
55　Kathy Mae in the eyes for this one. He shifted his guitar to the side and turned his husky frame as far as he could, until his marbled, twinkling brown eyes could look straight into hers.

"Honey, the music isn't sad. Life is sad ... sometimes. And the Blues is just how you get through it. It's hard for a young
60　'un to hear the Blues right because you haven't been through enough pain of livin' yet." My Uncle was smiling, looking in the rear-view mirror at Sis, trying to judge her reaction. She seemed to be partly insulted by the implication that she would not be able to "get" the Blues.

65　"Have you ever cried yourself to sleep?" B.B. asked. Sis tightened her lips in resentment. "Don't be shy. We all have. Didn't you feel better when you woke up?" Sis tentatively agreed.

B.B. explained, "it's because the pain is distant when you wake up. The Blues is how I cry myself to sleep. It puts a dream
70　in between me and the pain, just like a thick frosted window pane that muffles it and makes it fuzzy to see." Sis and I turned to each other, finding this pearl of wisdom difficult to digest and resigning to the fact that some things were not meant for kids.

75　Years later, I would find a deep appreciation for B.B.'s music. Whenever I hear him play, I can't help but to imagine a waterfall—the pressure of the falling water was the weight of the pain. The mournful verses he sung made me think of the space behind the waterfall, a calm place of imprisonment,
80　where a thundering curtain of water is all you see in front of you. And when he started his guitar solo, it was like I turned into a bird that flew out through the waterfall. The heavy water pounded my light, buoyant frame down as I passed through it, but, once through, I was able to feel the freedom of lift, the
85　droplets of water rolling off my wings as I soared up towards the clouds, and the waterfall was only something beautiful to behold in the distance.

21. According to the passage, which of the following events occurred last chronologically?

    A. The narrator meets B.B. in the hotel parking lot.
    B. The narrator develops a strong fondness for B.B.'s music.
    C. The narrator helps his uncle perform chores for parishioners.
    D. The narrator helps clean his uncle's car.

22. Based on the passage, how old was the narrator's sister when she met King?

    F. Six
    G. Ten
    H. Twelve
    J. Fifteen

23. As it is used in line 72, the word *digest* most nearly means:

    A. understand.
    B. stomach.
    C. memorize.
    D. study.

24. The point of view from which the passage is told is best described as that of someone:

    F. trying to learn more about Mississippi culture.
    G. vacationing with his sister and his Uncle Randy.
    H. recounting how he learned to play blues guitar.
    J. remembering fondly an encounter with B.B. King.

25. Through his description of his meeting with B.B. King, the narrator portrays King most nearly as:

    A. flashy.
    B. morose.
    C. undignified.
    D. modest.

26. King uses the simile in lines 70–71 to convey the ability of the Blues to:

    F. get the most emotion out of a musical instrument.
    G. dull the sharpness of suffering.
    H. transform complex feelings into simple ones.
    J. help people relax and get to sleep.

27. Based on the passage, the narrator's and his sister's initial reaction to meeting King is one of:

    A. warmth and informality.
    B. caution and anxiety.
    C. amazement and confusion.
    D. skepticism and disappointment.

28. The narrator compares the feeling created by King's guitar solos to the feeling of:

    F. "a thick frosted window pane" (lines 70–71).
    G. "the space behind the waterfall" (line 79).
    H. "a thundering curtain of water" (line 80).
    J. "a bird that flew out through the waterfall" (line 82).

29. It is most reasonable to infer from the passage that King believes a true appreciation of the Blues comes primarily from:

    A. an upbringing similar to King's in Mississippi.
    B. watching it performed live by musicians.
    C. recognizing the struggles of life.
    D. having deeply held religious beliefs.

30. It is reasonable to infer that, following King's explanation of the Blues to Kathy Mae, the narrator and his sister:

    F. resolved to listen to Blues music more in order to understand the meaning behind King's words.
    G. decided they would ask Uncle Randy more about the Blues once King was no longer in their company.
    H. accepted that the point King was attempting to communicate was beyond their level of comprehension.
    J. gained the newfound impression that Blues music is a response to, not a cause of, sadness.

Passage IV

NATURAL SCIENCE: The following is adapted from the article "Seeking an Intelligent Definition of Intelligence" by Clark Matthews (© 2010 by Clark Matthews).

Cognitive psychologists who study humans and other animals are perpetually attempting to understand the type and extent of intelligence possessed by their subjects. Hindering their efforts is the ongoing debate about how we should define
5 such a nebulous concept as 'intelligence' in the first place. A scatter-hoarder species of squirrel would probably define intelligence as the ability to remember and re-locate the thousands of caches of food it has burrowed in hiding places throughout its environment. A dog, on the other hand, may emphasize its
10 ability to trace the source of objects in its environment based on the direction of the air current containing that smell.

There is a risk of bias in how we define intelligence because each species has evolved very specialized abilities based on its unique environmental niche and the techniques and strategies
15 that niche requires for survival. If we use our concepts of human capacities to define intelligence, we may be creating a standard that other animals couldn't hope to meet. Conversely, if we only mean by intelligence "the most highly refined capacities of that species" we make intelligence something that can only
20 be compared within a species, not across species.

One definition of intelligence holds that it is "a wide range of abilities relating to learning from one's environment and experience, and combining that learning with abstract reasoning to solve problems." Scientists frequently begin assessing
25 an animal's intelligence based on its susceptibility to classical or operant conditioning. Both methods involve pairing either a stimuli or a behavior with certain consequences, and waiting to see if a subject learns to associate the two and act accordingly. The faster the animal appears to absorb and act on the
30 association, the faster we believe it has 'learned' it. This gives us one supposedly objective means of comparing intelligent behavior across species.

The other primary evidence of an animal's intelligence is its ability to solve novel and/or complex problems. A spider
35 that spins a web to solve the problem of trapping insects for food is not considered to be displaying intelligence because the problem (food gathering) and behavior (spinning webs) are both embedded in the evolutionary history of a spider's habitat. An elephant that picks a lock at the zoo is thought to be acting
40 intelligently, since elephants do not pick locks in their native habitat and hence have no instinctive knowledge of how do undo them. The veined octopus is seen as a tool-user, scouring the ocean for coconut shells, which it proceeds to bring back to its homestead for the sake of building shelter. Although many
45 other animals, such as crabs and ants will take shelter using nearby objects, animal psychologists consider the long-term planning involved in the veined octopus's behavior as better evidence that it can conceptualize a goal and then act on it.

As if defining intelligence weren't tricky enough, measur-
50 ing intelligence is also a tenuous task. Ultimately, scientists can only observe an animal's behavior. So how can they ascertain if the animal is just behaving instinctively or if it is actually conceptualizing, thinking abstractly, and aware of its problem solving process? Because understanding is a private experience,
55 observing an animal's external behavior and hoping to infer its level of understanding is always a guessing game.

Both "intelligent" behavior and "unintelligent" behavior can be deceiving. Irene Pepperberg's famous subject, the parrot Alex, showcased a variety of impressive problem solving and
60 communication abilities that suggested an internal awareness and capacity for intelligence was present. For instance, Alex correctly called a "key" a "key," no matter what size, color, or orientation a certain key was. This suggests Alex had grouped the individual keys used to train him into a general category that
65 could be applied to novel stimuli. However, sometimes Alex gave wrong answers to a task he had completed successfully many times before. This was interpreted as Alex's boredom and frustration at repeating a task he had already mastered. Although the behavior looked unintelligent, experimenters
70 believed it was not due to a lack of understanding. Conversely, there is also the perpetual concern of the Clever Hans Effect, in which seemingly intelligent behavior is not believed to be the result of genuine understanding. The name comes from a horse named Clever Hans who was paraded around Europe in
75 the early 20th century, supposedly a marvel of animal intelligence. Hans could indicate the correct solution to arithmetic problems by tapping his hoof the appropriate number of times. Ultimately, though, scientists realized that Hans was getting the answer by reading nonverbal clues from his trainer. The trainer
80 would unknowingly tense up as the correct number of taps was getting nearer, which signaled to Hans when it was time to stop tapping. So although Hans exhibited behavior that seemed indicative of underlying intelligence, scientists do not believe he was actually solving the problems conceptually in his mind.

31. The main function of the second paragraph (lines 12–20) in relation to the passage as a whole is to:

   A. explain the human bias that is the focus of the rest of the passage.

   B. advance the argument that intelligence should be defined in human terms.

   C. showing how certain types of definitions have undesirable consequences.

   D. provide background information about the evolutionary niches of species.

32. According to the passage, what is the primary problem with defining intelligence as "the most highly refined capacities" of a given species?

   F. It would be a standard that no species could hope to meet.

   G. It would not take into account each species' unique environmental niche.

   H. It would too closely mimic our concepts of human intelligence.

   J. It would not be a standard we could use to compare one species to another.

33. According to the passage, all of the following behaviors seem to be intelligent EXCEPT:

   A. a spider solving the problem of trapping insects by spinning a web.

   B. an elephant picking a lock at the zoo.

   C. a veined octopus finding coconut shells for its shelter.

   D. a parrot identifying keys of various shapes and sizes.

34. According to the passage, scientists often start their assessment of animal's intelligence by:

   F. analyzing its ability to solve new and complex problems.

   G. identifying the most highly refined capacities of that species.

   H. stimulating the animal and observing its behavior.

   J. seeing how much information the animal can absorb.

35. Suppose beavers typically gather sticks from the forest floor and bring them to a stream to construct a dam. One beaver that cannot find enough sticks on the ground begins to strip bark from dying trees. Based on the passage, the author would most likely describe the behavior of this gopher as:

   A. intelligent if the lack of sticks is a novel problem.

   B. unintelligent if there was long-term planning.

   C. impressive and the result of operant conditioning.

   D. deceptive and illustrating the Clever Hans effect.

36. The passage indicates that the shelters of the veined octopus differ from those of crabs and ants in that the octopus shelters:

   F. are more likely to be constructed from nearby objects.

   G. are made of much sturdier materials than are crab and ant shelters.

   H. have more architectural interest than those of the crabs and ants.

   J. seem more to be the result of a long-term plan.

37. The primary purpose of the passage is to:

   A. define intelligence as it applies to non-human species.

   B. explore some of the challenges, both conceptual and practical, involved in assessing intelligence.

   C. identify the criteria used to discriminate between intelligent and unintelligent behavior.

   D. compare and contrast how intelligence appears within human species versus how it appears in non-human species.

38. The author mentions the behavior of the parrot Alex in the last paragraph primarily to:

   F. demonstrate that poor performance does not necessarily indicate poor comprehension.

   G. illustrate the meaning of intelligent behavior as applied to parrots.

   H. highlight an animal believed to be unintelligent which nonetheless acted intelligently.

   J. supply proof that animals can indeed learn the meaning of a concept.

39. As it is used in line 54, the word *private* most nearly means:

   A. internal.

   B. secretive.

   C. subtle.

   D. shy.

40. In the context of the passage, the phrase "can be deceiving" (line 58) most nearly suggests that an animal's behavior:

   F. often is intended to trick other animals in its environment.

   G. is the hardest thing about an animal to measure in a scientific way.

   H. will fool observers who are not trained to know better.

   J. does not always serve as a reliable indicator of that animal's mental activities.

END OF TEST 3
STOP! DO NOT TURN THE PAGE UNTIL TOLD TO DO SO.
DO NOT RETURN TO A PREVIOUS TEST.

Chapter 15
Reading Practice
Test 3
Answers and
Explanations

READING PRACTICE TEST 3 ANSWERS

1.	A	21.	B
2.	F	22.	G
3.	B	23.	A
4.	G	24.	J
5.	A	25.	D
6.	H	26.	G
7.	B	27.	B
8.	F	28.	J
9.	C	29.	C
10.	J	30.	H
11.	A	31.	C
12.	G	32.	J
13.	C	33.	A
14.	F	34.	H
15.	C	35.	A
16.	J	36.	J
17.	A	37.	B
18.	J	38.	F
19.	D	39.	A
20.	G	40.	J

SCORE YOUR PRACTICE TEST

Step A

Count the number of correct answers: _____. This is your *raw score*.

Step B

Use the score conversion table below to look up your raw score. The number to the left is your *scale score*: _____.

Reading Scale Conversion Table

Scale Score	Raw Score	Scale Score	Raw Score	Scale Score	Raw Score
36	40	27	30	18	18
35	39	26	29	17	16–17
34	38	25	27–28	16	15
33	37	24	26	15	14
32	36	23	24–25	14	12–13
31	35	22	23	13	11
30	34	21	22	12	9–10
29	32–33	20	20–21	11	8
28	31	19	19	10	6–7

READING PRACTICE TEST 3 EXPLANATIONS

Passage I

1. **A**   Choice (A) refers to a detail that comes from the description of Jacob's job working for his uncle. During the tour guide job, Jacob pointed out completed buildings, not works in progress. Choice (B) is supported by the script the tour guide had him read. Choice (C) is supported by the fact that the tour mostly attracted *Civil War enthusiasts*. Choice (D) is supported by the phrase *fancying himself as cutting quite a figure in his clean, pressed uniform* (lines 33–34).

2. **F**   The first few sentences of the second paragraph establish that Gettysburg is a town that is stuck in the past, or at least doing very little to modernize. *This lack of innovation* affects Jacob and gives him the impression that *there was little of interest to be discovered outside Gettysburg* (lines 26–27). Choice (G) is incorrect because the passage never offers Jacob's ideas for improving old buildings. Choice (H) is incorrect because the passage never discusses Jacob having difficulty finding a job. Choice (J) is incorrect because the passage does not suggest Jacob planned to work for the railroad.

3. **B**   The passage is essentially narrating Jacob's thoughts the majority of the time, and otherwise providing exposition on Jacob's life. Choices (A) and (C) are incorrect because there is nothing in the passage that provides an inner thought from Erin. Choice (D) is incorrect because there is no dialogue in the passage.

4. **G**   The passage refers to a fantasy Jacob had about being called to Erin's house and impressing her parents, but the passage never indicates that it happened. Choice (F) is supported in the second sentence of the fifth paragraph. Choice (H) is supported in the last sentence of the fifth paragraph. Choice (J) is supported in the second to last sentence of the fifth paragraph.

5. **A**   The last sentence of the first paragraph says that Jacob's *ambition towards ascending in the field* (lines 12–13) was basically to be able to impress a *fetching girl on his arm* (line 14) by describing architectural features of their environment. Choice (B) is incorrect because the passage never mentions Jacob devising a new approach to plumbing. Choice (C) is incorrect because the passage never mentions a desire to redesign the Dobbin House. Choice (D) is contradicted by details in the first paragraph which state that Jacob went to Mount St. Mary's, *not because it had a renowned architectural program* (lines 6–7).

6. **H**   Although Jacob's high school is mentioned as being small in comparison to Mount St. Mary's College, the number of students is never provided. Choice (F) is answered in the first paragraph —Jacob's tennis scholarship and yearning for Erin are the main factors. Choice (G) is answered in the third paragraph. *As each tour began*, Jacob was disappointed to not see Erin, so she never came to his tour. Choice (J) is answered in the second paragraph—*this lack of innovation deepened Jacob's disinterest in personal or academic enterprise* (lines 25–26).

7. **B** The last sentence of the fourth paragraph (lines 48–52) indicates that it wasn't *until he left the job* that Jacob started thinking more about the buildings. Choice (A) is incorrect because it is the opposite of what the passage indicates. Choices (C) and (D) are incorrect because the passage provides no comparison between how historically noteworthy Jacob thought the buildings were during and after his job as a tour guide.

8. **F** The paragraph begins with Jacob's frustration regarding his inability to run into Erin at college. It ends with Jacob, *With a resigned sigh* (line 76), recounting a memory of his one date with Erin. His final thought is that they were on two different tracks, hers a fearless stride toward the future and his an attempt to get used to the present. These sad details support choice (F)'s notion that he and Erin had grown apart. Choice (G) is incorrect because, although Jacob was frustrated by the campus size in his efforts to run into Erin, there is not support for something so strong as anger. Also, this would only relate to the beginning of the paragraph and not address the rest of it. Choice (H) is incorrect because there is no attitude mentioned or suggested towards Jacob's marriage to Martha. Also, this answer would not address the majority of the paragraph. Choice (J) is incorrect because, although you would assume Jacob was happy to get the date, the details in the paragraph are largely relating to why a relationship with Erin failed. There is no wording in the passage that indicates Jacob's contentment.

9. **C** The wording *an indelible streak of humility* is used in the second sentence of the first paragraph (lines 2–5), attributed to Jacob's grandmother telling him that the rest of the world was under no obligation to think he was special. Choice (A) is incorrect because humility is never suggested by the passage to be a trait of working class communities. Choice (B) is incorrect because Jacob's humility is more the cause of his feeling that he won't be famous than it is a consequence. Choice (D) is incorrect because the passage never links humility to Jacob's pursuit of Erin.

10. **J** This statement is from the last sentence of the passage, which begins *With a resigned sigh, he remembered…*. Hence, all the details in the sentence are things Jacob remembers about his first date with Erin. Choice (F) is incorrect because this is Jacob's impression, not the author's. Choice (G) is incorrect because this detail is presented as part of Jacob's memory of his date with Erin, not as part of his struggle to find her at college. Choice (H) is incorrect because this is part of Jacob's reminiscence, not Erin's.

Passage II

11. **A** The statement from Jergensen compares the way in which Wells looked out for her siblings to the way in which she looked out for the rights of any humans suffering from racial inequality. Choice (B) is incorrect because the passage does not suggest that any of her family members *persuaded* her to be an activist. Choice (C) is incorrect because the passage does not suggest she learned any *lessons of equality* via taking care of her siblings. Choice (D) is incorrect because the passage doesn't suggest any family metaphor used by Wells in her speeches.

12. **G** The passage relays Aunt Georgine's comment that Ida wanted to be the grown up she knew her brothers and sisters needed. Ida mourned privately in order to keep a strong appearance. Choice (F) is incorrect because *frightened* goes against the portrayal of Ida stepping into the caretaking role. Choice (H) is incorrect because *relieved* goes against the sadness Ida felt over her parents' passing. Choice (J) is incorrect because *hopeless* is too strong to be supported by anything in the passage.

13. **C** The passage states that *domestic life didn't spell the end of Wells's struggle against inequality* (lines 60–61), and the passage proceeds to describe Wells's activism after she was married. While care for the family did become primarily her concern rather than her husband's, the passage does not say her efforts in the struggle for racial equality were diminished, so cross off (A). Choice (B) is incorrect because Wells met her husband in Chicago, not England. Choice (D) is incorrect because there is no implied connection between her husband and the book club, and, additionally, she didn't start the club with that name.

14. **F** The passage calls Wells a *hushed voice in the race debate* (lines 7–8) since she was saying things people didn't want to hear. People were unaccustomed in those times to hearing such things from a woman and often sought to deny her her voice. Choice (G) is incorrect because the word *hushed* is not referring to softer volume, but rather, metaphorically, to being told to "hush!" Choice (H) is the opposite of the impression given by the passage, which is that Wells *did* recognize her gender and race as an obstacle to getting her message across. Choice (J) is incorrect because although the passage mentions her writing under a pseudonym (line 12), it was to protect her identity and it certainly wasn't for a "mainstream" newspaper.

15. **C** The passage indicates that following the publishing of Wells's article, she became *a despised figure in Memphis* (line 21). Choices (A), (B), and (D) are all incorrect because the passage states and/or implies that these parties would be sympathetic to Wells's public outcry.

16. **J** The passage provides a positive treatment of Wells, discussing her bold outrage in the first few paragraphs and her techniques of persuasion in the fifth paragraph. All these details correspond well with this account. Choice (F) is incorrect because the passage never calls into question the *fairness* of Wells's objectives. Choice (G) is incorrect because the passage *does* mention, in the first few paragraphs, the danger Wells put herself in. Choice (H) is incorrect because there is nothing to support the author's *unflattering* portrayal of Wells.

17. **A** Two sentences prior to this one, the author mentions Wells's long toil with only occasional rewards, and then mentions women's suffrage in 1920 as one of these "rewards." The sense of change on a societal level that the sentence in question refers to is women achieving suffrage in 1920, so it supports choice (A). Choice (B) is unsupported by the passage, which never says that family motivated Wells's struggle. Choice (C) is unsupported by the passage, which does not ever suggest each generation brings significant changes to society.

18. **J** The passage states that Wells baited *her opposition into admitting certain core principles before challenging them* (lines 48–49) to apply those principles to racial inequality. Choice (F) is incorrect because, though Wells certainly must have had strong philosophical convictions and Socrates sought

to weaken the strong convictions of his opponents, a shared sense of certainty is not part of the comparison Jergensen makes to Socrates. Choice (G) goes against the passage since Wells definitely has an agenda to promote racial and gender equality. Choice (H) is incorrect because the passage never discusses Wells's thoughts on the limits of what oration can accomplish.

19. **D** The passage states in the last sentence of the sixth paragraph (lines 66–69) that the book motivated an audience of *progressive thinkers*, while the practical and statistical measures of the problem it addressed did not improve. Choice (A) is incorrect because "philosophical inconsistencies" are not mentioned or suggested. There is no support for calling the book "unusually" radical as choice (B) does. The author does not praise the "scope" of the book, mentioning only its purpose of documenting racially influenced lynchings.

20. **G** The last paragraph states that Wells *nobly walks a self-chosen path of monumental toil, with rewards few and far between* (lines 80–81). This agrees best with choice (G). Choice (F) is too pessimistic for the passage's overall heroic portrayal of Wells. Choice (H) is incorrect since the idea that Wells's steadfast struggle to attain equality was *confusing* is not justified. Choice (J) is incorrect because it goes against the passage's portrayal of Wells's life as being filled with challenge and strife.

Passage III

21. **B** The last paragraph begins *years later*, indicating that the narrator's explanation of his love for B.B.'s music developed years after the summer of 1953 trip. Choices (A) and (D) took place during the summer of 1953 trip. Choice (C) is suggested to have taken place before the summer of 1953 trip.

22. **G** In the eleventh paragraph (lines 47–57), the passage says *feeling particularly fearless for a ten year old, Sis asked ...* Choices (F), (H), and (J) are incorrect because they contradict the age given for the narrator's sister.

23. **A** Saying King's words are difficult to process is akin to saying they are difficult to understand. Choice (B) is a trap answer due to its similarity to the normal meaning of *digest*. Saying something is difficult to stomach means one is reluctant to accept its meaning, not that one does not understand its meaning. Choices (C) and (D) relate to the process of learning and understanding, but neither one itself is a good substitute for the concept of understanding.

24. **J** The narrator is retelling events from the summer of 1953 that involve him meeting B.B. King, and describes the effect B.B.'s music came to have on him. This best supports choice (J). Choice (F) is incorrect because, other than the fact that B.B. and Uncle Randy both lived in Mississippi, there is nothing in the passage about trying to learn that state's culture. Choice (G) is incorrect because, although some of the passage's events take place during a vacation the narrator took with his sister to see his Uncle Randy, the narrator is describing those events in the past tense, not currently on vacation with them. Choice (H) is incorrect because it is never implied that the narrator plays guitar or learned to from B.B. King.

25. **D**   B.B. is very polite with the narrator and his sister, having them address him informally by his first name. B.B. refuses to be acknowledged as *the world's best guitarist*, substituting instead the name of *T-Bone Walker*. And, in talking to the narrator's uncle about life on the road, he seemed *reluctant to boast* (line 44). These details all support choice (D). Choice (A) is not supported, other than by the fact that B.B. wore gold rings and his Sunday-best cologne. These are not necessarily flashy things, though, as any adult might wear such things. Choice (B) is not supported because, although B.B. plays the Blues and discusses times in his life where he is sad, the narrator describes him having a *youthful, joyous spirit* (line 40). Choice (C) is not supported by anything in the passage.

26. **G**   King explains that the Blues helps him put some distance between himself and his pain, like a *frosted window* that *muffles it and makes it fuzzy* (lines 70–71). This supports the idea of dulling one's suffering in choice (G). Choice (F) is incorrect because King is not referring to any particular instrument. Choice (H) is close, but too broad—King is speaking about one particular feeling, not multiple ones. Choice (J) is too literal. Although sleep is mentioned in the extended metaphor/simile King describes, he is primarily discussing the way the Blues softens the feeling of pain.

27. **B**   The passage states that the narrator and his sister *timidly accepted* (line 33) B.B.'s handshake. They *sat silently* (line 36) and peered *nervously*. These details support the adjectives used in choice (B). Choice (A) is incorrect because the kids were not warmly greeting him if they were timidly accepting his handshake. Choice (C) is incorrect because amazement and confusion both are more extreme than the general sense of curiosity and strangeness described in the passage. Choice (D) is incorrect because there is no support for either skepticism or disappointment in the passage.

28. **J**   The author says when B.B. *started his guitar solo, it was like I turned into a bird that flew out through the waterfall* (lines 81–82). Choice (F) refers to how King compared the effect the Blues has on making pain feel more distant. Choice (G) refers to how the narrator compared the verses of King's music. Choice (J) refers to how the narrator compared the pain felt by the musician or listener.

29. **C**   As King explains the Blues to Kathy Mae, he says she wouldn't *hear the Blues right* because she hasn't had enough *pain of livin' yet* (lines 60–61). Choices (A), (B), and (D) are incorrect because King never stresses his hometown, one's childhood upbringing, live versus recorded music, or one's degree of religious commitment.

30. **H**   The passage indicates that the narrator and his sister had trouble digesting King's wisdom and resigned themselves to the idea that it was beyond a child's understanding. Choice (F) is incorrect because by resigning themselves to the fact that King's words were beyond them, they are giving up on understanding it, not resolving to expend more effort to understand it. Choice (G) is incorrect because the passage does not suggest any intent to speak with Uncle Randy about it. Choice (J) is incorrect because this answer sums up King's main message, which the children did not seem to absorb.

Passage IV

31. C The paragraph explains that if we define intelligence in human terms, other species might be hopeless to meet human criteria. However, if we define intelligence relative to a given species, we can't compare intelligence between animals of different species. These are suggested to be undesirable consequences. Choice (A) is incorrect because "human bias" is not the focus of the rest of the passage. Choice (B) is incorrect because the author does not endorse any specific definition of intelligence, and in this paragraph he explains a problem that would result from defining intelligence this way. Choice (D) is incorrect because the paragraph only mentions a general statement that every species has an evolutionary niche. This is not really background information, nor is that the focus of this paragraph.

32. J The last line of the second paragraph states that if we adopted this definition, we make intelligence something that cannot be compared *across species*. Choice (F) is incorrect because animals of the "given species" could definitely meet the standard as defined for their species. Choice (G) is incorrect because this definition, in being defined in terms of a given species, would take into account that species' unique traits. Choice (H) is incorrect because this definition would not use human intelligence as a measurement, but rather the unique capacities of each species.

33. A The passage specifically states that a spider that spins a web *is not considered to be displaying intelligence* (lines 35–36). Choices (B) and (C) are presented in the fourth paragraph as intelligent, and choice (D) is presented in the fifth paragraph as indicative of some intelligence.

34. H The passage states that *scientists frequently begin assessing an animal's intelligence* (lines 24–26) by analyzing the animal's *susceptibility to classical or operant conditioning*, which involves providing a stimulus and observing the animal's behavior. Choice (F) is incorrect because this is identified by the passage as the *other primary evidence* (line 33) of intelligence. Although this is an important form of evidence, it doesn't address the wording in the question stem, which specifically asks about where scientists *start* their assessments. Choice (G) is given (lines 18–19) as an example of something problematic in determining intelligence. Choice (J) is incorrect because the passage never mentions testing an animal's capacity to absorb information.

35. A The beginning of the fourth paragraph states that one of the primary sources of evidence for intelligence mentioned in the passage is the ability to solve novel problems. So if the lack of sticks is a new problem and the beaver devises a solution to address it, the author would call that intelligent behavior. Choice (B) is incorrect because *long-term planning* (lines 46–47) is described in the passage as evidence of intelligent behavior. Choice (C) is incorrect because there is no reason to think the beaver's behavior is the result of *operant conditioning*. Choice (D) is incorrect because there is no reason to assume the Clever Hans Effect is involved.

36. J The passage makes a contrast between crab and ant shelters and octopus shelters, saying the latter's *long-term planning* is better evidence of some intelligence. Choice (F) is incorrect because this would apply to crab and ant shelters. The veined octopus scours the ocean floor for coconut shells, which indicates a more extended search for materials. Choices (G) and (H) are incorrect because the passage mentions nothing about *sturdiness* and *architectural interest*, respectively.

37. **B**   The passage spends the first four paragraphs (lines 1–48) discussing the conceptual difficulties involved in creating a definition of intelligence that would be applicable across a range of species. The rest of the passage describes the practical challenges involved in trying to measure intelligent behavior. Choice (A) is incorrect because the passage does not offer one clear definition for intelligence, but rather seeks a definition that would apply to human and non-human species alike. Choice (C) is incorrect because, although the passage describes some behavior as intelligent and other behavior as unintelligent, it does not identify specific criteria. Also, this answer is too narrow in terms of the passage's overall subject matter. Choice (D) is incorrect because the passage is not organized around a comparison between humans and non-humans. It is organized around the search for an understanding of intelligence that would relate to all animals.

38. **F**   The author begins the paragraph by explaining that intelligent and unintelligent behavior aren't always what they seem. The example with Alex getting problems wrong is intended to demonstrate that *although the behavior looked unintelligent, experimenters believed it was not due to a lack of understanding* (lines 69–70). Choice (G) is incorrect because the author has no clear definition of intelligence, so he couldn't possibly be applying it to parrots. Choice (H) is incorrect because the parrot example mainly illustrated the opposite of this answer. Even though the parrot is described having seemingly intelligent behavior, the passage never says that parrots are believed to be unintelligent. Choice (J) is incorrect because the word *proof* is too strong. The author said that Alex's behavior *suggests* that it learned a concept, not that it *proves* it did.

39. **A**   The sentence is making a contrast between the animal's private experience, which scientists can't observe, and the *external* behavior that scientists can observe. Choice (B) is incorrect because, although secrets are things that are hidden from some people, the adjective *secretive* implies an intention of hiding something, which is not present in the use of *private experience*. Choice (C) is incorrect because a private experience could be subtle or strong—either way it is something outsiders cannot perceive. Choice (D) is incorrect because *shy* implies being nervous or uncomfortable in the presence of others, and that is not what the passage implies about an animal's *private experience*.

40. **J**   This topic sentence (lines 57–58) for the last paragraph foreshadows a discussion of a parrot who behaved unintelligently despite researchers believing it knew how to behave intelligently, and a horse who behaved intelligently but ultimately seemed to not have an intelligent grasp of its behavior. Choice (F) is incorrect because the examples provided do not suggest the animals intended to trick others; this is a trap answer based on the normal meaning of "deceive." Choice (G) is incorrect because the question asks about animal behavior, and that would not be the *hardest thing* to measure. The passage does not state what is the *hardest*, but it is suggested that the mental state of the animal is *harder* to measure than is the animal's behavior (lines 49–56). Choice (H) is incorrect because the passage maintains that even trained researchers still can only hazard a guess as to the thought processes that exist behind an animal's behavior. This answer implies that one can be trained enough to not be fooled.

Chapter 16
Reading Practice
Test 4

READING TEST

35 Minutes—40 Questions

DIRECTIONS: There are four passages in this test. Each passage is followed by several questions. After reading each passage, choose the best answer to each question and blacken the corresponding oval on your answer document. You may refer to the passages as often as necessary.

Passage I

PROSE FICTION: This passage is adapted from the novel *Birds of Paradise* by Minnie Foroozan (©2002 by Minnie Foroozan).

As a young woman, Ani Kealoha had never dreamt of someday owning a hotel on her native island of O'ahu, but—as she would happily tell any of the hotel guests and staff at her 120-room "home away from home"—her outgoing and car-
5 ing nature, along with a strong work ethic and natural ability for organization, had practically made it her destiny. Ani had grown up in a small but happy family of limited means. Most days, Ani would help her parents with their market stall on King Kekaulike Street, where they served increasing numbers
10 of tourists and military personnel. If she ever had aspirations of wealth, it was just to have enough money to visit the faraway places these visitors would talk about—Los Angeles, Sydney, or even New York. They captured her imagination and filled her with a desire for adventure.

15 In the years before statehood, once her sisters were old enough to assume some of her duties at the market, Ani Kealoha's desire to help her family and teenage sense of adventure led her to find other work as well. Hawaii's grow-ing and near year-round influx of tourists allowed ample
20 opportunity for someone of her character. She was a skillful musician and naturally graceful; she would play ukulele and dance to the *hapa-haole* music for the frequent tourist hula shows, eventually acting as "manager" for several groups of musicians and dancers. Ani "The Fearless" would walk from
25 hotel to hotel, asking to see the manager and, more often than not, convincing him that he should invite her group to perform. It was during these frequent visits that she became familiar with the already world-famous Moana Hotel. During one of her visits, she learned of, and was eventually offered,
30 an opening for a staff position at the hotel, and she accepted without hesitation.

Although she started there as a chambermaid, Kealoha recalled her time at the Moana with nostalgia. The endless parade of visitors, from the obscure to the famous, never grew
35 tiresome for her, and her enthusiasm for her work soon saw her managing the entire housekeeping staff. After again proving her capability and resourcefulness as a manager, she was eventually to manage all guest services for the hotel.

With the arrival of statehood in 1959, everything changed.
40 Now a citizen of the United States, she, like her sisters and many of her friends, was eager to take advantage of the new opportunities citizenship offered. While her sisters chose to go to university on the mainland, Ani's experience qualified her to be employed as a civilian for the Quartermaster Corps,
45 helping to organize and distribute supplies to American units and troops still stationed throughout the Pacific.

Gazing out of her office window, listening to the sound of the surf and the ocean breeze in the palms, she often thought of her time as a clerk in the Quartermaster Corps, where she met
50 Lt. James Santos, to whose company she had been assigned, and with whom she would gradually fall in love and then marry a year later. In the days just after their marriage, they lived on the Army base in a small but neat bungalow-style home. When Santos, now "Jimmy," was later promoted to Lieutenant Colonel,
55 Kealoha left her clerking position and spent her time turning their little bungalow into a home—cooking meals in their tiny kitchen, adding a rug here, curtains there, and the big purchase, a brand-new radio. Then one day, Jimmy came home with a surprise: a tiny, half-starved, brown puppy, apparently orphaned.
60 They nursed him back to health, and gave him the grand name Pua Pua Lena Lena—after the beloved dog of Hawaiian myth—which was almost immediately shortened to "Pup."

Thinking about evenings at home with Jimmy, listening to programs like *Hawaii Calls* and with Pup sitting and staring
65 at the radio (looking for all the world like the dog on the RCA Victor label), Kealoha would smile and think about the first time she met Jimmy. Born in the Philippines and raised in Tacoma, Jimmy was young for his rank, being only 24 years old at the time, and newly-arrived in Hawaii. He was slightly-built and
70 fair-skinned, which made him look even younger than he was. As such, he made a special effort to maintain what he felt was the "proper" military bearing. At their first meeting, when she had reported to his office, he was terse, but not rude, and called her "Ms. Kealoha." She could tell that he was trying to make
75 his voice sound deeper than it actually was.

Lieutenant Santos was a tireless worker, and seemed to always find a reason to be at or near her desk, but at the same time, he would seldom speak to her or even make eye contact. Kealoha thought perhaps he felt that she, as a civilian, needed
80 extra supervision, and she made an extra effort to demonstrate just how capable she was.

1. The events in the passage are described primarily from the point of view of a narrator who presents the:

   A. thoughts of Kealoha, her customers, and her family as conveyed in dialogue.
   B. inner thoughts and sentiments of Kealoha only.
   C. inner thoughts of Kealoha and Santos only.
   D. inner thoughts and emotions of all the people in Kealoha's life.

2. The passage supports all of the following statements about the Moana Hotel EXCEPT that:

   F. it was one of the better-known hotels on the island of O'ahu.
   G. Kealoha worked there as a chambermaid.
   H. it had more rooms than the hotel Kealoha currently owns.
   J. its guests included celebrities as well as people who were not as well-known.

3. Which of the following questions is NOT answered by the passage?

   A. What kind of business did Kealoha's parents own?
   B. How long did Santos live in the Philippines before moving to Tacoma?
   C. How did Pup react when Kealoha and Santos listened to the radio?
   D. Under what circumstances did Kealoha first become aware of Santos?

4. One of the main ideas of the second paragraph (lines 15–31) is that:

   F. as a young woman, Kealoha often changed jobs because she quickly grew bored at each position.
   G. Kealoha's work as a musical group manager earned her the nickname Ani "The Fearless."
   H. working many jobs at once, Kealoha lost the opportunity to spend holidays with her family.
   J. because of her abilities and outgoing nature, Kealoha held a variety of jobs as a young woman.

5. According to the passage, all of the following were aspects of Kealoha's time at the Moana Hotel EXCEPT:

   A. cooking meals in the kitchen.
   B. working there as a chambermaid.
   C. receiving a promotion for her efforts.
   D. seeing celebrities.

6. In the passage, the statement that Santos appeared even younger than he was is best described as the opinion of:

   F. Kealoha that she expresses to him in an effort to compliment him.
   G. Santos that he states to the men in his command in hopes that Kealoha will overhear.
   H. Kealoha that she forms while working at Quartermaster Corps.
   J. Kealoha that replaced her earlier impression of him that he reminded her of someone she once knew.

7. The passage indicates that Kealoha's primary response to the events described in the fourth paragraph (lines 39–46) is:

   A. sadness due to her sisters' departure.
   B. concern about the loss of her heritage.
   C. optimism gained from new opportunities.
   D. dismay over the increased number of troops.

8. According to the passage, as a young woman, Kealoha made goals for herself that included:

   F. opening her own market.
   G. owning a farm on a different island.
   H. going to university on the mainland.
   J. traveling to different cities.

9. The passage indicates that compared to her work at her parents' market, Kealoha's job at the Moana offered:

   A. longer hours.
   B. shorter hours.
   C. fewer opportunities for advancement.
   D. more opportunities for advancement.

10. That Santos felt self conscious about his age was:

    F. a confession he shared with the men in his platoon to put them at ease with him.
    G. an insight Kealoha made based on the manner in which he spoke to her.
    H. a question Kealoha posed to him in the first private conversation the two shared.
    J. an opinion he held because he had been promoted so early in his career.

Passage II

SOCIAL SCIENCE: This passage is adapted from the article "A Mann for All Seasons" by Tiptan Held (©2007 by Brookvale).

Held is reviewing the biography *Lasting Vision* by Thomas Younger.

In 1837 the state of Massachusetts formed the first-of-its-kind State Board of Education, and the search began for someone to fill the role of First Secretary. Horace Mann, a state senator from Massachusetts, accepted the position, despite a
5 successful and promising political career and the lack of any demonstrated interest in public education prior to his appointment. He was supposedly drawn to the role solely because it offered a dependable salary, a perk not offered to state legislators. Whatever his motivation may have been, as Thomas Younger
10 writes in his new biography, "Once the reins of the school system were placed in the sure hands of Horace Mann, the landscape of education in Massachusetts, and indeed the United States, was to change forever." And so it proved: after accepting the position, Mann turned to his duties with an unexpected, almost
15 unbelievable zeal, foregoing all other interests, both political and private, in their pursuit.

Thus began the legacy of the man who would eventually become known as the "Father of American Public Education," a surprising epitaph for a man whose own education, at least
20 during his formative years, was not particularly exceptional. Mann was born in 1796 in Franklin, Massachusetts and was raised by his parents on their family farm. From the time he was ten years old until he was twenty, he never attended more than six weeks of school in any given year. Some years, he didn't
25 attend at all. However, his Yankee upbringing had taught him the value of hard work and self-reliance. With the support of a tutor and using the resources of the town library, he studied on his own. He enrolled at Brown University at the age of twenty and graduated three years later as class valedictorian.

30 Younger's biography paints a picture of Mann as one of the most visionary and energetic reformers of his time, as well as one of the most prolific. He had already reached the relatively advanced age of forty-one when he was named First Secretary of the Board of Education, making the quality and quantity of
35 his accomplishments even more impressive. In what Younger calls "an unprecedented and daringly progressive campaign," Mann implemented the "common school" model, in which children from all social classes attended the same school. He argued that the common school model benefited all of society
40 and insisted that the single most important responsibility of a civilized state is the education of its citizens. In his description of Mann's reforms, Younger seems to invite a comparison to the similarly "radical" notions of abolition—a cause Mann would champion with equal fervor upon his election to the U.S. Senate
45 in 1848—and the Civil Rights movement almost a century later.

Mann's considerable dedication to reform was certainly impressive, all the more so considering the hardships he faced along the way, both public and private. Then, as now, education reform was a hotly-contested subject, and Mann encountered
50 resistance at nearly every turn, not only from the institutions he was trying to change but also from students, parents, and teachers. His stance on nonsectarian instruction angered many parents and various religious groups, just as his controversial proposal for the disuse of corporal punishment displeased a
55 group of schoolteachers in Boston. Mann also met with difficulty in his personal life; his grief over his first wife's death in 1832 never wholly left him. At about the same time, he inherited substantial debts left by his only brother. Despite these difficulties (or perhaps because of them), Mann's tireless
60 pursuit of his vision for change continued unabated, fueled by his singular passion and boundless energy.

Younger's well-structured narrative of Mann's life and works goes far beyond a simple recounting of his actions and achievements. By following him from his beginnings as a
65 self-educated young man, through his personal and professional travails and triumphs, to his eventually being named President of Antioch University, a larger story than that of a single individual emerges. Mann's crusade for public education becomes the story of reform itself, of drive and determination,
70 of struggle and sacrifice, and how the vision of one person, pursued relentlessly and with sufficient vigor, can spark change for an entire state, a nation, and indeed the world. Within a year of his appointment as Secretary of the Board of Education, Mann had visited every schoolhouse in the state to assess
75 personally the condition and quality of each. In 1838, Mann instituted the "normal" school system (a school whose primary purpose is to train high-school graduates to be teachers themselves, thereby establishing "norms") in Massachusetts and founded *The Common School Journal*, a publication in
80 which Mann, acting as sole editor, laid down his principles for public education. During his tenure, he also published a series of annual reports, which were circulated widely and influenced other school systems to adopt similar measures. It was this commitment not only to ideals but also to action,
85 Younger seems to tell us, that made Horace Mann an example for others who seek to effect social reform.

11. The passage's author most strongly implies that Mann's interest in public education:

A. was the result of a lifelong passion for education reform.
B. gradually lessened after his appointment as First Secretary of the Board of Education.
C. began in earnest after his appointment as First Secretary of the Board of Education.
D. ended abruptly after his wife's death in 1832.

12. According to the passage, who disapproved of the proposal described in lines 52–55?

F. A group of Boston schoolteachers
G. Younger
H. Mann's parents
J. Mann himself

13. As portrayed in the passage, Mann's reaction to the personal hardships he faced is best described as:

A. angry and afraid.
B. uncaring and selfish.
C. surprised but confident.
D. saddened but resolute.

14. In the statement in lines 10–13, Younger most strongly emphasizes:

F. the significance and impact of Mann's leadership as First Secretary of the Board of Education.
G. the folly of Mann's decision to give up a promising career in the legislature.
H. how Mann's upbringing had prepared him perfectly for his new position.
J. the contrast between the state education in Massachusetts and other places in the United States.

15. According to the passage, Younger believes Mann sets an example for others who seek social reform because Mann:

A. never sought the approval of others for his efforts to reform public education.
B. recognized that education reform can come about only through increased legislation.
C. was relentless in the pursuit of his own education.
D. was committed not only to his ideals but also to action.

16. The passage most strongly suggests that Mann felt the use of corporal punishment in education was:

F. necessary.
G. improper.
H. motivational.
J. justified.

17. Lines 35–38 most nearly mean that Mann:

A. patterned his model for a new school system on one that existed elsewhere.
B. cautiously instituted small reforms, one at a time, in order to achieve his goals.
C. fearlessly challenged the accepted social norms of the period in his efforts to reform education.
D. was more concerned with cost-saving measures than was his predecessor.

18. The passage's author characterizes Mann in the U.S. Senate most nearly as:

F. boldly engaged in other important reforms affecting the nation.
G. obsessively focused on the issue of education.
H. surprisingly inconsistent in his voting record on education issues.
J. amazingly articulate about the role of the state in educating its citizens.

19. For the passage's author, lines 72–75 mainly serve to support his earlier point that:

A. Mann had left the state legislature in order to be able to travel more.
B. there weren't enough schoolhouses in Massachusetts in the nineteenth century.
C. Mann tirelessly pursued his goal of improving and reforming education.
D. Mann was not effective at his job due to his extensive travel.

20. Another reviewer of Younger's book sums up Mann in this way:

Perhaps the single most important figure in American education reform, Horace Mann devoted himself entirely to the cause of public education. Despite facing widespread criticism, Mann never wavered in his commitment to universal education, and the effects of his reforms can still be seen today.

How does this account of Mann compare to that of the passage's author?

F. This account emphasizes Mann's commitment to reform, while the passage's author debunks it.
G. Both offer a similar and complimentary summary of Mann's work as a reformer.
H. Both offer a similar and critical summary of Mann's work as a reformer.
J. This account mentions Mann facing criticism, while the passage's author doesn't.

Passage III

HUMANITIES: This passage is adapted from the memoir *Sewing Circles* by Maria Erica Soreno (©2008 by Maria Erica Soreno).

Ingrid Bergman was a popular actress in Hollywood films of the 1940s and 50s.

In the autumn of 1945, my older sister Ines and I lived with Tía Elena in her little house in Pasadena. There, working from her little shop on Paso Robles Street, Tía Elena had made quite a name for herself as a skilled *costurera*, sewing beautiful
5 dresses for the women in the surrounding neighborhoods. In fact, her work was of such quality that sometimes she would get special orders from some of the nearby film studios, where she had worked years previously.

It was one such order she had received from RKO Radio
10 Pictures that seemed particularly important to her: a gorgeous, flowing, beige crepe evening gown, so intricate that I knew it must be for something or someone special.

"It's the most beautiful dress you've ever done, *tía*," I told her.

Tía Elena looked at me and smiled. "*Sí, hija*, and so it
15 should be—it's for the most beautiful woman in Hollywood. Would you and your sister like to meet her?"

Ines and I exchanged glances and said nothing, uncertain if our aunt was making a genuine offer.

The next day, however, with the just-finished gown pack-
20 aged carefully in a deceivingly plain white box, Tía Elena called to Ines and me to join her on the trip to the studio to deliver the dress. Excited, but still a little doubtful, Ines and I climbed into the car, Ines in the front and I in the back, holding the box, with its delicate contents, on my lap.

25 We arrived at the studio lot, met by a guard at the gate who smiled at Tía Elena and winked at my sister and me. "Welcome to RKO," he said and raised the gate to let us in. We parked the car and began walking towards one of the many buildings on the premises. Ines and I looked about in amazement at the
30 bustling studio lot—workers, costumed actors, cameramen, and hundreds of other people of every description were walking, running, standing, shouting, and laughing in a riot of noise and color. Tía Elena took the package from me. "Hold your sister's hand, Maria," she said, "We need to stay together."

35 Despite the chaos and the fact that many of the large buildings looked nearly identical, Tía Elena walked steadily onward, leading Ines and me up to one of the buildings, indistinguishable from the others apart from a large sign with the number 20 over the entrance. Inside was much the same
40 as outside—people everywhere, moving equipment, shouting

directions, and generally appearing rushed. Apparently unfazed by all the activity, Tía Elena led us confidently through the maze of equipment and crowd of people until we arrived at a door with a star and the name "Ms. Bergman" on it.

45 After a quick, reassuring glance at my sister and me, Tía Elena knocked on the door, which was answered almost immediately by a woman so strikingly tall and beautiful that I could barely think to say anything. Tía Elena came to our rescue, however. "Ms. Bergman, these are my nieces, Ines and
50 Maria. I hope you don't mind visitors, but they were eager to hear your opinion about the dress."

Ms. Bergman smiled at us and crossed to where Tía was unfolding the dress for her. She gasped and exclaimed, "Oh, Elena—it's the most wonderful gown I've ever seen; I'm
55 afraid I'll never do it justice!" Tía Elena beamed with an artist's pride, but only replied modestly, "I'm so happy you like it, Ms. Bergman, but I could never have done it without help from Maria and Ines."

"Is that true, girls?" asked Ms. Bergman, and before we
60 could answer, said, "Well, your aunt is certainly lucky to have such helpful nieces. And please, enough of this 'Ms. Bergman' business; please call me Ingrid, and I'll call you Maria and Ines, just like friends should. Now, such expert work surely deserves a little reward." She took two photographs of herself
65 from a desk drawer and signed them. On mine she added, "For my friend, Maria," and then did likewise for Ines.

In my memory, our visit to the studio that day unfolds like a scene in my very own movie, full of spectacle and wonder and emotion. Ingrid was filming *Notorious* on the day of our
70 visit, and although I've seen all of her films, I still think of that particular film as "ours." Her masterful portrayal of the tragic character Alicia Huberman always makes me remember that day, if only because it stands in such stark contrast to the smiling, friendly, generous woman I met. She was to say, much
75 later, in an interview:

"I have no regrets. I wouldn't have lived my life the way I did if I was going to worry about what people were going to say."

I was only eleven when I met Ingrid Bergman and couldn't really understand the magnitude of her accomplishments, but as
80 I read those words now, spoken of a life lived on a stage, with successes and hardships alike in plain view for all to see, I can't help but recognize, and be inspired by, a truly independent spirit.

21. The point of view from which the passage is told is best described as that of someone:

    A. visiting a movie studio with her aunt and sister.
    B. wanting to become an actor like Bergman.
    C. trying to adjust to life in California.
    D. looking back warmly on meeting Bergman.

22. According to the passage, which of the following events occurred the last chronologically?

    F. The narrator feels inspired by Bergman.
    G. The narrator and her sister receive photographs from Bergman.
    H. The narrator visits a movie studio.
    J. Tía Elena finishes the beautiful gown.

23. Through her description of her meeting with Bergman, the narrator portrays Bergman most nearly as:

    A. snobbish.
    B. rushed.
    C. friendly.
    D. regretful.

24. Based on the passage, the narrator's reaction to being first addressed by Bergman is one of:

    F. fright and silence.
    G. envy and jealousy.
    H. awe and speechlessness.
    J. excitement and doubt.

25. It is reasonable to infer that, following their first meeting with Bergman, the narrator and her sister:

    A. instantly understood the impact that meeting Bergman would have on their lives.
    B. were too busy helping their aunt with her work to think much about it.
    C. continued to see Bergman's movies in order to recapture fond memories of meeting Bergman.
    D. sold the rare autographed photos to a collector so they could afford beautiful dresses.

26. The narrator describes the building they visit at RKO as:

    F. "a riot of noise and color" (lines 32–33)
    G. "full of spectacle and wonder" (line 68)
    H. "indistinguishable from the others" (line 38)
    J. "strikingly tall and beautiful" (line 47)

27. As it is used in line 68, the word *spectacle* most nearly means:

    A. marvel.
    B. performance.
    C. demonstration.
    D. extravaganza.

28. The narrator makes the comparison in lines 73–74 to describe Bergman's:

    F. ability to act in almost any kind of movie.
    G. portrayal of a character completely different from herself.
    H. appeal to fans of all ages.
    J. dramatic reaction to meeting the narrator.

29. Based on the passage, how old was the narrator when she met Bergman?

    A. Twenty
    B. Sixteen
    C. Thirteen
    D. Eleven

30. It is most reasonable to infer from the passage that the narrator gains an appreciation of Bergman's accomplishments primarily as a result of:

    F. the way Bergman treated her when they met.
    G. the influence of her aunt and sister.
    H. her perspective as an adult.
    J. finally seeing Bergman wearing the dress Tía Elena had made.

Passage IV

NATURAL SCIENCE: This passage is adapted from *What is Life?* by Harrison George (©2002 by Melman University Press)

Few people have difficulty defining biology as "the study of life," which is a practical enough definition and certainly true. It may seem contradictory, then, that one of the most difficult and controversial issues biologists have to contend with
5 is defining what life really *is*. Since the time of Aristotle, there have been any number of definitions of life put forth, but as yet, there has been none that is accepted by all. Modern science, and particularly space exploration, has added a new twist to the old debate: we now have the ability to explore other planets
10 and search for, among other things, life—or at least evidence of it having once existed there. So, the question becomes, what exactly are we looking for?

The very essence of a definition is to describe the complex in terms of the simple, but with a concept as vastly complex as
15 life itself, the use of simple terms can be problematic. Some of the more frequently-used conditions put forth for "alive-ness" are complexity, autonomy, self-reproduction, evolution, and metabolism, all of which are assuredly qualities possessed by entities we would recognize as "alive." However, is a forest fire,
20 which self-reproduces and consumes fuel to produce energy (and therefore can be said to possess a "metabolism") alive? How about a computer virus that can evolve or mutate according to its "environment"? Are the individual cells of our bodies, which contain extremely complex internal machinery for the conversion
25 of nutrients into energy, to be considered separate, living entities? Our definition, it seems, requires terms general enough to include all living things but specific enough to exclude the non-living.

Another problem in finding specific terms for a definition is how far we carry their requirements. Terms like self-reproduction
30 and autonomy are useful but also problematic. Viruses self-reproduce, but they aren't autonomous because they depend on the metabolic functions of their host cells. Mules are autonomous living creatures, but they cannot reproduce—they are born sterile. And what of autonomy? Humans (and mules) depend on plants
35 for survival, so are they truly autonomous? Even plants, which don't require other organisms for food, depend on bacteria to break down atmospheric nitrogen, converting it from its inert form into one that allows photosynthesis to take place.

Regardless of the criteria we use for a definition, especially
40 for something as multiform and sublime as life itself, we must always be aware of the limitations we introduce in doing so. One such limitation is philosophical in nature—virtually all of our understanding of life comes from our observation of life on Earth. It was only recently, with the discovery of alternative
45 biochemistries, that it has become clear that a general definition of life will need to be flexible enough to also include life that is *not* necessarily dependent on oxygen and water.

This expansion of the notion of what it means to be alive has led to lively debate, to be sure, and it has also caused many
50 biologists to re-examine not only the terms used to define life but also the term "life" itself. The Gaia theory, for example, is a system of thought that treats the Earth as a whole as a single living organism. While it may not be surprising that such a radical departure from traditional systems of thought has
55 sparked heated opposition, the debate surrounding the issue has brought to light the difficulty of arguing that something is *not* alive without a widely-accepted definition for what *is* alive.

Perhaps the answer eventually to be found in the quest for a definition of life won't really be an answer at all, but
60 rather a whole series of new questions—questions that will open up new areas of study and help scientists gain a broader understanding of life and its place in the universe. Any good scientist knows that the importance of searching for knowledge far outweighs that of any single discovery, no matter how useful
65 or ground-breaking. Remember that it wasn't so very long ago that scientists considered there to be only four "elements" in the universe: fire, air, water, and earth. Each of these is easily enough described—fire, for example, is hot, needs fuel to burn, gives off light, etc. However, it was through efforts to gain a
70 deeper understanding—to find a definition, if you will—of those four elements that scientists made monumental discoveries in physical and molecular chemistry. Scientists could finally define water, for example, as a compound composed of two hydrogen atoms bonded to a single atom of oxygen. Now,
75 such a straightforward and simple description of so esoteric a concept as life may be unrealistic, but that is a small matter. The process of learning, of hypothesis and experiment, of trial and error, of investigation and observation, all brought to bear in a unified effort to achieve a goal—this is the true aim of
80 science. Perhaps in the end, rather than leading us to an answer, it will be the search itself that brings us closest to understanding what it is to be "alive."

31. The primary purpose of the passage is to:

    A. discuss the reasons for, and the difficulty and complexity of, establishing a definition of life.

    B. analyze the criteria for defining life.

    C. differentiate between definitions that are philosophical and biological in nature.

    D. explain the difference between the Gaia theory and traditional systems of thought.

32. The main function of the second paragraph (lines 13–27) in relation to the passage as a whole is to:

    F. dispute the scientific basis of the search for a definition of life.

    G. offer instances in which specific criteria can be problematic.

    H. provide historical context for the process described in the remainder of the passage.

    J. discuss solutions to the problems scientists encounter defining life.

33. The author mentions humans and mules in the third paragraph (lines 39–47) primarily to:

    A. demonstrate some of the problems that the specific criteria we use for a definition can cause.

    B. establish a means of comparison between the two species.

    C. challenge any definition that would not include both as "alive."

    D. persuade the reader to try to discover a definition of life.

34. According to the passage, all of the following could be considered, in general terms, to be alive EXCEPT:

    F. a forest fire.

    G. a computer virus.

    H. an automobile.

    J. the Earth as a whole

35. According to the passage, what is the primary problem with the term "complexity"?

    A. It is subjective and based on arbitrary criteria.

    B. It may easily be applied to things that are not alive as well.

    C. It has limitations that are philosophical and biochemical in nature.

    D. It can be accepted only by proponents of the Gaia theory.

36. According to the passage, scientists have been seeking a definition of life:

    F. ever since space exploration has been possible.

    G. ever since the time of Aristotle.

    H. to settle finally the debate over the Gaia theory.

    J. with greater intensity now than in the past.

37. As it used in line 37, the phrase *break down* most nearly means:

    A. malfunction.

    B. explain.

    C. weep.

    D. reduce.

38. In the context of the passage, the phrase "what exactly are we looking for?" (line 11–12) most nearly suggests that a definition of life:

    F. is one of many answers biologists are trying to discover.

    G. can be found if the investigation is carried out in a precise manner.

    H. will open up an array of other questions, leading to further investigation and discovery.

    J. is an essential first step towards finding evidence of life on other planets.

39. The passage indicates that the Gaia theory differs from traditional systems of thought in that the Gaia theory:

    A. will bring us closer to finally understanding how to define life.

    B. treats the Earth as a whole as a single living organism.

    C. considers there to be only four elements in the universe.

    D. has led to monumental discoveries such as alternative biochemistries.

40. Suppose a philosopher were to lead an investigation with the aim of finding an objective definition for "love." Based on the passage, the author would most likely describe this undertaking as:

    F. interesting but unrealistic.

    G. pointless and unscholarly.

    H. worthwhile and straightforward.

    J. arbitrary and useful only to philosophers.

END OF TEST 3
STOP! DO NOT TURN THE PAGE UNTIL TOLD TO DO SO.
DO NOT RETURN TO A PREVIOUS TEST.

Chapter 17
Reading Practice
Test 4
Answers and
Explanations

READING PRACTICE TEST 4 ANSWERS

1.	B	21.	D	
2.	H	22.	F	
3.	B	23.	C	
4.	J	24.	H	
5.	A	25.	C	
6.	H	26.	H	
7.	C	27.	A	
8.	J	28.	G	
9.	D	29.	D	
10.	G	30.	H	
11.	C	31.	A	
12.	F	32.	G	
13.	D	33.	A	
14.	F	34.	H	
15.	D	35.	B	
16.	G	36.	G	
17.	C	37.	D	
18.	F	38.	J	
19.	C	39.	B	
20.	G	40.	F	

SCORE YOUR PRACTICE TEST

Step A
Count the number of correct answers: _____. This is your *raw score*.

Step B
Use the score conversion table below to look up your raw score. The number to the left is your *scale score*: _____.

Reading Scale Conversion Table

Scale Score	Raw Score	Scale Score	Raw Score	Scale Score	Raw Score
36	40	27	30	18	18
35	39	26	29	17	16–17
34	38	25	27–28	16	15
33	37	24	26	15	14
32	36	23	24–25	14	12–13
31	35	22	23	13	11
30	34	21	22	12	9–10
29	32–33	20	20–21	11	8
28	31	19	19	10	6–7

READING PRACTICE TEST 4 EXPLANATIONS

Passage I

1. **B** While a number of other people, including Kealoha's family, customers, and Santos, are all mentioned in the passage, they are all described from Kealoha's point of view, and only as she remembers them.

2. **H** The Moana Hotel is described as *world-famous* (lines 27–28), so it would have been well-known on the island as well, as choice (A) states. The passage mentions her working there as a chambermaid (lines 32–33) and the variety of people, *from the obscure to the famous*, (line 34) who stayed there. However, the number of rooms at the Moana is never given, making (H) the only choice *not* supported by the passage, and therefore correct.

3. **B** Kealoha worked at her parents' *market stall* (line 8). When Kealoha and Santos listened to radio programs, Pup is described as *sitting and staring at the radio* (lines 64–65), and the passage states that Kealoha met Santos when she began working at the Quartermaster Corps (lines 49–50). The only question of the four *not* answered by the passage is choice (B); Santos was *raised in Tacoma* (line 67), but no mention is made of the age at which he moved there from the Philippines, making (B) the correct choice.

4. **J** The paragraph lists the different jobs she held and relates them each to her personality, but there is no evidence to support the fact that this was due to her growing *bored* with them, as stated in choice (F). Choice (G) is supported by the passage but only talks about one of the jobs she held, so it's not a main idea. There is no mention of whether Kealoha lost the opportunity to spend holidays with her family, as choice (H) states, or how she may have felt about it.

5. **A** The third paragraph (lines 32–38) mentions Kealoha working as a chambermaid, seeing famous people, and being promoted for her work, supporting choices (B), (C), and (D). The fifth paragraph mentions her *cooking meals in their tiny kitchen*, not at the Moana, but in her own home. Since (A) is the choice that is unsupported, it is the correct answer.

6. **H** Kealoha, thinking about the first time she met Santos, remembers that he was *slightly-built and fair-skinned, which made him look even younger than he was* (lines 69–70). There is no dialogue in the passage as stated in choices (F) and (G), and there is also no evidence for choice (J), which states that Santos may have reminded Kealoha of someone she once knew.

7. **C** The fourth paragraph describes Kealoha as *eager to take advantage of the new opportunities citizenship offered* (lines 41–42). Although her *sisters* and *troops* are both mentioned, there is no evidence given for her feeling either *sadness* or *dismay*, as in choices (A) and (D). There is no mention of the *concern about the loss of her heritage* in choice (B).

8. **J** The first paragraph describes Kealoha's aspirations *to have enough money to visit the faraway places these visitors would talk about—Los Angeles, Sydney, or even New York* (lines 11–13). Kealoha worked in her parents' market (line 8), but there is no mention in the passage of her wanting to open one of her own or of owning a farm, as in choices (F) and (G). Kealoha's sisters *chose to go to university on the mainland* (lines 42–43), not Kealoha.

9. **D** Kealoha is described in the third paragraph (lines 32–38) as having been promoted twice while at the Moana Hotel, and there is no evidence to show she was ever given added responsibility or higher pay while working for her parents. The actual number of hours she worked at either her parents' market stall or at the Moana is not given in the passage.

10. **G** When Kealoha first met Santos, *he was terse, but not rude, and called her "Ms. Kealoha." She could tell that he was trying to make his voice sound deeper than it actually was* (lines 73–75) in an effort to appear older. Choices (F) and (H) both involve dialogue, of which the passage has none, and while choice (J) may seem plausible, there is no evidence given for how Santos may have felt about being promoted.

Passage II

11. **C** Mann accepted the position of First Secretary of Education *despite. . . the lack of any demonstrated interest in public education prior to his appointment* (lines 4–7), and carried out his duties with *an almost unbelievable zeal* (lines 14–15). This contradicts choices (A) and (B). The passage states that Mann continued his efforts for education reform after his wife's death (lines 58–61), eliminating choice (D).

12. **F** The *proposal* in lines 52–55 was for *the disuse of corporal punishment*, which *displeased a group of schoolteachers in Boston*, as stated in (F). There is no support in the passage that Mann, his parents, or the biographer Younger disapproved of Mann's proposal.

13. **D** The passage states that the grief Mann felt over the death of his first wife *never wholly left him*, and he not only lost his only brother at about the same time but also *inherited substantial debt*. Nonetheless, his *vision for change continued unabated* (lines 57–60). While he may have been *angry* about these events, there is no support in the passage for his feeling *afraid*, as in choice (A). Similarly, Mann is never described as *uncaring* or *selfish* as choice (B) states; in fact, he is consistently shown to be quite the opposite. There is evidence that Mann was quite *confident* but nothing to support the fact that he may have been *surprised* about either event, making choice (C) incorrect.

14. **F** The statement in lines 10–13 is talking about the positive effects Mann had on public education after he accepted the role of First Secretary of the Board of Education, not the *folly* of his decision to accept the role, as in choice (G). Choice (H) refers to his *upbringing* prior to that point, which hadn't prepared him for the position and there is no evidence for the comparison in choice (J) between Massachusetts and other places.

15. **D** In the last sentence of the passage, the author states that Mann was an example to others because of his *commitment not only to ideals but also to action*. There is no mention in the passage of him *seeking approval*, as choice (A) states. While some of Mann's reforms involved legislation, there is no evidence for the claim in choice (B) that he thought this was the *only* means of reform. Choice (C) is supported by the passage, but the pursuit of one's own education isn't what the author offers as *an example for others who seek social reform*.

16. **G** Mann's proposal was for the *disuse* of corporal punishment (lines 52–55), so he must have felt it to be *improper*. There is no irony on the ACT, and choices (F), (H), and (J) are all reasons to keep using corporal punishment.

17. **C** Lines 35–38 refer to Mann's campaign as *unprecedented and daringly progressive*. Duplicating an existing system would not make his campaign *unprecedented*, just as *cautiously instituting small reforms, one at a time* would not be daring, making choices (A) and (B) incorrect. Choice (D) mentions *cost-saving measures* and *his predecessor*, neither of which are talked about in the passage.

18. **F** Discussing Mann's passion for education reform, the passage refers to *abolition* (lines 41–45) as *a cause Mann would champion with equal fervor upon his election to the U.S. Senate*. This contradicts choice (G), as *obsessively* would mean he was focused on education only. Choice (H) can be eliminated because Mann's voting record is never mentioned. Mann certainly claimed that education was the responsibility of the state as choice (J) states, but he did so as First Secretary, not as a U.S. Senator (lines 38–41). Additionally, there is no evidence offered in the passage to support how articulate or amazing he may have been in doing so.

19. **C** Lines 72–75 state that the reason Mann visited every schoolhouse in the state in the first year of his administration was *to assess personally the condition and quality of each*. There is no mention of Mann's desire to travel being the reason he left the state legislature, as choice (A) states; the only reason given in the passage was *dependable salary* (lines 7–8). There is no mention of the number of schoolhouses being sufficient or not, so you can eliminate choice (B). Choice (D) contradicts the passage, which describes Mann as successful primarily because of the energy and personal attention he put into his job.

20. **G** Both accounts use the same general criteria to praise Mann for his reforms and are not *critical* in tone—eliminate choices (F) and (H). The passage's fourth paragraph (lines 46–61) recounts Mann facing criticism from various sources, making choice (J) incorrect.

Passage III

21. **D** The narrator does indeed visit a movie studio, as choice (A) states, but that is not the focus of the story; her meeting with Bergman is. The narrator never mentions wanting to become *an actress like Bergman*, and there is no support for *adjusting to life* in choice (C)—the narrator merely mentions the fact that they live in California.

22. **F**   Speaking as an adult, the narrator feels inspired by Bergman in the final paragraph (lines 78–82). Choices (G), (H), and (J) all occur when she was a child.

23. **C**   The narrator relates Bergman's insistence on calling each other by their first names *just like friends should* (line 63) and remembers her as *smiling* and *friendly* (line 74). Bergman's actions are not *snobbish*, so eliminate choice (B). The people on the movie studio lot are described as *rushed* (line 41). Choice (D) is contradicted by Bergman's quote, *I have no regrets* (line 76).

24. **H**   When she first meets Bergman, the narrator describes her as *so strikingly tall and beautiful that I could barely think to say anything* (lines 45–48). There is no evidence to show she was afraid, as choice (F) states, or felt *envy* or *jealousy*. The narrator describes herself and her sister as *excited* and *doubtful* (line 22) but not during her meeting with Bergman.

25. **C**   The narrator says that she has seen all of Bergman's films (line 70) and goes on to say how one film in particular *makes me remember that day* (lines 72–73). In the final paragraph (lines 78–82), the narrator says she was too young to fully appreciate meeting Bergman, so eliminate choice (A). There is no evidence in the passage for the sisters being *too busy to think about* meeting Bergman as stated in choice (B). Choice (D) is also unsupported since the photos clearly meant a great deal to the narrator and her sister. Additionally, the narrator never expresses a desire to purchase a dress of her own.

26. **H**   The narrator mentions that *many of the buildings looked nearly identical* (lines 35–36) before describing the building they approach as *indistinguishable from the others* (line 38). *A riot of noise and color* in choice (F) refers to the move studio lot in general, not the buildings specifically. The narrator uses *full of spectacle and wonder* in choice (C) to describe her memories of the entire visit. Choice (D) is a description of Bergman herself.

27. **A**   The narrator compares her memories of meeting Bergman to a scene in a movie, *full of spectacle and wonder and emotion* (lines 68–69). *Performance*, *demonstration*, and *extravaganza* also have similar meanings to *spectacle*, but *marvel* best fits the context of *wonder and emotion*.

28. **G**   The comparison being made in the twelfth paragraph is between the tragic character Bergman portrays in the film and *the smiling, friendly, generous woman I met*. There is no evidence for choice (F), as the narrator is referring to only one movie. Choice (H) is unsupported since Bergman's *appeal to fans of all ages* is never discussed. The narrator describes Bergman as *smiling, friendly,* and *generous*, which disagrees with choice (J).

29. **D**   In the last paragraph, the narrator states *I was only eleven when I met Ingrid Bergman* (line 78).

30. **H**   Speaking about the words Bergman used to describe her own life, the narrator states *but as I read those words now. . . I can't help but recognize, and be inspired by, a truly independent spirit*. Choice (F) can be eliminated because it is contradicted by the narrator's statement *I was only eleven when I*

met Ingrid Bergman and couldn't really understand the magnitude of her accomplishments (lines 78–79). There is no proof for the claim in choice (G) that the narrator's aunt and sister had any *influence* regarding her appreciation of Bergman, and no mention is ever made of seeing Bergman in the gown Tìa Elena made—eliminate choice (J).

Passage IV

31. **A**   The passage as a whole is a discussion of not only how scientists define life and the difficulties they encounter but also the reasons it is important for them to do so. The *criteria* used for defining life are discussed, but that is not the primary purpose of the passage. Similarly, the notions of *philosophical* and *biological* criteria in choice (C), and the *Gaia theory* and *traditional systems of thought* in choice (D) are discussed, but they are not the main focus of the passage.

32. **G**   The second paragraph states *with a concept as vastly complex as life itself, the use of simple terms can be problematic* (lines 13–15) and offers some examples of specific criteria, as well as some examples that fit the criteria, but not the definition. However, there is no evidence that the intent is to *dispute* the *scientific* basis of this definition, as choice (F) claims. Choices (H) and (J) are incorrect, as there is no *historical context* given nor *solutions* offered in the second paragraph.

33. **A**   In the third paragraph, the author uses humans and mules as two examples of autonomous life forms and questions whether they technically fit that criterion since both species *depend on plants for survival*. While the two species certainly share that trait, there is no proof in the text that a *means of a comparison between the two species* is being established. There is no *challenge* offered in the text, as choice (C) states, nor is there evidence that author is trying to persuade the reader to take any sort of action—eliminate (D).

34. **H**   The second paragraph (lines 13–27) lists a *forest fire*, which *self-reproduces* and could be said to have a *metabolism*, and a *computer virus*, which *evolves according to its "environment,"* as examples of phenomena that meet at least some of the criteria for life. The *Gaia theory* in the fifth paragraph (lines 48–57) considers *the Earth as a whole* to be a *living organism*. The only example not offered by the passage is choice (H), an automobile, making it the correct answer.

35. **B**   The author uses *the individual cells of our bodies* (lines 23–25) as an example of entities that are complex but may still not be considered strictly to be alive. There is no mention of the term *complexity* being either *subjective* or *arbitrary*, as choice (A) states, nor is there a discussion of its *limitations*. *Complexity*, as a defining term, is not discussed in connection with the *Gaia theory*, making choice (D) incorrect.

36. **G**   The passage states that *since the time of Aristotle, there have been any number of definitions of life put forth* (lines 5–7). *Space exploration* is offered as a reason why scientists are so interested in finding a definition (lines 7–11). The debate over the *Gaia theory* (lines 48–57) is described as a result of the

search for a definition, not the reason behind it. There is no comparison in the text between the intensity of the present-day search and that of scientists in the past, so choice (J) can be eliminated.

37. **D** In lines (35–38), the author uses the phrase *break down* to describe a chemical process. Choices (A), (B), and (C) do not fit this context.

38. **J** The author poses the question to emphasize his earlier point about space travel and the ability to seek life on other planets (lines 7–11). The author does not mention the *many other answers* sought by biologists in choice (F), and there is no mention of the *investigation* needing to be carried out with a certain level of precision. In the sixth paragraph (lines 58–82), the author discusses the search for a definition leading to further *investigation and discovery*, but that is a different point from the one he is making in the first paragraph.

39. **B** The author states that the *Gaia theory is a system of thought that treats the Earth as a whole as a single living organism* and refers to the theory as *a radical departure from traditional systems of thought*, so that must be the difference. The author offers the theory as an example, not a solution, so eliminate choice (A). The universe being composed of *only four elements* is mentioned later in the passage (line 66), but not in conjunction with the Gaia theory, making choice (C) incorrect. *Monumental discoveries* (lines 71–72) and *alternative biochemistries* (44–45) are also mentioned in the passage, but also not in connection with the Gaia theory, so choice (D) is incorrect.

40. **F** It is reasonable to infer that the author of this passage would attach the same importance of finding a definition for *love* to philosophers as he would that of a definition of *life* to biologists, and anticipate the same benefits, which directly contradicts choice (G). He gives several examples of the complexities of finding a single definition, saying *the use of simple terms can be problematic* and *the answer . . . won't really be an answer but rather a whole series of new questions*. This is the opposite of *straightforward*, so eliminate choice (H). There is no support in the passage for the notion that the author would find such an investigation *arbitrary*, which eliminates choice (J). The author would agree that such an investigation was *interesting*, as choice (F) states, and he also makes it very clear that an objective definition is *unrealistic* by suggesting several times that a single answer won't be found. *Perhaps in the end, rather than leading us to an answer, it will be the search itself . . .* shows that he doesn't expect there to be a clear answer at the end of the search. Both parts of choice (F) are supported, leaving it as the best answer.

Part IV
Paying For
College 101

If you're reading this book, you've already made an investment in your education. You may have shelled out some cold, hard cash for this book, and you've definitely invested time in reading it. It's probably even safe to say that this is one of the smaller investments you've made in your future so far. You put in the hours and hard work needed to keep up your GPA. You've paid test fees and applications fees, perhaps even travel expenses. You have probably committed time and effort to a host of extracurricular activities to make sure colleges know that you're a well-rounded student.

But after you get in, there's one more issue to think about: How do you pay for college?

More Great Titles from The Princeton Review
Paying for College Without Going Broke
The Best 377 Colleges

Let's be honest: College is not cheap. The average tuition for a private four-year college is over $33,000 a year. The average tuition of a four-year public school is about $6,695 a year. And the cost is rising. Every year the sticker price of college education bumps up about 6 percent.

Like many of us, your family may not have 33 grand sitting around in a shoebox. With such a hefty price tag, you might be wondering: "Is a college education really worth it?" The short answer: Yes! No question about it. According to a 2010 report by the College Board, the median earnings of full-time workers with bachelor's degrees were $55,700 in 2008—$21,900 more than those of workers who finished only high school.

Still, the cost of college is no joke. It's said that a college education ultimately pays for itself; however, some pay better than others. It's best to be prudent when determining the amount of debt that is reasonable for you to take on.

Here's the good news. Even in the wake of the current financial crisis, financial aid is available to almost any student who wants it. There is an estimated $177 billion—that's right, billion!—in financial aid offered to students annually. This comes in the form of federal grants, scholarships, state financed aid, loans, and other programs.

We know that financial aid can seem like an overwhelmingly complex issue, but the introductory information in this chapter should help you grasp what's available and get you started in your search.

How Much Does College Really Cost?

When most people think about the price of a college education, they think of one thing and one thing alone: tuition. It's time to get that notion out of your head. While tuition is a significant portion of the cost of a college education, you need to think of all the other things that factor into the final price tag.

Let's break it down.

- Tuition and fees
- Room and board
- Books and supplies
- Personal expenses
- Travel expenses

Collectively, these things contribute to your total Cost of Attendance (COA) for one year at a college or university.

Understanding the distinction between tuition and COA is crucial because it will help you understand this simple equation:

Check Out Our Financial Aid Library
PrincetonReview.com/ scholarships-financial-aid .aspx

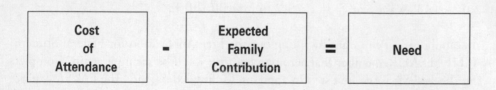

When you begin the financial aid process, you will see this equation again and again. We've already talked about the COA, so let's talk about the Estimated Family Contribution, or EFC. The EFC simply means, "How much you and your family can afford to pay for college." Sounds obvious right?

Here's the catch: What you think you can afford to pay for college, what the government thinks you can afford to pay for college, and what a college or university thinks you can afford to pay for college are, unfortunately, three different things. Keep that in mind as we discuss financing options later on.

The final term in the equation is self-explanatory. Anything that's left after what you and your family have contributed still needs to be covered. That's where financial aid packages come in.

WHAT'S IN A FINANCIAL AID PACKAGE?

A typical financial aid package contains money—from the school, federal government, or state—in various forms: grants, scholarships, work-study programs, and loans.

Let's look at the non-loan options first. Non-loan options include grants, scholarships, and work-study programs. The crucial thing about them is that they involve monetary assistance that you won't be asked to pay back. They are as close as you'll get to "free money."

Grants

Grants are basically gifts. They are funds given to you by the federal government, state agencies, or individual colleges. They are usually need-based, and you are not required to pay them back.

One of the most important grants is the Pell Grant. Pell Grants are provided by the federal government but administered through individual schools. Amounts can change yearly. The maximum Federal Pell Grant award is $5,550 for the 2012–2013 award year (July 1, 2012 to June 30, 2013).

You apply for a Pell Grant by filling out the Free Application for Federal Student Aid (FAFSA). Remember that acronym because you'll be seeing it again. Completing the FAFSA is the first step in applying for any federal aid. The FAFSA can be found online at www.fafsa.ed.gov.

There are several other major federal grant programs that hand out grants ranging from $100 to thousands of dollars annually. Some of these grants are given to students entering a specific field of study and others are need-based, but all of them amount to money that you never have to pay back. Check out the FAFSA website for complete information about qualifying and applying for government grants.

The federal government isn't the only source of grant money. State governments and specific schools also offer grants. Use the Internet, your guidance counselor, and your library to see what non-federal grants you might be eligible for.

Scholarships

Like grants, you never have to pay a scholarship back. But the requirements and terms of a scholarship might vary wildly. Most scholarships are merit- or need-based, but they can be based on almost anything. There are scholarships based on academic performance, athletic achievements, musical or artistic talent, religious affiliation, ethnicity, and so on.

Believe It or Not...
The Chick and Sophie Major Memorial Duck Calling Contest, held annually by the Chamber of Commerce of Stuggart, Arkansas, gives out college scholarships totaling $4,250 (in 2011) to those high school seniors who can master hailing, feeding, comeback, and mating duck calls.

When hunting for scholarships, one great place to start is the U.S. Department of Labor's "Scholarship Search," available at www.careerinfonet.org/scholarshipsearch. It includes over 5,000 scholarships, fellowships, loans, and other opportunities. It's a free service and a great resource.

There is one important caveat about taking scholarship money. Some, but not all, schools think of scholarship money as income and will reduce the amount of aid they offer you accordingly. Know your school's policy on scholarship awards.

Check Out the Scholarship Search Page
PrincetonReview.com/scholarships.aspx

Federal Work-Study (FWS)

One of the ways Uncle Sam disperses aid money is by subsidizing part-time jobs, usually on campus, for students who need financial aid. Because your school will administer the money, they get to decide what your work-study job will be. Work-study participants are paid by the hour, and federal law requires that they cannot be paid less than the federal minimum wage.

One of the benefits of a work-study program is that you get a paycheck just like you would at a normal job. The money is intended to go towards school expenses, but there are no controls over exactly how you spend it.

Colleges and universities determine how to administer work-study programs on their own campuses.

The Bottom Line? Not So Fast!
It is possible to appeal the amount of the financial aid package a school awards you. To learn more about how to do that, check out "Appealing Your Award Package" at PrincetonReview.com/appealing-your-award.aspx

LOANS

Most likely, your entire COA won't be covered by scholarships, grants, and work-study income. The next step in gathering the necessary funds is securing a loan. Broadly speaking, there are two routes to go: federal loans and private loans. Once upon a time, which route to choose might be open for debate. But these days the choice is clear: *Always* try to secure federal loans first. Almost without exception, federal loans provide unbeatable low fixed-interest rates; they come with generous repayment terms; and, although they have lending limits, these limits are quite generous and will take you a long way toward your goal. We'll talk about the benefits of private loans later, but they really can't measure up to what the government can provide and should be considered a last resort.

Stafford Loans

The Stafford loan is the primary form of federal student loan. Loans can be subsidized or unsubsidized. Students with demonstrated financial need may qualify for subsidized loans. This means that the government pays interest accumulated during the time the student is in school. Students with unsubsidized Stafford loans are responsible for the interest accumulated while in school. You can qualify for a subsidized Stafford loan, an unsubsidized Stafford loan, or a mixture of the two.

Stafford loans are available to all full-time students and most part-time students. Though the terms of the loan are based on demonstrated financial need, lack of need is not considered grounds for rejection. No payment is expected while the student is attending school. The interest rate on your Stafford loan will depend on when your first disbursement is. The chart below shows the fixed rates set by the government.

First disbursement made on or after	Interest rate on unpaid balance
July 1, 2008 to July 1, 2009	6.0 percent
July 1, 2009 to July 1, 2010	5.6 percent
July 1, 2010 to July 1, 2011	4.5 percent
July 1, 2011 to July 1, 2012	3.4 percent

As with grants, you must start by completing the Free Application for Federal Student Aid (FAFSA) to apply for a Stafford loan.

PLUS Loans

Another important federal loan is the PLUS loan. This loan is designed to help parents and guardians put dependent students through college. Unlike the Stafford loan, the PLUS has no fixed limits or fixed interest rates. The annual limit on a PLUS loan is equal to your COA minus any other financial aid you are already receiving. It may be used on top of a Stafford loan. The interest rates on PLUS loans are variable though often comparable to, or even lower than, the interest rates on Stafford loans. Your PLUS Loan enters repayment once your loan is fully disbursed (paid out).

To become eligible for a PLUS loan, you need only complete a Free Application for Federal Student Aid (FAFSA). There are no other special requirements or forms to fill out.

Perkins Loans

A third and final federal loan you should be aware of is the Perkins loan. Intended to help out students in extreme need, the Perkins loan is a government-subsidized loan that is administered only through college and university financial aid offices. Under the terms of a Perkins loan, you may borrow up to $5,500 a year of undergraduate study, up to $27,500. The Perkins loan has a fixed interest rate of just 5 percent. Payments against the loan don't start until nine months after you graduate. Apply for Perkins loans through your school's financial aid office.

Private Lenders

We said it before, and we'll say it again: DO NOT get a private loan until you've exhausted all other options.

That said, there are *some* benefits to securing a private loan. First off, many students find that non-loan and federal loan options don't end up covering the entire bill. If that's the case, then private lenders might just save the day. Second, loans from private sources generally offer you greater flexibility with how you use the funds. Third, private loans can be taken out at anytime during your academic career. Unlike most non-loan and government-backed financial options, you can turn to private lenders whenever you need them.

All private lenders are not the same! As the old song says, "You better shop around." Every lender is going to offer you a different package of terms. What you need to do is find the package that best fits your needs and plans. Aside from low interest rates, which are crucially important, there other terms and conditions you will want to look out for.

Low origination fees   Origination fees are fees that lenders charge you for taking out a loan. Usually the fee is simply deducted automatically from your loan checks. Obviously, the lower the origination fee, the better.

Minimal guaranty fees   A guaranty fee is an amount you pay to a third-party who agrees to insure your loan. That way, if the borrower—that is you—can't pay the loan back, the guarantor steps in and pays the difference. Again, if you can minimize or eliminate this fee, all the better.

Interest rate reductions   Some lenders will reduce your interest rates if you're reliable with your payments. Some will even agree to knock a little off the interest rate if you agree to pay your loans through a direct deposit system. When shopping for the best loan, pay careful attention to factors that might help you curb your interest rates.

Flexible payment plans   One of the great things about most federal loans is the fact that you don't have to start paying them off until you leave school. In order to compete, many private lenders have been forced to adopt similarly flexible payment plans. Before saying yes to a private loan, make sure that it comes with a payment timetable you can live with.

IT'S YOUR CALL

No matter what the state of the economy, it is always a good idea to research thoroughly the assortment of low-interest federal assistance programs available to you. Weigh your financing options (loans, grants, scholarships, work study, etc.) against the overall cost of your college education. Remember that this is a personal choice with potentially long-term ramifications, and that what your peers are doing may not be right for you. Talk it over with your parent(s) or guardian(s). With thoughtful planning (and a lot of form-filling!) it's possible to pay your way though school without breaking the bank.

NOTES

NOTES

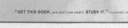

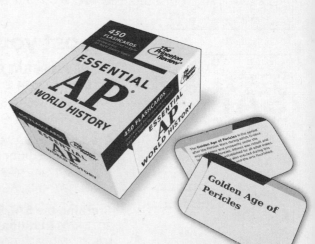